Graduate School
in the Sciences

Graduate School in the Sciences:
Entrance, Survival, and Careers

JACK G. CALVERT

Professor of Chemistry
The Ohio State University

JAMES N. PITTS, JR.

Professor of Chemistry and
Director, Statewide Air Pollution Research Center
University of California, Riverside

GEORGE H. DORION

Director of Advanced Projects
Bacardi Corporation

WILLEY—INTERSCIENCE
a division of John Wiley & Sons, Inc.

New York   London   Sydney   Toronto

Copyright © 1972, by John Wiley & Sons, Inc.

All rights reserved. Published simultaneously in Canada.

No part of this book may be reproduced by any means, nor transmitted, nor translated into a machine language without the written permission of the publisher.

Library of Congress Cataloging in Publication Data

Calvert, Jack George, 1923-
    Graduate School in the sciences.

    1.   Science—Study and teaching (Higher)—U. S.
2.   Science as a profession. I. Pitts, James N.,
joint author. II. Dorion, George Henry, joint author.
III. Title
Q181.C328   507'.11'73   72-572
ISBN 0-471-13080-X

Printed in the United States of America

10 9 8 7 6 5 4 3 2 1

Preface

This book was conceived, as are so many things, while two old friends, colleagues, and neighbors were quaffing a few mint juleps on a hot summer's night some seven or eight years ago and rapping about their students—past and present.

This book is dedicated to students—those of the original fathers' of the idea, as well as those of the authors who finally translated that idea into a reality.

One of the two original "idea men" is Professor L. Metcalf who during that period was chairman of the Department of Entomology and vice chancellor of the University of California, Riverside. Subsequently he left to join the faculty of the Urbana Campus of the University of Illinois where he is presently head of the Department of Zoology. While Bob Metcalf did not participate in the actual writing of the text, he gave us his blessing, some excellent ideas, and a thorough review of the final product. We give him our warm thanks!

The actual writing started about two years ago when one of us spent a sabbatical quarter at the University of California, Irvine and the other two were close at hand in Riverside. Our purpose was to "tell it like it is" (but of course from our viewpoint!) by organizing and putting in writing our thoughts on some student-oriented matters that had concerned us for years; for instance, "How do I pick a graduate school?" "What do I do, pick a hotshot, a well known research man who may see me only briefly and rarely in the lab, or a young assistant professor who will be a lab mate but may not be recognized nationally?" "What is a copyright?" "Now that I have my Ph.D., what kind of a job should I take—if I am lucky enough to have some options?" We hope our experiences will be of some assistance to you in answering such questions for yourself.

The sum of the authors' background experiences is multicolored. It includes a total of four decades in various aspects of teaching and administrating in universities on the part of two of the authors, and well over a decade in industrial and military research and management on the part of the other author. The two academic authors were lab mates in grad school just after World War II working for "The Chief", Professor F. E. Blacet of the University of California, Los Angeles. Both have been chairman of departments, one at a large, established state university, the other at a new campus of a state university. One has served as chairman of the National Air Pollution Manpower Development Committee and the National Air Pollution Research Grants Advisory Committee of the Office of Air Pollution Control of the Environmental Protection Agency. The other directs the University of California's Statewide Air Pollution Research Center. Both have enjoyed teaching undergraduate and graduate students and have directed the research of graduate and postdoctoral students for over two decades, and they continue today in these efforts. The "industrialist" author has headed a research team in a major chemical company, has been president of a small company devoted to the educational and research aspects of environmental pollution, and presently is director of Advanced Projects for a major corporation.

We cite these statistics not in the attempt to impress or awe you; youth today, happily, are neither awed nor impressed by mere titles. However we cite them as evidence that we have campaigned over many battlefields of academia, industry, and government, and thus speak from experience— some sweet, some bitter—but none of it dull! We plead guilty here and now to being biased in some areas and opinionated in others, but we hope that our bias is toward the direction of improved graduate education. We have tried to be candid without being negative. We also say mea culpa—we don't pretend to have lived up to all of the advice we give in this book, but generally we have tried to do so.

The various drafts have been read and criticized by Professor Metcalf as well as a number of undergraduate, graduate, and postdoctoral students, colleagues in various branches of the natural sciences, and by two anonymous reviewers for John Wiley. They have all been very frank and helpful in their evaluations.

You will note from the acknowledgment list that several of our women colleagues and students offered their comments and criticism. Although these were not in the "accepted" "women's lib" style, they were even more effective in seeing that "male chauvinism" (as one reviewer put it) did not permeate the book.

The text was read by our wives, who suffered with the authors in the hard work that goes into the preparation of any book. Some of their pet ideas are included—and a good thing, because they too, like students, have a sage perspective we need.

While many people indeed have participated in the ideas and writing of this book, special thanks are due to Miss Barbara Finlayson, a graduate student at U.C.R., who expended a substantial amount of time, effort, and imagination this summer in reorganizing and editing the first draft for final publication. Previously the authors' working schedules and time tables looked like a literary "pull out from Viet Nam"—would it never end? She saw to it that it did.

We thank our many other colleagues and students who contributed to our effort in one way or another: Drs. Charles Badcock, Ken Callahan, Karen Darnall, Richard Daubendieck, Alan Lloyd, Charles Nicol, Fred Wampler, Katherine Wilson, Professors J. Alistair Kerr (University of Birmingham) and Benjamin Linsky (University of West Virginia), and Mr. Kenneth Demerjian, Mr. Jeff Gaffney, Mr. Mike Hovanec, Mrs. Judy Hughes, Mr. Robert Metcalf, Jr., Miss Billie Perry, and Miss Judy Scott.

Four secretaries toiled long and hard over the various drafts of the present book and offered useful comments, based on their intimate view of life in the academic salt mines. They are Mrs. Connie Bennett, Mrs. Mae Minnich, Mrs. Elizabeth Ballantine Haire, and Mrs. Elizabeth Sutter. Our thanks for a job well done.

Finally, we acknowledge with pleasure the professional assistance and genuine enthusiasm of Dr. Robert Badger, editor for John Wiley and Sons. It is a pleasure working with him, and "joint venturing" with the Wiley-Interscience Company.

We hope you will read this book in the same spirit in which it was written, relaxed but considerate of the questions raised. We hope that you will send us your comments and criticisms. We may wince, but we won't be mortally wounded—we of the "establishment" do *need* your input.

Good luck and good hunting.

Jack G. Calvert

James N. Pitts, Jr.

George H. Dorion

Contents

List of Appendix Tables

1

Academic Gamesmanship: The Art and Science of the Graduate Student

1. Introduction

"The Days of Wine and Roses" are over, not only in the cinema and song, but in a very real sense for all of us who are deeply involved with fundamental research, whether it be in industry, government, or that scientific Valhalla, the university. It was a great trip. Today, the hangover hurts. American society is going through an agonizing reappraisal, not only involving those incredibly complex societal problems of race, environment, and indeed of the relationships of men and women to themselves, but also delving into an area that to date has been virtually sacrosanct—basic research. The ramifications are staggering to all of us who have been involved with, and passionately committed to, this our intellectual mistress.

The purpose of this book, then, is to "tell it like it is," but in the additional context of the way it *was* and the way we think it *will* be. Specifically, we hope that we can provide enough facts, figures, and philosophy that we can help undergraduate and graduate students, fledgling faculty and researchers, and indeed anyone interested in the American science scene, to make rational and rewarding decisions in that critical area of their lives—their professional careers.

Times have changed. In the fifties and sixties even a relatively mediocre undergraduate science student could be assured of a place in a graduate school and financial support. Indeed, if accepted, he could be reasonably confident of at least a master's degree and at the end of the line, a job. Today this is no longer true. While the seventies may be the age of Aquarius and of ecology, we have nevertheless returned to the tough and the competitive academic and industrial

3

worlds of the thirties and forties. Financial support in graduate school and subsequent employment are no longer to be taken for granted.

We are addressing this book, then, to the several strata of scientists, from student to independent researcher, that comprise our profession. We hope that the experience and knowledge offered here will provide some insight into the various problems which must be resolved as one winds his way along the path from graduate student to mature scientist. Thus, each of the three parts of the book deals with a separate stage of one's career development in science.

In Part I, we deal with the often traumatic decisions facing the college senior as he approaches graduation:

"Should I go on to graduate school?"

"If so, into which area of science should I venture?"

"Which university should I attend?"

"What are my chances of earning a Ph.D. degree?"

The science major asks these and related questions at some point, too often quite late, in his undergraduate career. In fact, every potential bachelor's degree recipient in the sciences and engineering must one day evaluate his ability and his future aims in life, and he must decide for or against continuing his formal education at the graduate school level. Unfortunately, most students make this vital decision with minimal help and little knowledge of the alternatives. It has been our experience that the undecided student may often be misled by an "old pro" graduate student of questionable qualifications and experience. In many cases, the student determines his future direction in science after only a few minutes of discussion with his academic advisor. During our past two decades of teaching and counseling students, we have continued to be amazed and often embarrassed by the superficial planning and consideration often devoted to such crucial matters even by good students and, alas, sometimes by us, their advisors.

Part II discusses, in what we hope is a realistic light, life in that "academic salt mine," the graduate school. Our discussion runs the gamut from entrance to exit, including master's and doctoral studies, as well as that phenomenon which flowered in the fifties and sixties, the postdoctoral student.

Part III is the payoff. We consider the various career alternatives of industrial, academic, and government employment for the scientist, including the often unrecognized options which may unfold as his career emerges, such as administration, sales, and product development. In fact, the great majority of researchers ultimately become involved with these latter aspects of contemporary science.

Sexual discrimination in hiring has been as commonplace in the sciences as elsewhere in our business world. We have devoted a chapter in Part III to the unique position of the woman in science today. At this point we should warn our women readers that we have continued a common but questionable discriminatory practice in our presentation: for convenience the graduate student and the scientist are usually referred to as "he" only; "he or she" becomes extremely cumbersome when used continuously.

While we have tried to stress the practical "facts of life" associated with a scientific career, we must admit in all honesty to some personal prejudices in their presentation and to some boundary conditions which limit the scope of the book. Nevertheless, even though this book is directed specifically to the natural scientists and engineers, we believe that the philosophy extends to other areas. Because the authors' experience is primarily in the United States, some parts of our discussion will be of limited value to scientists in other countries; however, we hope that it might serve to introduce people in other parts of the world to life in American graduate schools.

We ask our many friends in the university, industry, government, and the business world who have either directly or indirectly helped us in the preparation of this book to be tolerant of this effort and to continue to educate us on the strengths and weaknesses of career offerings for scientists. We welcome your advice and criticisms.

2. "To Be or Not to Be"— The Decision to Attend Graduate School

It has become the "in thing" to proceed to graduate school after completion of the undergraduate science curriculum. Many factors influence the student's decision to enter a graduate program: his desire to further his intellectual prowess and to insure his future financial position, pressure from parents, relatives, and counselors alike, as well as in some cases the desire of the male student to avoid involvement with the armed services. However, today's student should not be so easily convinced that he *must* go to graduate school. It is essential that he make a sensible evaluation of his career goals and his individual abilities and interests.

A. INTELLECTUAL REWARDS

Charles F. Kettering once said that his interest was in the future because he was going to spend the rest of his life there. If you are about to graduate from college and are seriously thinking of graduate work, then your interest and goals should be focused on a spot in the future a decade or more hence. Here is the analytical justification for this: after proceeding

7

from your undergraduate college to graduate school, it will take you three to five years in graduate school before you obtain your Ph.D. If you then enter industrial life, you will start planning your research and development (R&D) programs for the subsequent five to eight years from the moment you reach the door of industry. It is well established that this five to eight year period is required to deliver a new product starting from a new idea; the average time is about seven years. Therefore, if you start R&D programs when you enter industry, you will probably not see the fruits of your labor, or at least the company won't see the fruits of your labor, for this period of time.

Interestingly enough, the situation will not be much different if you go into academic work. *Your* first graduate student will probably not finish his Ph.D. until four or five years after your arrival at the university. Add to this academic product lag, or the industrial product lag we mentioned previously, your four or five years in graduate school, and you can see that even as an undergraduate, you should be planning your career on the basis of research and products in a future world. Pause and look at the world a decade from now. Try to get an idea of what you would like to be doing then.

What will be the problems ten years from now? While it's difficult to know, you should, as you consider your future career, critically examine some of your interests and long-range goals. A recent report for General Electric that was circulated among its management was designed to get better input for its future growth. Eight forces for possible social change in the United States over the next ten years were identified:

(1) Increasing affluence
(2) Economic stabilization
(3) Rising tide of education

(4)   Changing attitudes towards work and leisure
(5)   Growing independence of institutions
(6)   Emergence of the "postindustrial" society
(7)   Strengthening of pluralism and individualism
(8)   The Negro-urban problem

These major social changes will certainly affect you as an individual as well as your future career in science. Think, then, about a decade hence in planning your graduate program and in choosing your area of employment.

Recently there has been a great change in national and international priorities in response to the public demand for a better quality of life on an individual as well as on a societal basis. The public is no longer willing to watch its tax dollars being poured into technological advancements while societal problems, which have been ignored too long, increase daily. It is demanding immediate action on these issues. This has caused a large shift in the research politics of government, industry, and the university. Consider, for example, the recent announcement in the United States of almost unlimited funds for cancer research, while support for the previously well-endowed aerospace industry has fallen to a new low.

Dr. Kenneth S. Pitzer, Professor of Chemistry at the University of California at Berkeley and former president of Rice and Stanford Universities, has recently commented on this change in science policy:[1]

> In spite of these clear successes, there has been since about 1964 a new questioning and criticism of science. In part this was a natural response to the pressure of the Vietnam war expenditures; the greatly increased science budgets were already targets for possible savings; nevertheless, the previously accepted rationale for the support of science has been questioned by some and sharply attacked by other . . . . Scientists themselves are raising new questions about the social value of their

work, and more particularly, about the new products which business or government may develop on the basis of scientific discoveries. I believe that we need to review the relationship between science and society.

There are a great many ramifications of this change in the support of various areas which have appeared, and these will continue to grow. Multidisciplinary research teams composed of researchers from the natural and social sciences, engineering, medicine, and law, will be necessary to tackle such problems as environmental pollution and urban planning. Such teams will require members who have a firm and very thorough background in one particular area, whether it be for example, economics or chemistry, but who are capable of expanding their specific knowledge to problems of wider scope.

Such a multidisciplinary attack is demonstrated by the recent activities of the University of California through its Statewide Air Pollution Research Center and Project Clean Air. Faculty are coordinating their efforts in air pollution within the framework of an overall system as shown in Figure 1. This involves researchers from a variety of fields and all of the University of California campuses. The critical feedback from legislation to research and development is indicated by the dashed lines in this figure. This is symbolic of the interdependence of "rules and research." Good legislation in the field of pollution is based on good fundamental and applied research. By the same token, the course of research in university, industry, and government is dictated to a great extent by legislation.

The need for multidisciplinary research efforts was recognized recently by the National Academy of Sciences in their announcement of a plan to expand the Academy over the next five years to include people in clinical research and in the social and behavioral sciences. NAS President, Dr. Philip Handler, commented that this action was ". . . the symbol of

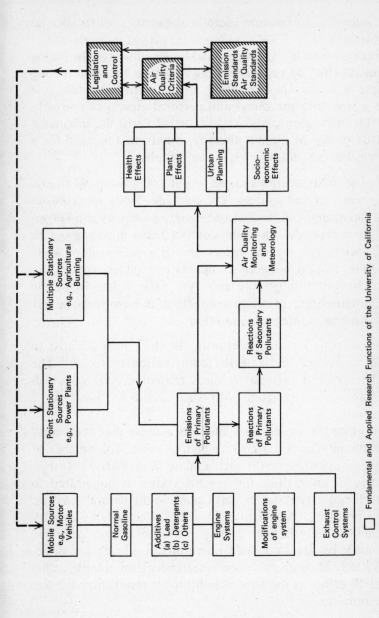

Figure 1: A model for the air pollution "system": Relationship between legislation, control, and research in a multidisciplinary attack on air pollution problems by the University of California.

☐ Fundamental and Applied Research Functions of the University of California

▨ Functions of Federal, State, and Local Legislative Bodies and Control Agencies

our intention to become usefully engaged . . ." in societal problems.[2]

Such a trend has great personal implications for the young scientist. The "do-your-own-thing" attitude for many young people is an attempt to establish a totally integrated life style into which both the career and personal aspects of one's life will blend harmoniously. Dr. Frederick Perls, the originator and developer of Gestalt therapy, points to this need for a homogeneous outlook in his autobiography:[3]

> The best solutions come about, of course, when the needs of self and society coincide. While the conflict between the individual and society is obvious and known to everybody, while the conflict between selling out to society and making one's own bed is nothing new, while the division between compliers and rebels remains unchanged through the ages, yet little is known of the internalizing of these conflicts and how to go about finding an integrative solution.

Here, then, is a real opportunity for the young scientist to make a genuine and relevant contribution to society. The intellectual and personal rewards gained may far outweigh the problems associated with such a break from "pure" science.

However, it would be foolish to assume that "relevant" multidisciplinary research is a bed of roses. The number of problems associated with such a many faceted attack is large. Firstly, in universities the reward system is not geared to multidisciplinary research, particularly in the natural sciences. Since problems that might be attacked effectively by a multidisciplinary approach are usually in themselves very complex, no quick results, or indeed no results at all, are promised. This often discourages young researchers from joining such a research effort as the lack of publishable results may damage his future career.

Secondly, even if his team obtains publishable results, the article must appear in a journal dealing with problems of wide scope, cutting across a number of academic boundaries. Often one's departmental peers downgrade or even frown on a young faculty member for publishing in journals which lack prestige. The authors can personally testify to this problem. One of us has recently had to fight for the promotion to tenure of a young scholar who produced an excellent piece of research within a multidisciplinary team but which, by its very nature, could not and should not have been published in a "class" journal of pure research.

Thirdly, a good deal of time and patience and coordination within the research team itself is required for the necessary communication between members of the group. However, it would seem that in the near future such difficulties must be surmounted if the multidisciplinary research effort is to fulfill its potential in solving the problems of society.

The past few years have also seen the advent of intense competition between basic and applied research. The swing has come quickly from "pure" research that at the time of publication has little practical, immediate application to applied research of more direct utility. In the opinion of the authors, such extreme oscillations will eventually do great harm to both science and society. While applied research is urgent and necessary to solve many contemporary societal problems, basic research will remain as the backbone of scientific progress. If our lack of foresight allows basic research to grind to a halt, we will suffer the consequences in a few short years. A balance between the two—basic and applied research—is critical.

There is much more than just the personal satisfaction the scientist may experience in attacking a socially relevant problem; there are untold intrinsic intellectual rewards to be gained from pitting all of one's creativity and ingenuity against Mother Nature's stubborn streak in any type of research. The thrill of that final experimental breakthrough or sudden flash of insight cannot be matched. These most rewarding experiences usually, but not always, follow the months or even years of frustration and hard work in scientific research. You, as young scientists, have undoubtedly had at least a taste of both the bitter and the sweet rewards of scientific work.

B.   THE EMPLOYMENT SITUATION

Throughout the sixties, leaders in industry, government, and the universities were crying "wolf" and pointing out serious deficiencies in the numbers of trained scientists and engineers. However, a drastic change in the employment situation occurred in 1969, making the future of the Ph.D. or M.S. not so rosy. In that year Nelson[4] noted that the job market for scientists was tightening. Federal grants for the training of scientists were cut by about twenty-five percent. A budget official commented, "Why do we have to keep giving added inducements to train people when we were having trouble placing the people we did train . . . . The need for scientists has been exaggerated across the board." Nelson concluded then that, "The days of a salary and security 'gravy train' for the scientists of only average abilities seem to be drawing to a close. Unless the tendency to cut back on federal science spending is reversed, it may well be that the scientific profession will be winnowed to those able scientists who are driven primarily by love of their work."

Nelson's predictions have indeed come true. All areas of science have been hit by the employment squeeze; as of June 1971[5] about 3.0% to 3.5% of all scientists and engineers in the United States were unemployed. However, particular areas such as physics and aerospace engineering are suffering more than others. Unemployment in physics as of May 1971 was 4%, and it was predicted that this could soon rise above the national unemployment level of 6.1%.[6] As of March 1970 in Los Angeles and Orange counties in Southern California alone, aerospace employment had fallen off 22% to 338,000 from a peak of 435,000 in December of 1967.[7]

In chemistry, the unemployment level in May 1971 was 2.7% but when one includes those chemists who are temporarily employed, employed part-time, or underemployed, this figure rises to 7.3%.[6] Recruiting on campuses in 1971 by chemical companies was down by as much as 50%, while hiring of new graduates was down by about 45%.[8] Furthermore, the situation is expected to get worse before it gets better.

The situation in university hiring of Ph.D.'s is also grim. Table 1, taken from an article by Cartter[9] gives the relationship between projected needs for new Ph.D. teachers and the expected supply, based on Cartter's doctoral projections. Note that the ratio of supply to needs in the period 1960 to 1969 was approximately 2:1, whereas by the early 1980's this ratio is predicted to be about 10:1. Hiring rates are already down. For example, the hiring rate of physics faculty has dropped to a rate of 1% to 2% in 1970 compared to one of 6% to 8% in the 1960's.

There are many causes for this turn in scientific fortunes. Dr. Frederick E. Terman has attributed the sudden change in the employment situation to three factors:[10] a decrease in the number of openings for Ph.D.'s in the universities, a leveling off of government financial support of academic research, and the shift in emphasis away from defense and space technology. These factors probably reflect changing public opinion as well as the economic situation.

The results of this bleak employment picture are fourfold. Firstly, salary levels are decreasing. The range of 1971 Ph.D. salary offers is from $9,500 to $16,000 a year, as compared to a range in 1970 of $10,000 to $18,000;[6] at the B.S. level the lower end of the pay scale decreased from $6,000 a year

TABLE 1:   New Ph.D.'s and New College Teachers with Doctorate Required to Maintain Quality of Faculty, 1960-1989.[a]

	Number (Thousands)		
	(1)	(2)	(3)
Period	Ph.D.'s Awarded	New Teachers (with Ph.D.) Required	Ratio (1)÷(2)
	ACTUAL		
1960-64	59.3	33.9	1.8
1965-69	103.6	41.5	2.5
	PROJECTED		
1970-74	157.6	47.7	3.3
1975-79	204.1	44.2	4.6
1980-84	258.0	27.1	9.5
1985-89	?	-0.4	

[a]From reference 9.

in 1970 to $5,760 in 1971.[6] Secondly, because employers now have a wide range of applicants from which to choose, they are demanding much better quality in their employees. Thirdly, industrial employers are in many cases choosing the B.S. graduate over the Ph.D. with the rather peculiar justification that the number of actual course credits required for the B.S. are not too far below that required for a Ph.D., with the emphasis of the latter degree on research.[6] Since industry often retrains the scientists anyway, the lower cost of the B.S. may be the deciding factor in his hiring. Finally, in Cartter's words:[9]

> The price of surplus of Ph.D.'s (surplus in terms of traditional jobs) is not unemployment, but rising underemployment. Associated with it frequently are personal disappointments and a gradual erosion of hard earned skills and intellectual agility. There is a social cost (about

$50,000 is directly invested in the individual with the Ph.D., plus an equivalent amount in others who began but did not complete the degree), but the human cost in unfulfilled expectations and discouragement may be even more important.

Even in the field of environmental sciences, the employment situation is, at best, only holding its own. According to recent estimates, the *need* for environmental professionals will triple by 1980.[11] Figure 2 shows the number of professional environmentalists that will be required "to make significant improvement in environmental quality in 1970, 1975, and 1980."[11] However, today we see little evidence that, in fact, this *need* will be satisfied. While there has been much talk, little hard cash has been poured into either the environmental sciences or elsewhere in the sciences. However, while the present situation even in this area is not optimistic,[8] it holds some promise for the future.

We see then that the existing need for graduate Ph.D. and M.S. students in science is for high quality rather than great quantity. A person who is neither highly qualified nor highly motivated should not proceed to graduate school. While it is true that the marginally qualified student will probably be able to find a university somewhere which will accept him, he must recognize that some graduate departments will accept almost any average college graduate to fill their pressing needs for the cheap labor of a teaching or research assistant. However, entrance into a program merely because one can be accepted insures neither the receipt of the advanced graduate degree nor success in science. Even if the degree is awarded through kindness or default of the faculty and/or perseverance on the part of the student, the borderline Ph.D. or M.S. graduate will face the frustrations and difficult challenges of competitive interactions with reputable products of legitimate graduate schools. This experience has proven to be very destructive to both the employee and the employer in many

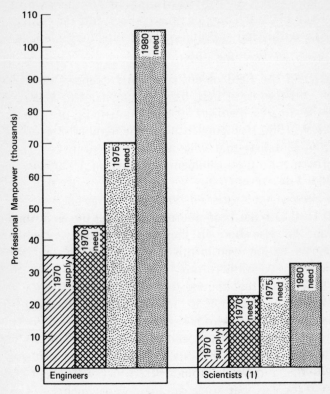

Figure 2:   Present supplies and predicted future requirements for professional engineers and scientists in environmental work, 1970, 1975, and 1980.

cases familiar to the authors. We estimate that a substantial number of the Ph.D. graduates of many universities today are inadequately endowed and improperly motivated to pursue the demanding career of the Ph.D. Their lives may indeed be less personally rewarding than those of a B.S. scientist, a good bricklayer, or a talented television repairman.

The awarding of a Ph.D. obviously does not insure a successful career in scientific research, education, or administration. However, it is clear that the chance of succeeding in a specific task favors the prepared mind. Dr. Alfred B. Garrett of Ohio State University has stated often that the success of a person in science can be attributed in large part to his serendipity. Certainly one cannot recognize and capitalize on the importance of many scientific observations without considerable insight and feel for the area of study. Scientists such as Charles F. Kettering or Thomas A. Edison, who had rather limited higher educations and yet contributed so significantly to the applied science areas, are rare today indeed.

There is no question that the choice of a graduate education is a sound one for the highly qualified person. It allows the student to review the fundamental principles of his own and related areas of science and to grasp, often for the first time, an overview of his general scientific knowledge. Through his graduate program, he can reach the threshold of published knowledge in his chosen specialty, and contribute significantly to the advancement of knowledge at the frontiers of that area. He works to develop some new and significant experimental or theoretical finding in his area. He then defends this finding before the established scientists within his area or in allied fields in his own university and, through the medium of his publications, among the international members of his scientific area.

It must be realized by the potential graduate student in science that graduate education is very different from that obtained at the undergraduate level. While it is true that there are some necessary courses and seminars as well as examinations, the unique accomplishment of the graduate student is his original and significant research contribution to his field as evidenced by his Ph.D. dissertation.

The Ph.D. graduates of the University of California are continually reminded of their specific qualifications for the Ph.D. degree. The Ph.D. diploma from the University of California, Los Angeles, reads in part as follows:

THE REGENTS OF THE UNIVERSITY OF CALIFORNIA
on the Nomination of the
Council of the Graduate Division, Southern Section
Have Conferred Upon

SAMUEL A. SCIENTIST

*Who Has Proved His Ability by Original
Research in Chemistry*
The Degree Doctor of Philosophy
With All of the Rights and Privileges Thereto Pertaining

· ·

Note that there is no mention made of the candidate having completed certain required courses, having passed qualifying examinations, or having satisfied other prerequisites to the degree.

The potential graduate student should carefully evaluate his interest in and potential ability to do independent research. Perhaps the best guide that the student can have in this matter is the opinions of his professors at his undergraduate school, particularly in the laboratory-oriented courses and his summer or part-time employer in science areas. These men can often recognize the desired research talent in a student through their observations of his attitude, integrity, perseverance, ingenuity, desire to learn, and ability to report ideas both orally and in written form. The student should seek the honest advice of both his teachers and employers.

The Ph.D. candidate must be as prepared for the continual frustrations of scientific failure as well as he is prepared for success in his research. In our own experience and that of many of our colleagues, we estimate that as few as 25% of the first attempts to solve a problem can be expected to be completely successful. The graduate research project is conceived in the human minds of the graduate student and his preceptor; it is only one potential route to the unraveling of some scientific problem. The plan may work well up to a point, but there will be necessary modifications and alternatives which must be developed as the real problem is faced. The power to recognize and observe carefully the unexpected as well as the expected results is fundamental to the true understanding of a problem and the attainment of a proper interpretation of a phenomenon. In the long run, the occurrence of the unexpected may prove to be more interesting and significant than the expected. If the scientist cannot work under these conditions, the Ph.D. degree is not for him.

C.   FINANCIAL REWARDS

As a group, scientists are not overpaid when one takes into account the very high intellectual capacity and the years of formal training required. This is clear if a comparison is made of the ratios of the median annual income of persons in specific professions to their mean years of schooling.

It is a common belief that today's mature undergraduate student is less interested in the financial rewards of his career than he is in the intellectual challenge and the feeling of social accomplishment which he might derive from it. Well schooled in this concept, one of the authors in speaking to a group of undergraduate science majors at a large university, accented the intellectual challenge and social accomplishment of scientific careers. After forty minutes of considering these intrinsic benefits, the first question (as well as the two succeeding ones) addressed to the discussion leader concerned the starting salary and the expected salary growth for workers in the various scientific areas. The simultaneous recognition, by both the professor and the students, of the obvious emphasis on the presumably mundane subject of salary compelled the embarrassed students and professor to justify the apparent interest. Some agreement was eventually reached that the ideal future position is one which would provide sufficient financial gain to allow a comfortable living for the person and his family, but more important it would give the scientist a sense of accomplishment in planning, designing and/or producing some concept, equipment, or material to improve the intellectual or physical well-being and enjoyment of the populace. However, it is interesting to note that some administrators believe that a definite price tag can be attached to some young scientists.*

It can be shown easily that the financial rewards of a graduate education are quite generous. In the years that are required to obtain a Ph.D., a minimal stipend is usually provided for the graduate student. Integrating over a forty-year period of employment, however, one sees that this frugal graduate school life reaps tremendous dividends. For example, a Bachelor of Science student in chemistry may start his career at about $5,000 per year more than the teaching assistant or research assistant in graduate school. If we assume a period of four years to earn a Ph.D., the bachelor's student who goes directly to industrial employment will earn about $20,000 more than his colleague who went to graduate school in this period. However, the Ph.D. scientist quickly recovers from his relatively poor financial position. For example, consider the published annual salary data for chemists, summarized in Figure 3. These data suggest that during the forty-year working lifetime of the average B.S. and Ph.D. chemists in industry, the Ph.D. chemist will earn approximately $132,000 more than the B.S. chemist. There is no question that the advanced degree is a financially sound investment. Therefore, the major concern

*An eminent authority in air pollution control, with considerable experience in hiring young scientists and engineers for his state control agency, recently said to us: "The difference between a student working for me as an air pollution 'ecologist' and going to work for the 'polluter' industry is about $1,000. If I offer him $11,000 and industry offers no more than $12,000, he'll take the cut; otherwise he generally goes with them."

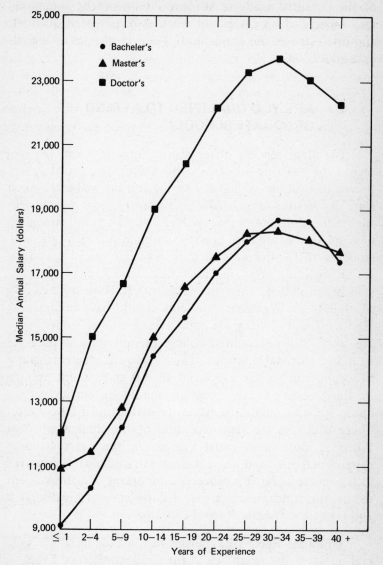

Figure 3: Chemists' median annual salary for 1969 as a function of years of service. (Data from ref. 12.)

of the potential graduate student should not be the monetary aspects of his career but whether or not he is qualified and interested in the opportunities and challenges of a graduate education.

D.   ARE YOU QUALIFIED TO ATTEND GRADUATE SCHOOL?

Graduate schools differ significantly in their requirements for entering students. The prestigious, privately endowed institutions of higher learning and the well-established state universities are usually significantly more selective in their admissions policy. Many older institutions and struggling new universities are hard pressed to obtain sufficient graduate students to fill the slots in their graduate teaching and research assistant programs, and these schools tend to lower standards to satisfy their manpower needs. However, as a rule of thumb, undergraduate students should have obtained at least a 3.0 out of 4.0 grade point average in their undergraduate work at an accredited college or university if they are to have a reasonable chance of success in a graduate program. Students who receive a 3.5 out of 4.0 grade point average in their undergraduate program should be encouraged to apply for either national, state, or institutional fellowships. There is always the rare exception of the student who has taken a more than usual interest in the extracurricular campus activities and has not demonstrated his full potential in his course work. It is especially important that this student review the fundamental areas of knowledge of his discipline and take the Graduate Record Examination.[13]

Graduate Record Examinations.   Academicians in general question the reliability of the Graduate Record Exam as a complete guide to the student's ability to do graduate work. However, nearly all graduate departments require that the

Graduate Record Exam, or some other similar institution-designed test, be taken by those candidates for graduate school who have a grade point average below 3.0. It is not uncommon to admit the academically questionable student if he has placed high on the Graduate Record Exam, in the belief that some independent proof of his qualifications for further training is necessary in lieu of an outstanding undergraduate record. It is not only the applicant with the questionable record who should be encouraged to take the Graduate Record Exam, but also the outstanding student who plans to apply for national fellowships. In our opinion, every student who plans to enter a graduate program in the sciences should take these examinations. The review which the student makes prior to the examination will benefit his grasp of the subject matter, and the results of the examination will provide the student, as well as the university, with some feeling for the student's chances of success in graduate school.

In many respects the Graduate Record Examination is similar to the aptitude tests encountered at entrance to the university undergraduate programs. It is designed to measure both the educational background and the general scholastic ability of the student. The test is divided into several sections. The aptitude test measures both verbal and mathematical ability; it is neither an intelligence test nor an achievement test. There are questions that involve such facets as verbal reasoning, reading comprehension, arithmetic reasoning, and interpretation of graphs and diagrams. In the aptitude portion of the Graduate Record Exam, a period of two and one-half hours is allowed.

The second part of the Graduate Record Examination is the advanced test. This is designed to measure comprehension of the basic material in the student's field. Students are expected to be familiar with all of the basic undergraduate subject matter of importance in that particular area. Advanced tests are offered in the scientific areas of biology, chemistry, economics, engineering, geology, mathematics, physics, philosophy, psychology, and sociology. A period of three hours is allowed to complete the advanced test.

The Graduate Record Exam is given several times a year throughout the country and also at selected centers outside the United States. It is important that the student apply to take the examination early in his senior year. A formal application with the Educational Testing Service is made, and a modest examination fee is required. The forms are available through most university administrative departments and graduate schools. The Educational Testing Service returns a ticket of admission to you which indicates the exact address to which you should report and the time the examination will be given. This ticket of admission is needed in order to enter the examination room. A report of your scores will be sent to you and, without additional fee, to three graduate or professional schools if you designate them on your original application. The authors suggest that the potential graduate student read the more detailed resume of the Graduate Record Examination in such publications as that of Gruber.[13] These publications give sample examinations and some sage advice to which the concerned student may wish to refer on the psychology and preparation for the examinations.

E.   CHANGING VIEWS IN EDUCATION—THE MASTER OF SCIENCE AS A TERMINAL DEGREE VERSUS THE DOCTOR OF PHILOSOPHY

In some institutions an immediate choice of ultimate career goal, M.S. or Ph.D., must be made by the new graduate student. In the older educational system, obtaining an M.S. degree was considered to be a necessary prerequisite for acceptance to the Ph.D. program. There are still some scientists steeped in the rich traditions of the past who maintain that this practice continues to have real virtue. They argue that the student proves himself through selected course work and the completion of a minor, but not trivial, research problem. The year or two required for this allows the preceptor to judge the likelihood of the student's success in the Ph.D. program. However, this is not the current philosophy with most large graduate science departments offering both the M.S. and Ph.D. programs.

It is common practice today for the student to enter the graduate program without specifying the final degree sought. (However, in some cases the graduate school of the university may require the student to record his initial degree choice.) After required course work and/or examinations have been completed, the decision is made by the graduate faculty as to which degree the student should pursue. In most institutions, the master's degree program is required of those students who have performed with less than success on the preliminary courses and tests and yet have an overall B average or better which allows them to remain in graduate school. The master's degree is a terminal award in many of these cases, and the student is thus labeled as not being Ph.D. material, at least at that institution. Thus the M.S. degree in the sciences today is most often a consolation prize which is awarded in lieu of a Ph.D.[14]

However, it should be emphasized that there are still several smaller universities and colleges which offer only the master's degree. Many of these are fine institutions with high requirements and excellent research programs. The Master of Science degree is a very legitimate reward for study at these institutions. In fact, in some cases, particularly in mathematics, an M.S. may be more desirable than a Ph.D., in that the M.S. is qualified to teach in academic institutions such as junior colleges which, until recently, have had difficulty in attracting and holding qualified Ph.D.'s.

The graduate student should consider carefully his alternatives in the graduate program. In the opinion of the authors there is little, if any, benefit in obtaining a master's degree

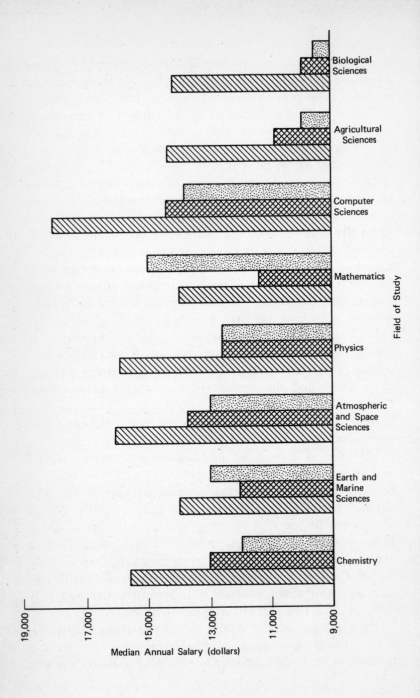

Median Annual Salary (dollars)

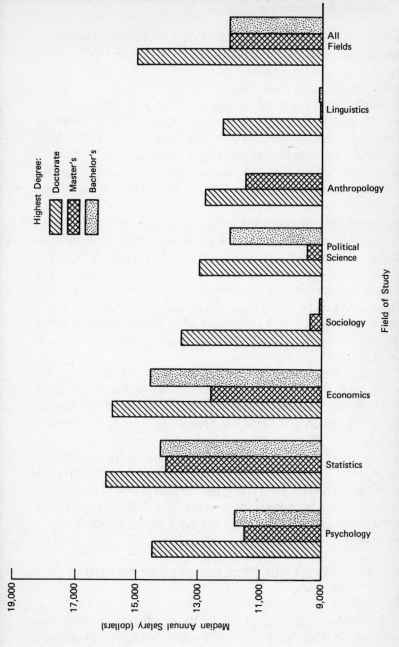

Figure 4: Median annual salaries for full-time employed civilian scientists for various fields of study, 1968. (Data from ref. 15.)

in most of the sciences today. This conclusion is based on several facts. In the first place, the extra year or two which the B.S. student may spend in receipt of the master's degree will provide little financial reward. This is evident in Figure 4 which gives the median annual salaries for full-time employed civilian scientists in various fields of study. Note for example, that in physics the B.S. scientist and the M.S. scientist have exactly the same median annual salary. Perhaps more surprising is that M.S. scientists in the earth and marine sciences, economics, mathematics, psychology, political science, and statistics, have a lower median annual salary than B.S. scientists in the same area. Surely this reflects, at least in part, the genuine distrust of the qualifications and abilities of the scientists whose highest degree is the Master of Science. It appears that there is a tendency to look on a person with a master's degree as one who tried but failed to obtain a Ph.D. This view prevails regardless of the fact that there are many extremely capable M.S. scientists who, for financial or other reasons, were forced to terminate their graduate education short of a Ph.D.

Under the present circumstances, the student must be advised of the limited usefulness of the master's degree in most of the sciences. There is at least one exception to this reasoning. When a student has been away from the university and the use of scientific principles for some time, he may feel the need for extensive review of his basic discipline and for recovery of his self-confidence in his ability to do graduate work. In this case, where the motivation is one of ultimately improving one's chances of success in a Ph.D. program, the extra year or two spent in a master's program can be most beneficial.

F. THE GAMBLE ON SUCCESS IN GRADUATE SCHOOL

There are a great many variables which determine success or failure in graduate education. Even if you have an excellent undergraduate record and an extensive knowledge of your field, you are not assured of success in a graduate program. While you must maintain a satisfactory performance in your courses, pass the qualifying examinations, and fulfill the language requirements, the true test is the successful completion of an original piece of research which adds significant new knowledge to your particular field. Unfortunately, the graduate student cannot, with any degree of certainty, tell his spouse or other long-suffering benefactors that his research work will be completed after one, two, three, or more years. The completion of the Ph.D. student's research depends very strongly on his imagination, originality, diligence, productivity, and pure good fortune as a research scientist. Even the best classroom academician among the graduate students can be a complete failure as a research scientist. However, this is certainly the exception; the academically sound student has the most reasonable chance of success in his research, especially if he applies himself to his work diligently. The most common source of problems in graduate school is the failure of the borderline student to meet the academic standards of the department. But don't fool yourself; you cannot expect to spend a quiet year or two in course work and then one or two years of casual research effort and still be successful in your program. Hard, long hours and many frustrations, as well as the most gratifying successes, are to be expected in working at the frontiers of scientific research.

Data are available which reflect the chance of success of the chemistry B.S. student in a graduate program. In Figure 5 we can trace the educational path of the B.S. chemist as derived from our various data sources.[16] Note that in the case of the chemist, about 34% of all B.S. graduate chemistry majors enter graduate programs. The other 66% go to immediate employment, the majority in industry and government work. Of those entering graduate school, about 25% enter the Ph.D. program and are ultimately awarded this degree. About 42% are either required or choose to enter the master's

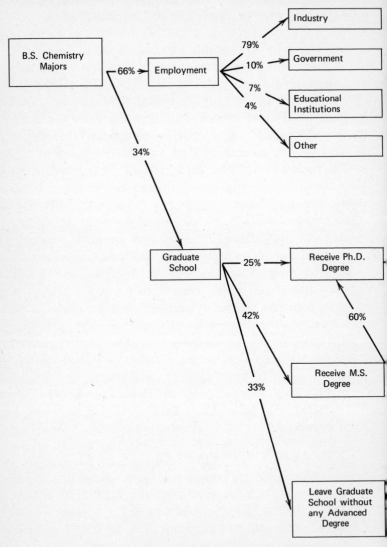

Figure 5: The educational and occupational paths of chemists in the United States. Data are only approximate and based on the author's extrapolation.

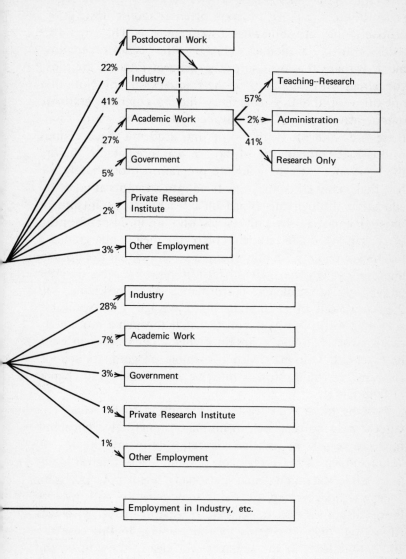

program. Some 60% of those who receive the M.S. degree proceed into the Ph.D. program often at another institution, probably one with somewhat lower standards. The other 40% enter industry, academic work, or other types of employment. Perhaps the most surprising data of Figure 5 are those concerned with the failure of the graduate student. Note that one-third of the B.S. chemistry majors entering graduate school leave without any advanced degree. In many cases, these are students with borderline academic backgrounds whose high probability of failure was predictable before their entrance into the graduate program. Unfortunately, we feel that many students are enticed into attempts at graduate education through the award of a teaching assistantship or other financial aid by universities who are in desperate need of cheap graduate student help in their undergraduate teaching programs. An honest appraisal shows that the borderline student is often offered false hopes of success. If your undergraduate academic performance was borderline, say 2.8 to 3.0 out of a 4.0 grade point average at a responsible academic institution, yet you feel that through a more dedicated effort you can maintain higher quality work in graduate school, you may wish to gamble on graduate school. However, if you do so, you must be warned that your chance of failure is great.

Perhaps there is at least one exception to the rule. The student may do very well in his major in natural science, but for one reason or another he can't, or won't, hack that "Humanities 1A," German, or alas and alack, English grammar. While the student may personally regret poor performances in these humanistic fields they generally will not seriously affect his research career, at least in the earlier stages (they well may affect his overall career). In this case the student's talents in the sciences will clearly show up in the Graduate Record Examinations and understanding deans and departmental advisors may waive the usual requirement of an overall B average.

G. THE ROLE OF YOUR SPOUSE IN YOUR GRADUATE EDUCATION

While a discussion of the role of your spouse in your graduate career may seem a statement of the obvious, it is the authors' personal experience that too often your spouse's attitude to your graduate career is overlooked, when in fact it can be a major factor in determining your success. Your wife or husband can literally make you or break you in graduate school, and it is essential that you have his or her full support at all times during this especially difficult period. It requires a great deal of understanding, patience, and maturity on your spouse's part to accept that you must put in unusually long hours at work. Even when you are at home, your mind may be occupied with the strange results of that last experiment or with planning the next one. They must also be willing to accept meager pay and the frustrations of not being able to plan on a set number of years in graduate school. All of these factors require a rather special marriage partner if your graduate career is to be a happy and successful one. In making the decision to attend graduate school, we urge you to be sure to take this into account.

3. The Crucial Questions: What, Where, Why, and How?

Once you have made the final decision to enter graduate school, several crucial questions arise which will have far-reaching effects on your scientific career: What will be your area of concentration? Where should you do your graduate work? Why? How will you support yourself financially? Let's consider these and other related questions now.

A. WHAT AREA? THE EVALUATION OF FUTURE OPPORTUNITIES

At this point you probably have a fairly firm conviction of the area of science of greatest interest to you. However, regardless of the past history of your interests, this is the time to make a careful evaluation of your goals in life. What do you want out of life? What do you want to be doing ten years from now—twenty years from now? How important to you is your economic status in years ahead? How available to you are opportunities for administration, teaching, research, and service? A point well made by Moore is that the first and continuing responsibility of the scientist is self-appraisal.[17] Too often a person chooses his vocation by chance, only to discover later that he is dissatisfied and would like to try something more challenging, dynamic, or rewarding.

In considering what field to enter, an evaluation of future opportunities is essential. One can gain some measure of the degree of employment activity in the various areas of science through a study of the numbers of scientists employed in the various scientific fields as shown in Figure 6. In 1968 the National Science Foundation poll showed that chemists represent about 32% of all United States' scientists with either a B.S., M.S., or Ph.D.; about 26% of all Ph.D. scientists in the United States have their degree in chemistry. Of the total of all Ph.D. scientists, those in various other major areas amount to about 20% in the biological sciences, 13% each in physics and psychology, 6% in mathematics, 5% in economics, 4% each in the earth and marine sciences, and smaller percentages in other areas of science. While these are taken from 1968 data and employment activity has changed somewhat since then, they should give a reasonable estimate of the relative activity in various scientific fields today.

However, one should bear in mind the earlier comments made on the present state of flux in the employment situation. There is an obvious tendency towards research activity in all fields bearing on environmental and societal problems, and the effects of this will be felt in the near future. See Figure 2, for example.

Don't feel that it is necessary to take advanced study in exactly the same area as that of your undergraduate training, although this has been the common practice. For example, if you majored in physics or mathematics, you may wish to investigate the opportunities for graduate study in biophysics, theoretical chemistry, or other attractive areas which build on the rich mathematical background of your undergraduate training. There are many examples of very successful scientists who changed areas of study at the point of entering graduate school. The highly regarded theoretical chemist,

Professor Leland C. Allen of Princeton University, received his undergraduate degree in electrical engineering, with practically no formal course work in chemistry. He entered graduate school in chemistry and overcame the deficiencies in his undergraduate chemistry largely through his own study. His prowess in mathematics was his most important prerequisite for success in theoretical chemistry. There aren't many Leland Allens in the scientific world, but you may be one, and you should seriously consider alternative paths in your graduate study.

Write to the headquarters of the national societies which represent potential areas of interest to you. Ask that career opportunity booklets be sent to you. However, recognize the fact that there is much pure propaganda in such information. The national societies which represent the various science areas have become good public relations men in their efforts to expand their influence and the affluence of their members. You can sort out the obvious trash and learn a lot about areas of possible interest from such publications. Don't stop with this, but also seek out a local practicing scientist or two in these areas, and test the statements made in the career booklets. They probably are right, but they may be colored a bit towards the rosy side. A list of sources of career materials for most scientific areas is given in the Table A-1 of the Appendix.

While it should play a minor part in your choice of an area of concentration, you may wish to consider the salary structure in the various scientific fields when making your decision. Data from the N.S.F. *American Science Manpower, 1968* indicate that then the highest median annual salary among the full-time employed civilian scientists was in the area of computer sciences (see Figure 4). Ph.D.'s in atmospheric and space sciences and statistics ranked next in salary, while Ph.D.'s in physics and economics received the next highest compensation. The lowest paying fields were those of political science, anthropology and linguistics. (See the Appendix,

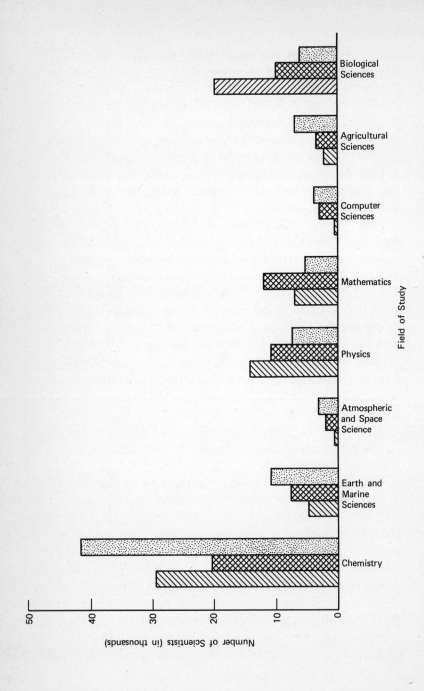

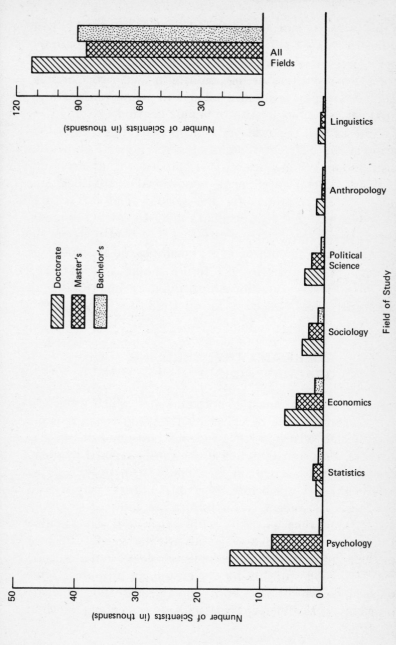

Figure 6: Distribution of United States scientists by field and highest degree held, 1968. (Data from ref. 15.)

Table A-2, for more complete salary data of scientists with different employers.) Although the salary is certainly not the only factor one must consider, it does tend to reflect the competitive position of the graduate in that particular area. The law of supply and demand acts to maintain a relatively low salary structure in areas of limited demand.

Note as well the availability of opportunities for employment in the different types of agencies. Figure 7 shows the distribution of the scientists employed in industry and business, federal government, educational institutions, and nonprofit organizations for the various fields of science. In Table A-3 of the Appendix, a more complete resume of these data is given. It appears that if you plan to pursue graduate study in anthropology, linguistics, or sociology, for example, your plans for the future should anticipate employment in an educational institution as opportunities in the other areas, at least as of 1968, are very limited.

B.   WHERE AND WHY? CHOOSING YOUR GRADUATE SCHOOL

Probably the most important factor which influences the student's choice of university for graduate study is the counsel and advice of the student's undergraduate faculty advisors. Unfortunately, this advice can be colored by prejudices which are based on very limited experiences of the advisor many years before. A graduate advisor may seek to send his best student to his former preceptor or to a close associate at some university with which he is very familiar. Universities often make a vigorous attempt to enlist the help of the faculty of small undergraduate colleges in the procurement of good students for their graduate programs. Some universities which have both undergraduate and graduate programs work out reciprocal trade agreements in which at least an attempt is made to trade budding Ph.D. candidates like commodities on the stock market.

It is important that the potential graduate student thoroughly investigate the quality and reputation of the available graduate programs. Listen to the advice of your colleagues, but do some serious study, planning, and thinking on your own as well. You may want to take into account a number of personal considerations, such as a desire not to throw yourself into a very large impersonal institution after undergraduate training at a smaller, more personal college or university. On the other hand, you may wish to avoid a small university in that its very limited staff and equipment may not allow you access to all of the important research tools which are available at the larger institutions. Such considerations will vary from person to person and no general advice can be given. Therefore, we will overlook such factors and consider only the more practical and universal aspects of examining potential graduate schools. Your selection of a list of potential graduate schools can be initiated through literature which is available in most university libraries.

Let's consider briefly some of this literature. One rather widely used and significant document is the Cartter report, on *An Assessment of Quality in Graduate Education.*[19] Cartter has wisely indicated that quality in a graduate school is not easily subjected to measurement. However, there are some common features of graduate schools which suggest the presence of quality: the size of the endowment, the number of books in the library, the publication record of the faculty, the level of faculty salaries, the number of Nobel Laureates, Guggenheim fellows, or members of the National Academy of Sciences on the faculty who participate actively in the graduate program, and the number of Woodrow Wilson, National Science Foundation, National Institutes of Health, and other similarly honored fellows in the graduate school. However, these measures of quality were not used

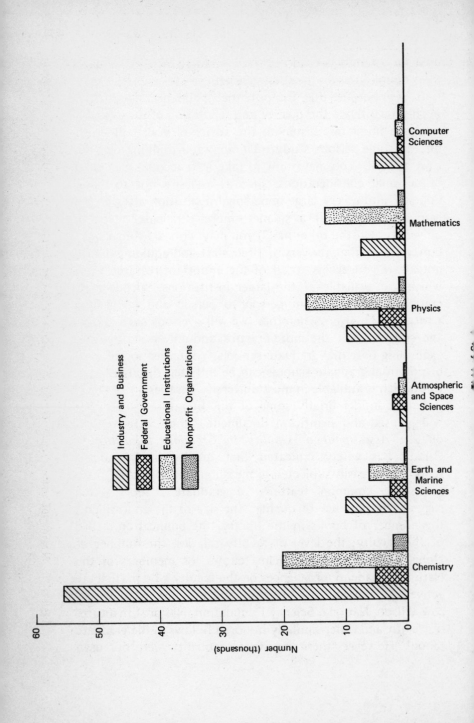

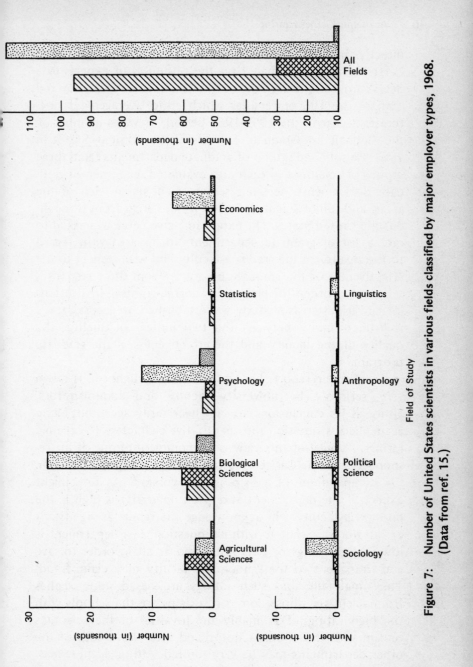

Figure 7: Number of United States scientists in various fields classified by major employer types, 1968. (Data from ref. 15.)

directly in the evaluation of Cartter and his associates. Cartter's report was based on the responses of experts to a detailed questionnaire sent out in 1964. This report covered each of the 106 universities which either averaged ten doctorates a year in the 1953-1962 period, or was a member of the Council on Graduate Schools in the United States in 1961. He solicited ratings of graduate departments from three groups of scientists in each area evaluated: chairmen of graduate departments, selected senior scientists in each of the areas, and junior scientists in the various areas from throughout the United States. The expert in a given area was asked to rate a list of graduate departments in his area with regard to the quality of the graduate faculty and with respect to the effectiveness of the graduate program. From these responses a "pecking order" of prestigious degree-granting institutions in the various areas of study was established. In general, there is little disparity between the two indices of quality: the quality of the faculty and the effectiveness of the graduate program.

The Cartter report, because of its thoroughness, is taken very seriously by university faculty and administrators, although its conclusions are not necessarily accepted. Many academicians question the quantitative character of academic ratings. Typical of this view is the comment of one of the respondents to the Cartter questionnaire; quoting Dr. Johnson, "A compendium of gossip is still gossip." As one might expect, if the department at a given university is high in the rating, its faculty will acknowledge the report as significant or, at worst, accept it without question. If a department is low in the ratings or it is not listed at all in order to save embarrassment to the school, the faculty may claim fraud. They maintain that such ratings are based upon replies from scientists whose dominant origins are the schools with the high ratings. Presumably the loyalties of the scientists remain with their home schools, and their knowledge of the other departments may be very limited. Although there may be some element of truth to this suspicion, the fact remains that the commission which designed the sampling and statistical methods of the Cartter report used careful planning and sound methods in deriving their ratings. Sincere attempts were made to overcome the objections mentioned.

The most serious difficulty with the use of these ratings, in our opinion, is the rather large lag which must occur between the time of the report and the time at which the impressions of the respondents were formulated regarding the quality of the graduate programs in the various departments. Many new universities which have just started graduate programs have not had the opportunity to demonstrate the effectiveness of their graduate programs and the quality of their graduates. Furthermore, all universities are continuing to undergo significant changes both in faculty and in graduate programs. The outstanding scientists in each area receive attractive offers to join other faculties, and there is a significant movement of many of the best scientists between the universities. Likewise, the unimpressive faculty who have not received tenure are often dropped. In spite of these and other deficiencies which are inherent in all rating systems, they are a convenient guide to the potential graduate student.

You can be sure that the competition is very keen for the entering slots in the graduate programs at the top-rated institutions. If your undergraduate academic qualifications are outstanding, you may expect to compete favorably for the top-rated departments. If your qualifications are marginal, it is unlikely that you will be accepted by the departments rated as "Distinguished," "Strong," or "Good." There is some question as to your chances of acceptance even in departments rated as "Adequate Plus." Of course, if the results of your Graduate Record Examination and your recommendations from the undergraduate faculty reflect a high potential for success in graduate school, exceptions to these generalizations will occur.

We suggest that you check the information on your area of interest which is contained in the report of Cartter (1966)[19a] and the more recent report of Roose and Anderson, *A Rating of Graduate Programs* (1970).[19b] These lists should provide some counsel for you in your graduate school selection process. In the tables are the top universities as picked by leading scientists in some particular field. If you decide on a department for graduate study which is low or not on the list at all, you should satisfy yourself that the department has now become better recognized nationally or that there are other circumstances that make the logic of your decision sound. It is a good idea to apply for admission to one school which you would very much like to attend but for which your qualifications seem to be somewhat lacking. You may underestimate your potential and be accepted; it doesn't hurt to have tried.

Obviously, there are many possible alternative rating systems of graduate science departments. Let's consider one such system which may be used. Since 26% of all the Ph.D. scientists employed in the United States are chemists, it is of interest perhaps to consider the attractiveness of the chemistry Ph.D. granting institutions from this alternative point of view. We may illustrate by means of this system a few of the many criteria which are presumably student oriented and which the Cartter and Roose and Anderson reports do not consider. The considerations given here, of course, are applicable to other areas where detailed information can be collected to make such an analysis. In Table 2, a comparison is made of the most prolific chemistry Ph.D. granting universities in the United States and Canada (1965-1967).[16d] It is interesting that more than one-half of the Ph.D. degrees granted in chemistry in the United States in 1966-1967 came from only twenty nine of these departments. However, we should not deceive ourselves into thinking that bigness is greatness or that quality in the product is necessarily maximized by maximizing the number of degrees granted.

There are many factors which the graduate student may weigh in the determination of the university in which he will do his graduate work. The following are seen as particularly significant to us:

(1)   He would like to spend his time efficiently in graduate school and receive his degree after thorough study and experience, but without prolonged delay.

(2)   He would like to attend a graduate school in which there is a faculty to graduate student ratio which allows him to have a significant, meaningful interaction with his professors.

(3)   He wants to attend a university at which the graduate faculty and research work are of high quality; he wants his thesis work to have an excellent chance for recognition by the scientific community through publication in a reputable journal.

(4)   He would like to attend a graduate department which has sufficient money for research equipment, supplies, fellowships, or research assistantships.

(5)   He would like to attend a graduate school where the faculty members not only know their subjects well, but where they communicate their knowledge well to the students; in other words, the student would like to have a faculty of excellent teachers.

From the American Chemical Society's published data for graduate faculties in chemistry[16d] we can derive some qualitative tests for quality of the department as measured by the first four of the above factors. Since these data are several years old at the time of this writing, conclusions based on their use may not be valid for the conditions which exist at these institutions today, but they can be used to illustrate this student-oriented rating method. You may, however, ap-

TABLE 2: Comparison of the Most Prolific Chemistry Ph.D. Granting Universities in the United States and Canada (1965-1967).[a]

University	(1) Ph.D. Degrees Granted 1965-66	(2) Ph.D. Degrees Granted 1966-67	(3) No. Full-Time Staff as of 9/67	(4) No. Full-Time Grad. Students Enrolled as of 10/66	(5) No. Postdoctoral Fellows as of 10/66	(6) No. Publications of Faculty 1965-67	(7) Fed. Support to Science Depts. (Other than R&D) 1967; dollars $\times 10^{-3}$	(8) $\frac{(1)+(2)}{(4)}$	(9) $\frac{(3)+(5)/2}{(4)}$	(10) $\frac{(3)+\frac{3}{4}(4)+(5)}{(6)}$	(11) $\frac{(7)}{(3)} \times 10^{-5}$	(12) $(8)\times(9)\times(10)\times(11) \times 10^{-4}$
Univ. Illinois	51	57	45	363	50	381	13,786	0.30	0.19	1.04	3.1	1.8
Univ. Wisconsin	50	55	38	311	36	218	12,136	0.34	0.18	0.71	3.2	1.4
Univ. Calif., Berkeley	43	52	48	279	70	303	14,449	0.34	0.30	0.93	3.0	2.8
Purdue Univ.	35	50	46	405	36	280	8,260	0.21	0.16	0.73	1.8	0.4
Mass. Inst. Technol.	48	40	39	255	87	310	5,710	0.35	0.32	0.98	1.5	1.7
Ohio State Univ.	36	36	37	281	46	234	10,474	0.26	0.21	0.80	2.8	1.2
Northwestern Univ.	17	35	26	151	46	241	4,880	0.34	0.32	1.30	1.9	2.7
Iowa State Univ. Sci. & Technol.	33	33	34	229	36	215	4,823	0.29	0.23	0.89	1.4	0.8
Harvard Univ.	19	30	28	152	76	226	13,132	0.32	0.43	1.04	4.7	6.8
Univ. Texas at Austin	30	30	42	237	49	203	8,814	0.25	0.28	0.75	2.1	1.1
Univ. Florida	20	29	32	155	43	152	6,629	0.32	0.35	0.80	2.1	1.9
Indiana Univ.	34	28	33	180	34	173	9,314	0.34	0.28	0.86	2.8	2.3

Polytech. Inst. Brooklyn	27	27	252	16	112	c	0.21	0.14	0.48	----	----
Cornell Univ.	35	27	182	68	287	9,736	0.34	0.38	1.19	2.7	4.2
Univ. Washington	27	27	205	10	107	13,333	0.26	0.16	0.56	4.8	1.1
Univ. Minnesota	24	25	174	46	158	15,644	0.28	0.31	0.76	5.0	3.2
Columbia Univ.	23	24	137	37	107	10,101	0.34	0.37	0.66	4.8	4.0
Univ. Pennsylvania	21	24	174	34	138	11,025	0.26	0.24	0.73	4.6	2.1
Wayne State Univ.	16	24	203	19	130	4,226	0.20	0.18	0.66	1.6	0.4
Case-Western Reserve Univ.	12	23	206	24	202	> 6,937d	0.17	0.23	0.94	> 1.9	> 0.7
Penn. State Univ.	27	23	168	9	95	7,233	0.30	0.24	0.56	2.0	0.8
Univ. British Columbia	21	22	126	18	260	c	0.34	0.41	1.67		
Univ. Kansas	18	21	152	14	131	6,661	0.26	0.20	0.87	2.9	1.3
Univ. Maryland	12	20	182	12	73	8,313	0.18	0.18	0.42	3.2	0.4
Stanford Univ.	15	20	130	48	227	12,310	0.27	0.35	1.36	5.9	7.6
Calif. Inst. Technol.	16	19	158	58	236	2,527	0.22	0.44	1.09	0.6	0.6
Univ. Delaware	16	18	135	10	65	c	0.25	0.16	0.51	----	----
State Univ. Rutgers	19	18	187	16	62	4,578	0.20	0.15	0.35	2.3	0.2
Univ. Calif., Los Angeles	20	17	179	58	227	10,458	0.21	0.38	0.98	2.7	2.1
Univ. Chicago	18	17	203	35	241	10,755	0.17	0.23	1.11	3.6	1.6
Ill. Inst. Technol.	15	17	105	11	74	c	0.30	0.27	0.65	----	
Univ. Iowa	8	17	106	3	83	6,077	0.24	0.19	0.81	3.2	1.2
McGill Univ.	20	17	135	35	124	c	0.27	0.35	0.75	----	
Univ. Michigan	18	17	136	20	114	12,921	0.26	0.35	0.71	3.4	2.2
Univ. Arizona	5	16	97	26	126	3,403	0.22	0.42	0.99	1.2	1.1
Univ. Colorado	19	16	132	17	135	10,095	0.27	0.30	0.92	3.3	2.5
Georgia Inst. Technol.	8	16	102	7	69	c	0.24	0.29	0.63	----	----
Kansas State Univ.	20	16	93	1	63	3,355	0.39	0.24	0.68	1.5	1.0
Univ. New Hampshire	8	16	69	3	38	c	0.35	0.27	0.53	----	----
Oregon State Univ.	16	16	160	5	72	3,441	0.20	0.15	0.49	1.6	0.2
Univ. Pittsburgh	16	16	118	23	113	8,296	0.27	0.34	0.80	2.9	2.1

TABLE 2 (Continued)

University	(1) Ph.D. Degrees Granted 1965-66	(2) Ph.D. Degrees Granted 1966-67	(3) No. Full-Time Staff as of 9/67	(4) No. Full-Time Grad. Students Enrolled as of 10/66	(5) No. Postdoctoral Fellows as of 10/66	(6) No. Publications of Faculty 1965-67	(7) Fed. Support to Science Depts. (Other than R&D) 1967; dollars $\times 10^{-3}$	(8) $\frac{(1) + (2)}{(4)}$	(9) $\frac{(3) + (5)/2}{(4)}$	(10) $\frac{\frac{(3)+3(4)+(5)}{4}}{(6)}$	(11) $\frac{(7)}{(3)} \times 10^{-5}$	(12) $(8)\times(9)\times(10)\times(11)$ $\times 10^{-4}$
Princeton Univ.	26	16	30	98	50	236	2,857	0.43	0.56	1.53	1.0	3.7
Univ. Alberta	12	14	30	131[b]	40	189	c	0.20	0.38	1.13	----	----
Univ. Cincinnati	16	14	17	100[b]	4	44	4,280	0.26	0.17	0.41	2.5	0.5
Michigan State Univ.	15	14	28	182	12	112	6,753	0.16	0.19	0.63	2.4	0.5
Univ. North Carolina	14	14	24	111	22	85	10,009	0.25	0.32	0.66	4.2	2.2
Univ. Notre Dame	16	14	24	86	25	120	2,720	0.35	0.42	1.05	1.1	1.7
Rensselaer Polytech. Inst.	14	14	23	91	18	96	3,292	0.31	0.35	0.88	1.4	1.3
Univ. Utah	13	14	19	71	18	180	7,067	0.38	0.39	2.00	3.7	11.0
Yale Univ.	30	14	23	124	31	43	8,742	0.38	0.39	0.29	3.8	1.2
Univ. Calif., Riverside	12	13	18	72	20	104	c	0.35	0.31	1.13	----	----
Inst. Paper Chemistry	8	13	21	41	3	54	c	0.51	0.55	1.00	----	----
Louisiana State Univ.	14	13	28	99	15	83	c	0.27	0.36	0.71	----	----
New York Univ.	12	13	28	97	18	70	11,948	0.26	0.38	0.59	4.3	2.5
Univ. Rochester	10	13	18	86	10	46	5,742	0.27	0.27	0.49	3.2	1.1
John Hopkins Univ.	11	12	16	77	21	106	12,515	0.30	0.34	1.12	7.8	8.9

University											
State Univ. N.Y., Buffalo	11	12	27	120	9	114	3,716	0.19	0.26	0.90	1.4	0.6
Rice Univ.	11	12	15	58	24	65	1,148	0.40	0.47	0.78	0.8	1.2
Carnegie-Mellon Univ.	13	11	35	70	7	111	>2,119^e	0.34	0.55	1.17	>0.6	>1.3
Florida State Univ.	10	11	27	145	32	161	3,027	0.14	0.30	0.96	1.1	0.4
Univ. Massachusetts	14	11	39	125	6	83	c	0.20	0.34	0.60	---	---
Oklahoma State Univ.	6	11	20	76	3	73	4,280	0.22	0.28	0.91	2.1	1.2
Univ. Toronto	18	11	30	165	30	199	c	0.18	0.27	1.08	---	---
Univ. Akron	7	10	17	157	2	26	c	0.11	0.11	0.19	---	---
Fordham Univ.	9	10	14	75	4	69	c	0.25	0.21	0.93	---	---
Univ. Missouri, Columbia	6	10	19	60	1	61	9,586	0.27	0.33	0.94	5.1	4.3
Univ. Montreal	5	10	19	65	8	70	c	0.23	0.35	0.92	---	---
Univ. Nebraska	11	10	26	112	6	57	5,418	0.19	0.26	0.49	2.1	0.5
Syracuse Univ.	5	10	17	90	2	21	4,150	0.17	0.20	0.24	2.4	0.2
Univ. Virginia	6	10	19	69	10	61	5,520	0.23	0.35	0.75	2.9	1.8

[a] Data of columns 1–5 from the "Directory of Graduate Research," American Chemical Society, preparation by the A. C. S. Committee on Professional Training, 1967.[6][d]

[b] There are 30 part-time students as well. One-half this number was added to the number of full-time students to derive the 115 total students used in all calculations.

[c] Not available. Not in list of 100 United States universities with largest federal support.[20]

[d] Data for Case-Western Reserve University not available.

[e] Data for Carnegie-Mellon University not available.

ply this technique to schools of interest to you, using more recent data.

Let us define first an "efficiency factor" which reflects the tenure of the graduate student in the university. In Table 2, a total of the Ph.D. degrees granted during the 1965-1967 period (the sum of columns 1 and 2) divided by the number of full-time graduate students enrolled as of October, 1966 (column 4), is shown in column 8 of Table 2. The relative magnitude of the number is a function of the number of years that the graduate student spends in the university, and the failure rate of the entering graduate students. Presumably, the larger the number, the more efficient is the training of the graduate student at the given university and the greater is the chance of the receipt of a Ph.D. degree.

Most of us would accept as sound (but expensive) educational policy the often quoted analogy of the ideal education system—the student at one end of a log and the teacher at the other. In this light, we may define a second quality measure, the "faculty to student ratio." This is shown in column 9 in Table 2. By our treatment it relates to, but is not simply, the teacher to graduate student ratio at the university. Today, in most universities, postdoctoral fellows play an important part in the guidance of graduate students in the Ph.D. program. The postdoctoral student does full-time research in the university to gain additional experience before embarking on his scientific career. He is usually of the same intellectual caliber as his professor. He has already demonstrated his ability to do significant and independent work in obtaining his Ph.D. degree. It is an obvious advantage to the Ph.D. graduate student to have postdoctoral students associated with his laboratory. In fact, graduate students we have trained claim that the advice of our postdoctoral students is at least as significant and helpful as our own advice in the pursuance of graduate research. However, reflecting the prejudice of the established academician, we rate the postdoctoral student as equivalent to one-half of a full-time faculty member in his contribution to the graduate program of the student.

With this assumption, the data presented in Table 2 have been calculated for the most prolific chemistry Ph.D. granting universities. The sum of the full-time faculty (column 3) and one-half of the number of postdoctoral fellows (column 5) divided by the number of full-time graduate students (column 4) is a qualitative measure of the actual "faculty to student" ratio at the universities (column 9). Obviously, the higher this number, the more personalized and hence more attractive becomes the educational program of the graduate student. Basic to our reasoning is the assumption that there is an equal mix of students and good communication between all the different research groups which occurs in the department. Obviously, this is a generalization to which many exceptions exist. In reality, the well-established graduate faculty members often have more postdoctoral students than graduate students, so that this individual group could have a high "faculty to student" ratio, but in turn, it could have a significantly less favorable ratio than that calculated by the procedure adopted here. However, the qualitative significance of this ratio is retained.

The third of the quality measures may be defined as a "research productivity" factor. One qualitative measure of productivity of the faculty is shown in column 10 of Table 2. This represents an attempt to measure the number of scientific publications per research scientist in each department. In our count of publications, we have included for each department only those publications which resulted from work done in the given department. Joint publications of two faculty colleagues were counted only once. In calculating this ratio we assumed that only three-fourths of the graduate students enrolled are involved in active research programs (the other one-fourth being involved in course work and library work prior to the selection of a preceptor). The sum of the full-time staff, plus three-fourths of the full-time graduate students, plus the number of postdoctoral fellows provides a measure of the graduate researchers in the department. The number of scientific publications which resulted from work done at that university divided by the total scientific researchers is the ratio shown in column 10. The magnitude of this number reflects the quality of the graduate program as measured by the efficiency with which the research culminates in publication.

Publication of your research is at least qualitative evidence that it is a significant piece of work as judged by the scientific peers who acted as referees for the journal. Obviously, the number of publications alone does not reflect the true variable which we wish to measure. Some scientists are prone to publish a given finding first as a "communication" or "letter" to a journal and later in more complete form as an "article." Obviously, if it is the same work which is being reported in both cases, these two publications should be counted but once in our calculations. Time and our limited patience did not permit this refinement in our method. Furthermore, journals of very different quality exist in every area, and a proper evaluation of the literature from a given department would involve a weighting factor to allow for the variation in the quality of the journal. In general, the scientific journals which are published by the professional societies of the given area have legitimate refereeing systems which manage to discriminate reasonably well between the trivial and the important contributions. Although there are serious complications to the counting procedures which have been employed in deriving the data of column 10 of Table 2, it is still a qualitative measure of the significance and efficiency of the graduate research in the various departments.

A fourth factor, the "financial factor" may be defined to judge the degree of support available to the particular science program at the university. In most major state and private universities, the burden of graduate research is carried in large part through federal grants and contracts. These are awarded to specific members of the graduate faculty after extensive review and rating of the proposed research by highly trained experts in the specific area of the proposal. These grants and contracts provide the lifeblood for graduate research; they make possible the purchase of equipment and supplies needed by the graduate student in the pursuance of his research work. Unfortunately, data for the chemistry departments are not available to us at the time of this writing, therefore the federal support to the science departments of the individual universities (excluding R & D and R & D plant categories of support) was used in this treatment.[20]   In column 11 of Table 2, a measure of the scientific competence and acceptance of the university science graduate faculty on the national level is indicated through the ratio of the federal support of the science programs (column 7) to the number of full-time staff members (column 3). Obviously, the larger this number, the more attractive the university from the standpoint of graduate research support for needed equipment, supplies, research assistantships, etc.

Certainly one of the most important criteria of the quality of a graduate school is the teaching of its faculty. This is difficult, if not impossible, to measure without the direct exposure to the faculty in lectures and laboratory work. This is one important phase of your evaluation procedure which you alone can make through your personal interviews and discussions with faculty of the universities which you choose to visit.

Some arbitrary combination of these four factors, weighted according to the student's personal preferences, along with other factors important to him, provide a basis for a comparison of the various graduate schools. Each student would probably weight these factors somewhat differently. Thus, if he has an assured fellowship from the university or from the federal government, he may be concerned primarily with the quality of the faculty and the efficiency of graduate student training, while the financial support would not be weighted as heavily. It is interesting to calculate for equal weighting of the above factors an overall "attractiveness factor" as shown in column 12 of Table 2. In this treatment the departments are penalized heavily for any weakness in the different quality measures. A product of the "efficiency factor," "faculty to student ratio," "productivity factor," and "financial factor" is taken in deriving the "attractiveness factor."

Although there are some notable exceptions to the order of the top departments derived by this procedure, generally the order is in qualitative agreement with that derived by the Cartter and Roose and Anderson committees.

Such a detailed analysis of the graduate program in universities is more than an academic exercise, but it has only qualitative value in recognizing serious weaknesses or outstanding virtues of certain departments. If a department in a university is extremely low or extremely high in these quality factors, a serious weakness or a striking strength is indicated. However, the data of the type used in the preparation of Table 2 are continually undergoing change as departments recognize weaknesses and try to overcome them.

Until now we have assumed that you would choose a department and then select from within that faculty a research director. There is an alternative approach oftentimes used by students who have a clear understanding of the type of research they want to do in graduate school; this is generally gained while doing research as an undergraduate. In this case, your choice may not be based on your evaluation of the department's strengths and weaknesses but rather on one or two faculty members who have carved a niche for themselves in their field. Statistical analyses of the type presented here represent no more than that—statistics—and should be judged in this light. In the final analysis you may want to ask yourself where the best man in the country is who is doing research that "turns you on." You may find that for one reason or another he is not at one of the top universities but instead is in a small but acceptable department. Find out all you can about this man, his personality, his student success ratio, and his research before making the final decision. Maybe you'll want to go with him. Rarely are all the faculty in any department first-class researchers across the board, and rarely indeed is the department nationally recognized in all subdisciplines of its field.

Let us say, by the use of suitable documentation and evaluation paths, as attempted above or otherwise, that you have selected a number of universities which have graduate programs that appeal to you. You should write to each of these departments and ask for department brochures, fellowship announcements, and any other information which they might provide to an interested student. Make sure that your final decision is based upon a solid judgement formulated after serious study of the potentially interesting faculty of each of the departments. Often the departmental brochure will list critical information such as the recent publications and research interests of all the graduate faculty. Plan to spend several evenings in the library with the original literature, reading first-hand the research articles of several staff members in the departments in which you are interested. You should not necessarily decide at this stage on a preceptor; this choice should be made after a personal interview with several possible preceptors. Furthermore, you have no assurance of acceptance by the graduate school, the department, or any of the group of preceptors of your choice at this stage. What you wish to establish, however, is that there are several potential preceptors whose work is of primary interest to you at each of these universities. You should be fair to the universities and indicate to each of those with whom application is filed that you have also filed applications at other universities, which you name. This will not hurt your competitive position at any of the institutions and will allow the administration of each university to make an objective evaluation of their offer to you of financial support.

Let us assume that your qualifications for graduate school are reasonably good and that you receive offers from more than one university to join their graduate program. There is a very important step which you should take now, if possible; that is, a visit to each of these graduate schools.

Schedule before your visit, by written request, a meeting with several of the faculty members in whom you have an interest as a potential preceptor. Make sure that you take a close look at the major research facilities within the department, including the library. Meet the librarian and ask about the library holdings. Which journals are incomplete or entirely absent? Are graduate students given access to the library at all hours? Make a note of any special equipment or facility which would be particularly attractive to you in your graduate research.

If you cannot visit all of the universities from which you have received offers, make sure that you write again to those which you cannot visit, and receive answers concerning any potential problem areas. What is the availability of the special equipment in which you have an interest and that you know exists in some of the other universities that you have visited? It is our opinion that one of the most important criteria which you should use in determining your choice of universities is the quality of the research faculty and the attractiveness of the available research facilities. Of secondary concern should be the magnitude of the financial support which the university offers to you.

There is one final point concerned with the timing of the acceptance of offers which every potential graduate student should understand. Don't be pressured into a decision between alternative offers before you are very sure of your choice. The Association of Graduate Schools, which includes many of the major graduate degree-granting institutions in the United States, has a gentleman's agreement between the graduate school deans of its member universities, which is designed to remove, or at least lessen, the pressure on the student for a quick decision on offers. Usually fellowship offers for the following summer or fall quarter are not given out until March 21 of that year, so you certainly don't want to accept any offer until you have heard about your success in receiving a fellowship. Teaching assistantships may be offered earlier in some cases. In any case, the potential graduate student is not bound by any decision until April 15 of the year he is to enter graduate school. He could conceivably accept at one school, reverse his decision, and then accept at another school as long as it is before the April 15 deadline. Obviously it is a much fairer practice to wait until you are very sure of your choice. You are, however, a free agent only until April 15. If you change your mind for any reason after this time, you must get the permission of the school which has your "acceptance." Until this release is obtained, other schools cannot accept you. Don't let some aggressive administrator or faculty member pressure you for a very early acceptance unless you are very sure that this school will remain your first choice.

C.   HOW? FINANCIAL SUPPORT THROUGH FELLOWSHIPS AND TEACHING AND RESEARCH ASSISTANTSHIPS

Most graduate students today in the sciences have financial support through university or government funds; such support usually accompanies acceptance at a responsible university. The student who has done exceptionally well academically in his undergraduate school and who has obtained outstanding marks on the Graduate Record Examination often qualifies for a federal or university sponsored fellowship. These fellowships pay the minimal stipend, about

$2,600 per year. In certain cases, a small allotment of approximately $500 per dependent is included. As these fellowships are very limited in number and the competition is keen, it is certainly an honor to receive one. A person who feels he qualifies should apply and accept such a fellowship if it is offered. A number of sources of graduate student fellowships are summarized in Table A-4 of the Appendix. Figure 8 gives the relative importance of the various types of support of full-time graduate students in engineering, the mathematical sciences, and in the physical sciences, as taken from reference 22. The data are based on information over a period of three years, 1967-1969, from 2,338 doctorate departments. It indicates that while the supply of fellowships and traineeships declined over this period, the amount of self-support by graduate students increased. Due to the recent financial cutbacks at the time of this writing, it is probable that this trend toward increased self-support has continued.

There is one aspect in the training of a fellow in graduate school which should be emphasized. There is, in the opinion of the authors, a very great deal to be learned from the experience gained in teaching in the department. The fellow should volunteer to accept some significant teaching responsibilities during his tenure as a graduate student. At least one or two quarters of teaching experience will be extremely valuable.

The great majority of graduate students are supported with the granting of a teaching assistantship or research assistantship for the first year. Others allow one to two quarters for the graduate student to become acclimated and trained in some of the important aspects of his teaching responsibilities; his teaching duties are then assumed starting the third quarter or later.

Some schools have found that it is possible to guarantee support of the entering graduate student by dividing his time between teaching and research activities during his entire tenure. Usually one quarter per year during each of the four

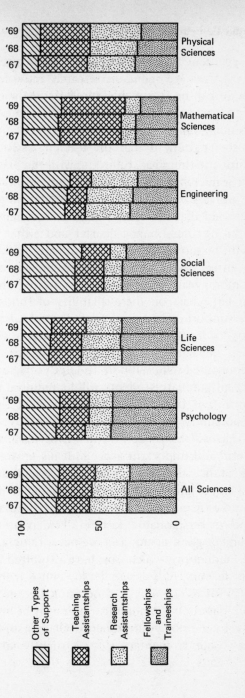

Figure 8: Percent distribution of types of major support of full-time graduate students in doctorate departments by area of science, 1967-1969. (Reproduced from ref. 22.)

years is spent in teaching. The other two quarters and the summer quarter are spent on research activities. Guarantee or not, you can be reasonably sure of some sort of financial aid in most reputable graduate programs in the sciences, provided you maintain a good record.

The usual pattern is that the teaching assistantship is appointed for the first year, full-time, with the exception of the summer. Some extra stipend for the summer may be available in some universities without additional teaching responsibilities, provided that the teaching assistant remains at the university during the summer quarter and either continues or initiates his research effort. A few students are kept one, two, possibly three, and, in a very limited number of cases, even four or more years, as a teaching assistant. This timing depends in large part on the availability of funds for research assistant support, which is under control of the student's preceptor, or on the success of the graduate student in obtaining a department, university, government, or other agency-sponsored fellowship in his later years.

Nearly all graduate students will be required to participate to some extent in the teaching program at the university. This opportunity should not be scorned by the graduate student. He will look back on this experience as one of the most useful and important aspects of his university training. The importance to the student lies in several areas. Perhaps the most important of these is the experience he gains in his attempt to organize and present materials to students in a clear and understandable fashion. Undergraduate students are extremely good critics and are never reluctant to tell you of some inadequacy which you have exhibited in the preparation or delivery of your material. Praise from students is more difficult to come by, but occasionally one of your finer efforts in classroom communication might be commented on favorably by one of your students. Of course, even in these rare cases, your momentary glory is slightly tarnished. Is the student speaking from conviction, or as a politician seeking psychological aid in the future establishment of his grade?

Also, the teaching assistant must develop the attributes of leadership in handling the students under a variety of circumstances. You may be in charge of a freshman laboratory session and find that one of your students has encountered difficulty and has been injured seriously in a violent explosion or fire. Your immediate corrective action may save the student's life. A group of protestors may march through the classroom during some crucial argument of your lecture or during an examination. You may discover that one of your students is using some unauthorized memory aid during an examination. Your ability to meet such situations with prompt and intelligent action must be developed if you are to survive with your self-respect and gain leadership attributes.

These and many other challenges are somewhat peculiar to the teaching assistant, and they are certainly excellent training, regardless of your choice of future employment. Remember that one of the major decisions which all graduate students face is a choice between accepting academic work in a university on one hand, and employment in industry, government, or other areas on the other hand. Your experience as a teaching assistant will help you to decide whether the life of a university teacher-researcher will be gratifying to you and whether you are sufficiently motivated and qualified to pursue this goal.

Even if you choose to work in industry or government, this teaching experience will be valuable in many tangible ways. One of your major responsibilities as a scientist in these areas is to express yourself well in oral and written reports to management and other scientists in your organization. Your experience as a teaching assistant will be invaluable in this regard. Remember that a scientist who does excellent work but is unable to communicate the value of this work to his colleagues and superiors, has wasted a large part of his effort.

Continued support for your endeavor is based on what your superior can understand and appreciate among your efforts and accomplishments.

In addition, the teaching assistant gains a fresh and valuable insight into the subject matter of his area. He must describe it to others; this means that he must understand the subject in considerable depth himself. The teaching assistant is stimulated to learn each of the areas with a perspective that is quite different from that which he gained in a similar course in his undergraduate career.

It is usually apparent to the professors serving on the graduate student oral examination committees those among the students who have had experience as a teaching assistant. Not all teaching assistants turn out to be sparkling performers under pressure, but they most often exhibit a poise, a self-confidence, and a clarity of presentation that is far superior to the graduate students who have missed this important experience.

In summary, we recommend strongly that you accept assignment as a teaching assistant during your tenure as a graduate student for at least one or two quarters. We feel that any small amount of additional time which this requires will be more than compensated for by the important gains made.

It is well to remember that the teaching assistant has some significant responsibilities which he must assume. Accepting a teaching assistantship does not mean that you will simply show up at class time and do little else but "baby-sit." If you are to be of help to the students who are assigned to you, you must take time to prepare your discussions, lectures, or laboratory activities. In most universities a teaching assistant in the sciences is assigned full responsibility for a freshman recitation section and the supervision of the corresponding laboratory section. A smaller number of teaching assistants serve in laboratory supervision in the sophomore, junior, or senior courses. It is likely that you will spend about fifteen hours per week in preparation, grading, and actual contact with your students. If it is anything less than this, you will not be fulfilling your responsibilities to your students. Many schools have a grading program which rates the teaching assistant according to his performances. Sometimes some financial bonus is given to the most highly qualified teaching assistants in the second or subsequent quarters of their teaching. In any case, the professor to whom you are responsible in your teaching assignment will note your attitude and abilities and refer to these in his all-important subsequent letters of recommendation and discussions with future employers.

Don't forget, even though you are a teaching assistant, your concurrent responsibilities as a graduate student include the graduate course work and the active pursuance of graduate research. You must plan to schedule your time carefully so that you do not shortchange any aspect of your graduate career. During your first year, you should spend fifteen to twenty hours per week on your teaching, ten to fifteen hours per week on your course work outside of classes, and another fifteen to twenty hours per week either on the recent literature of your faculty in preparation for your choice of preceptor or in laboratory work, once this choice has been made. On top of this, you will undoubtedly spend a substantial amount of time preparing for departmental graduate examinations. In short, don't spend all your time on teaching duties. A teaching assistant who spends forty hours per week in preparation and execution of his teaching duties is signing his death warrant as a successful graduate student. If you take this much time to accomplish your assignments, you should question the professor who is supervising your course as well as yourself. Is he expecting too much of you? Are you inadequately prepared for graduate school? Find out.

Most graduate students spend the majority of their student careers as a research assistant. They work on their Ph.D. dissertation research during this period except for the time spent in attending a few classes and seminars, taking examinations, study, and a very few other pressing responsibilities. The research assistant has a firm responsibility to work "full-time" on his research during his tenure. The preceptor spends his own research money and expects some action. We have seen several cases where this responsibility was taken lightly, and the frugal research preceptor decreased the stipend paid to the student to be more consistent with his effort. Pressures are very great upon the professor to obtain results which are meaningful and, hopefully, publishable within a reasonable period of time. He must have something significant from you to show his granting agency as justification for the funds spent in your support. Otherwise, his future support from this agency is in jeopardy. This affects not only you but all the other members of his research team. It is very important that you do not spend your time as a young research assistant studying for your examinations and course work during the regular day.

The graduate student who has been fortunate and received the reward of a fellowship has as large a responsibility as the teaching assistant or the research assistant. He feels the special pressure that he must continually demonstrate his exceptional qualifications as a graduate student. The fellow is expected to be at the top of his class in the academic subjects. If he isn't, that fellowship may not be renewed. Like the research assistant, the fellow is expected to work diligently on his thesis research during the majority of his time as a student. Study for examinations and courses should not be carried out during the usual working hours in the laboratory of his preceptor. Both the research assistant and the fellow can gauge the working hours which are expected of them through observation of the hours kept by their preceptor. He expects you to be in the laboratory, except for classes and other such responsibilities, whenever he is there—and some of the time when he is not. If you have any doubt of what he expects of you, ask him. He will not be reticent to share his feelings on this matter with you.

In many universities today, the salary structure for the teaching assistant is fixed above that of the research assistant. The reasoning behind this practice is twofold. The competitive position of the teaching assistant has to be improved to compensate for the nonthesis research time which his teaching requires. Furthermore, many universities are striving to improve the quality of their undergraduate instruction and a higher teaching assistant salary attracts better people.

In other universities, stipends which both the teaching assistant and the research assistant receive are comparable to that of the research fellow. From $250 to $350 per month is the common magnitude of the stipends in the physical and biological sciences. In some areas of engineering, such as electrical engineering, graduate research assistants have received much more than this. Presumably such lucrative support reflected the availability of large contract support, exceptional competition for available graduate students in the area, and very great pressures to produce in a very short time period. In any case, you will receive offers stating the financial rewards of your assistantship or fellowship, and you can determine from a comparison of these whether any one of them is out of line. In making your choice, it is important that you do not weigh too heavily the differences in stipend, but be sure to check what your actual stipend is. In some universities, tuition is waived for the teaching assistant and/or research assistant; in others, tuition must be paid from your stipend. You may also have to pay federal, state, and local taxes on the total stipend.

The report of Carter and his committee on "Professional Training of the American Chemical Society" indicates that graduate students can be "bought," but they suggest that an unusual stipend opens a weak school to the charge of bribing students to accept an inferior education.[23] The extent of this salary practice may be judged by comparing assistantships advertised in news magazines in your field and in various departmental bulletins. Carter states that these comparisons sometimes suggest an inverse correlation between stipends and excellence. However, if your proposed stipend is unusually high or unusually low, you might question the administration of that school as to their motivation in arriving at this stipend structure. Something may be wrong.

II

Life in the
Academic Salt Mines

4. Meeting the Formal and "Informal" Graduate School and Departmental Requirements

A. INITIATION RITES OF GRADUATE SCHOOL

In some respects, the most critical time in the entire professional life of a scientist is his first year in graduate school. It is the toughest form of academic "boot camp." An incoming graduate student lays it all on the line during this period; he must work under great mental and physical strain. In addition to having a number of new and important specific responsibilities such as serving as a teaching assistant and passing a battery of graduate courses and examinations, he must often adjust to an entirely new academic, cultural, and geographical environment. For example, the student from a small town who matriculates at a small college or university and then enters a large urban university for graduate work, may find that his success or failure during the first critical few months depends significantly upon his becoming rapidly adjusted to a completely different manner of living. The authors have seen otherwise well-qualified first-year graduate students succumb as much to "cultural shock" as to academic rigors.

In addition to the customary academic responsibilites imposed by the university, today's graduate student has, in general, a keen sense of responsibility toward society's problems. The male student has also had to face the hazards imposed by the Vietnam war as well as the possibility (and indeed, probability) of being drafted as compared to the alternatives of leaving graduate school to flee the country, accepting a job in industry or government which promises deferment, or joining the reserves. There is also the personal struggle involved in attempting to reconcile the compelling sociological needs such as the urban and racial crises, with the propriety and relevance of one's living in a somewhat cloistered academic atmosphere for the next four years and working on problems which could often be construed as esoteric.

Specific challenges to the entering graduate student include placement examinations, duties as a teaching assistant, and remedial courses and/or introductory graduate courses. Other responsibilities include initiating the "quest" among the faculty for a thesis research director, preparing for the written predoctoral examinations, attending the weekly departmental seminar, and reviewing for the required language examinations.

B.   YOUR DEPARTMENT

Having arrived on campus as a new graduate student seeking a doctorate, you should recognize that your home away from home for at least the next three or four years is "the department." The university, through its graduate dean and graduate study council provides an overall structure for your graduate program, but in most first-class universities, each department has a high degree of autonomy in setting up and running the essential detailed elements of its own particular graduate curriculum. These include writing and giving the graduate examinations and placement examinations, administering the teaching functions of the graduate teaching assistants, and, perhaps most important of all for the doctoral program, creating and maintaining a scholarly atmosphere conducive to imaginative research.

Thus one of the key university administrators with whom you will come in contact is your department chairman. Actually, while the dean of the graduate school is ultimately responsible for broad university-wide policies and crucial procedural matters such as admission, in most specific items involving individual students he acts on the recommendation of others, particularly the department chairman, the department graduate study committee, the doctoral committee, and another key person, the department graduate advisor. The latter person is the faculty member with whom you will generally conduct most of your formal departmental business; he or she is a most important person for you to get to know. A strong measure of the success of a first-rate department can be attributed not only to its faculty, students, and chairman, but also to a perceptive and diligent graduate advisor and a hard-working, dedicated graduate study committee.

You should realize that although these individuals are generally busy, they will be available at almost any reasonable time for help and consultation. Under ordinary circumstances, you should respect the tight schedule of these people and make formal appointments to see them. On the other hand, the chairman or graduate advisor is not only willing, but considers it a compliment if a student having unusual difficulties, academic or personal, seeks their advice *at any time* if the situation is urgent. This holds true even after a graduate student has chosen his research preceptor. Even if there is a close relationship between you and your research director, it is still a good idea for you to go out of your way to interact with the departmental administrators. They, just as well as your research director, will get to know you—your faults and virtues—and be better prepared to assist you in evaluating yourself. The interaction with departmental administrators is helpful to your own progress in graduate school, but also it will add substance to their judgment of you when the great day comes and you join the ranks of the job hunters. Thus, employers will seek recommendations from your research director, but often they will solicit additional evaluations from your department chairman, your graduate advisor, and other faculty members.

In addition to the importance of the relationship between the director and graduate student, which we will consider in detail later, it is very important that you maintain good personal relations with all of the faculty, staff, and fellow students with whom you have regular contact. Once a graduate student has entered a department and spent some significant part of his life there, the department's overall evaluation of him will have a profound effect on his professional advancement, not only while he is in graduate school, but for the rest of his life. Often students feel that the only criteria on which they are judged are their academic performance and research productivity. These are certainly very important factors. In addition, your personal qualities may influence significantly the critical decision in some important job opportunity that may occur years or even decades after you leave graduate school: your attitude, your loyalty to your colleagues and your department, and your ability to get along with fellow students, faculty, and (equally important) the nonacademic staff of your department. We are not implying that each student should be a "Pollyanna," but we are saying that life in a department of a major university is complex, challenging, and competitive; obviously, individuals, faculty members, or students who make an extra effort to promote harmonious relationships will be making a genuine contribution to the department. They will also be insuring their own future. Faculty, administrators, and research directors don't forget any more easily than you do.

In addition to becoming acquainted as soon as possible with the department chairman and graduate advisor, it is wise for the novice graduate student to expend a certain amount of time and energy talking to the experienced graduate students in the department. One can learn some helpful information from these senior graduate students—some fact, some fiction. Of course, you should make a careful assessment of the validity of their comments; "snowing" the newcomers has been one of the enjoyable pastimes for generations of academic veterans. However, generally this is without malice, and with a little time, effort, and perception, one can usually get the straight "scoop" on many matters from understanding vets.

To reiterate: handle with care and perception the information you pick up in these bull sessions with other students. File it away, but start immediately to build up your own personal store of information regarding "this course," "that professor," or "the hangups of the storeroom keeper on the third floor." More often than not, you will find that your opinion will change with time, so preliminary judgments based solely on the casual statements of others must be treated with caution. When we were graduate students, we frequently got the straight scuttlebutt on a particular professor, including, for example, what a tough S.O.B. he was in grading, and how he had miserable personal relationships with students. Subsequently, on the basis of working relationships with the professor as a senior graduate student, or later as a fellow academician, we found that the judgments of some of the old graduate student pros and our own first impressions were totally wrong. In the long run, judgments of this type which are based in a large part on departmental gossip really do more harm to the student than to the faculty or staff member.

Finally, it behooves the entering graduate student to get on good terms, or at least establish working relationships, with the nonacademic staff of the department. These include department secretaries, storeroom keepers, glassblowers, machinists, electronic technicians, purchasing agents, janitors, and others. These are the "troops" who really keep the place going and, in a good department, deserve the utmost cooperation and respect of both the faculty and the students. All too often we have seen entering graduate students come in and treat such staff with a haughty and superior air. All this does is to annoy the staff member who, in fact, can retaliate readily. He or she can see to it in many ways, all of them legal, that the special chemical you need for that crucial experiment, that piece of apparatus that must be repaired to complete the experiment, or the test which you want to have typed quickly, is handled on a routine basis, but *not* as an emergency.

Universities have rules about rules. You will be amazed to see the great complexity and the extensive nature of the administrative manual of most departments and universities. This manual is the bible, and, at times, the curse of the department chairman. It is a sobering experience to leaf through the hundreds of pages of rules and regulations. This and related red tape explains in part why faculty, administrators, and their staff are at times short-fused and preoccupied. Although "The Book" was not designed for this purpose it, provides a mechanism whereby, if a staff member decides to slow things down because he is confronted by a smart-aleck graduate student, he can do so with no trouble at all by deliberately invoking red tape while staying well within the legal framework of his responsibilities.

C.   GRADUATE EXAMINATIONS

While the characteristic feature of the Ph.D. degree is the requirement of a dissertation based on original research, during the first year or two the graduate student must prove his qualifications as a potential Ph.D. through written examinations. Thus the success or failure of the student depends on his completing satisfactorily a prescribed set of courses and passing a series of written predoctoral qualifying examinations. These examinations are viewed in a quite different light by the faculty than by the students. The latter tend to regard all graduate examinations as being obstacles thrust in their paths by a generally sadistic faculty. The faculty, on the other hand, sometimes blithely refer to the examinations as simply "learning experiences" or "just a comprehensive review of the fundamentals." Some research directors go so far as to deprecate these examinations, pointing out to the student that he shouldn't study too long and hard for them, and suggesting "you really must get on with your research; we don't want to be scooped."

The best advice, as is so often the case, encompasses both viewpoints. It is highly desirable for a well-qualified graduate student to initiate his research program sometime during the second half of his first year. In this way he can be thinking about his research problem, setting up his laboratory, and preparing to make a sustained effort at research during the first summer. The research director is naturally interested in seeing how the new student handles himself on a "hot" research project. Incidentally, all of a professor's research projects are, by definition, "hot"; it is the research of the other professor which may be "conventional." In any case, there is good reason for the student to get research under way if his course background is adequate. On the other hand, it is also true that even a brilliant student researcher who neglects his studies and repeatedly fails his qualifying examinations will be asked, regrettably, to leave or at best to depart with a terminal master's degree. In short, all students must pass the examinations. They know it, and the faculty know it.

This leads to a key question: "How much time should I spend preparing for these damned examinations?" The variety of examinations includes the placement, qualifying, cumulative, preliminary, oral, language, and final oral examinations. However, that age-old question remains yet to be answered. It requires a great deal of maturity, not to mention a certain element of luck, to schedule properly on a relatively long-term basis, a study program which will culminate in your best understanding of the specific material at a time which coincides with the date of each of these various examinations. The graduate student may consider himself an old pro at this game. After all, he has survived four years as an undergraduate. He may also have served as a graduate teaching assistant and in that capacity advised and counseled undergraduates on the practice of "examinationship." Unfortunately, all too often a graduate student's false confidence leads to a rude awakening.

While there are no set rules or advice we can offer, we have made two general observations: (1) excessive and late cramming can be fatal, and (2) starting to review or to prepare too soon can take the edge off a subject and leave the student overtrained and frankly bored. In some cases, if he starts too soon, by the time he gets to the examination, he may have already forgotten much of the factual material he reviewed earlier. Perhaps the best we can do is to re-emphasize the need on your part for a conscious, clear recognition of what your challenges will be, particularly during your first year. You should candidly appraise your own resources—mental and physical—and then lay out a schedule which will include study in your on-going graduate courses along with a detailed review in preparation for the general qualifying examinations and the language examinations. Your study program should permit enough time to participate in other activities such as initiation of your research, as well as to just plain relax. Otherwise you may go "stir-crazy." However, any schedule which totals up to an effort of less than about sixty hours per week on all aspects of the graduate study, including your teaching assistant responsibilities, is either unrealistic or is a program capable of being followed successfully by only a small percentage of the brightest and most highly organized students.

While speaking of the sort of work effort required of the typical graduate student in the sciences, we should point out that after completing his required examinations, the typical successful and dedicated graduate student generally attacks his research with a vengeance. A sixty-hour work week represents an almost relaxed pace. This may seem to be overstating the case. It is true today that among some graduate students a forty-hour work week is considered a nonnegotiable right. However, you can't have it both ways. If you are an average graduate student and want to turn out a good, definitive piece of research which within three or four years will lead to a dissertation of which both you and your research director can be proud, then you must plan to work for longer than the regular work week. On the other hand, if you (and your preceptor) are willing to settle for a pre-Ph.D. period of five years or more, then you must be prepared to expect reference to your prolonged graduate career in letters from the department administration and your research director which will go out to your prospective employers:

> Mr. Sam Scientist is a pleasant, intelligent person who, overall, has done a good academic job during his stay here. However, there appears to be one regrettable attribute of the candidate; he showed a lack of initiative and industry in attacking his doctoral research problem. As a result, it took at least a year longer than would otherwise have been necessary to complete his dissertation. . . .

Your letters of recommendation will be very honest. You may choose the forty-hour week, but be prepared to accept public disclosure of this choice.

The Departmental Placement Examinations.   It is common practice among many science departments in the country today to give orientation or placement examinations at the time of registration. These examinations are designed to test the background of the incoming graduate student in the fundamental areas of his or her discipline. For example, an entering student in chemistry would take examinations in organic, physical, inorganic, and, in many schools, analytical chemistry. Deficiencies in the background of the incoming students are then remedied by their taking selected undergraduate courses.

Your standing on these examinations relative to the other entering students provides a useful frame of reference for yourself as well as the graduate advisor and your potential research director. If they are carefully designed examinations, your performance can be a reasonably good indication of the quality and depth of your training as an undergraduate and of your native ability.

Actually, if a student is bright and industrious but, for one reason or another, is deficient in his undergraduate background, placement in undergraduate courses at the outset of his graduate work is often a blessing in disguise. Thus on the positive side, taking such remedial courses not only provides a sound foundation for the graduate courses, but also builds up the basic background needed to complete the written qualifying examinations and pass with some distinction the preliminary oral. On the negative side, a poor performance generally means that the student has to take at least an additional half year or possibly one full academic year to complete his degree beyond that required for the incoming student who passes all of his placement examinations.

It is important to note that there is no stigma attached to a poor performance on the placement examinations; most faculty take a sympathetic attitude. However, they do critically review the student's course grades at the end of the first term. If he gets A's or B's in the remedial undergraduate courses, fine. It's on to graduate courses and qualifiers! On the other hand, a grade of C or less in an undergraduate course is a failing grade for a graduate student. The first-year graduate student can ill afford many, if any, failing grades in his undergraduate make-up courses.

Often we are asked how one prepares for these placement examinations. Some students walk in and take them cold, or arrive at the university a few days early and cram for them. Others, at the beginning of the summer lay out a systematic review program covering the key areas in their discipline. If they maintain their study schedule throughout the summer, such students generally wind up making a considerably better showing than if they had used the cramming technique. Incidentally, in many departments, the graduate advisor will furnish, well in advance of the examinations, material describing the areas to be covered. It is a good idea to take careful note of this material and to study accordingly.

The Graduate Courses and Accompanying Examinations. Little needs to be said here concerning the nature of graduate courses in the sciences except to point out that they generally require a greater level of maturity on the part of the student than do the undergraduate courses. The professor assumes that you enter with a solid background in the prerequisites to the course and that he can proceed at an advanced level. He further assumes that you intend to become a professional scientist and that you will accept the responsibility of tackling difficult material diligently, if not enthusiastically. You will not be "spoon fed."

Most of your fellow graduate students will take their course work seriously; poor course grades are grounds for flunking out. Furthermore, your grades in graduate courses are an important factor in determining which students will be awarded the prestigious and, in some cases, lucrative predoctoral fellowships that are often available to second and third-year graduate students. The student's rank in the qualifying or cumulative examinations is also taken into account here. As well, your grades are a permanent record available for all to see in later years, and, as such, have an impact on your future employers.

Having made this point, we want to re-emphaszie our opinion that while graduate course work is important, it is not the critical feature of the Ph.D. degree. As we have noted earlier and will continue to stress, its distinguishing requirement is outstanding research and scholarly activity. In our opinion, many departments overstress the amount of required course work, usually at the expense of the quality and quantity of research for the dissertation. We feel this is a tragic error and leads to a perversion of the true concept of the Ph.D. degree.

However, the basic courses in your graduate study are important and you should work hard on them. Highly specialized courses are for the very few who are planning to work in the specific sub-area of the course. Don't take these courses unless you and your preceptor agree on their real importance to your graduate study. If your study in the basic areas is thorough, then through your own reading and study, you can pick up easily the material which is important to the specialty areas if you should desire to work in one of them.

It is interesting to note that new types of doctoral degrees have recently been proposed. These are generally characterized by *not* requiring a doctoral dissertation based on original research. For example, some of the University of California campuses now award a Candidate in Philosophy degree for those people who have been advanced to candidacy in the Ph.D. program but who have not completed the research requirements for a Ph.D. There has been a great deal of debate, concerning the merits of these proposed degrees. We must admit that we are not enthusiastic about them. However, they may provide a useful function. Professor William G. Young, former vice chancellor at U.C.L.A., discussed this educational innovation in his Priestly Medal Address of 1968:

> Although most of my friends in science disagree with this approach (the Candidate in Philosophy degree

. . . ed.), nevertheless, many teachers of chemistry in junior colleges may soon come from this background. Some of these teachers will be very capable students who have taken this new degree by choice. Others will be those who have been unsuccessful with their Ph.D. thesis but who automatically qualify for the new degree if the department recommends it. Although some of these unsuccessful students may go into teaching today, many more will in the future with a new degree as an enticement.[24]

The Foreign Language Requirement.   A traditional requirement for the Ph.D. degree in one of the natural sciences has been passing grades in written examinations designed to test the ability of the graduate student to read scientific literature in each of two foreign languages. Generally, a science major will take German as one of his languages and either Russian or French as his second language.

The manner in which the language requirements are fulfilled varies from university to university and, in fact, from department to department. Thus, for example, in some departments the use of dictionaries is allowed during the examination; in other departments, they are not. Because of the wide variation in the interpretation of what constitutes a reading knowledge of scientific German, French, or Russian, we shall not go into detail about these examinations except to make a few general points.

The first is that it is advisable to get these examinations out of the way as soon as possible. It is generally a good idea for you to attempt to satisfy at least one of the foreign language requirements during your first term. Having just left undergraduate school, you are probably reasonably proficient in reading at least one foreign language, and with a moderate amount of hard study, you should be able to pass an examination of average difficulty. There are some excellent books available to test and develop your scientific reading ability in foreign languages.[25]

A second point is that there is often a great deal of just plain "luck of the draw" when it comes to the specific material you will be asked to translate. It is a common practice for a faculty member to select several articles from scientific literature in a particular language and have each graduate student translate a different article. Just as in the case of articles written in English, some of the articles may be written by authors who have a clarity of style, while other authors not only muddle up their science but also muddle up their grammar.

There is also an element of chance as to whether or not the article you are asked to translate lies within your sphere of interest. You might be lucky and have a reasonable scientific background in the subject of the article. Often a knowledge of the subject matter in the particular article is almost as valuable as having a reasonable reading ability in the foreign language. Two of the authors can testify to this last point. We both entered graduate school shortly after the end of World War II. One of our first trials as graduate students in chemistry was to pass the reading examination in French, yet neither of us had ever studied the subject as an undergraduate. Along with several other "vets" we enrolled in a freshman French class. One of us took the course for credit, the other audited it. Another one of our prewar friends in undergraduate school had come back from serving in France as a tank captain. He, too, was working for a Ph.D. degree in chemistry and joined us in this class. A fourth buddy, who had never taken French and had never left the United States, said, "To hell with taking a formal class in French, I'm going to pick up a book on scientific French, study it a while on my own, and gamble that I get assigned a subject in organic chemistry that I know something about. Maybe I can bluff my way through."

Perhaps you can anticipate the outcome of the story. Three of the four chemistry graduate students passed the examinations: the vet who took it for credit, the vet who simply audited the course, and the student who gambled and boned up on his own. The only person to flunk the French examination in that group was, alas, the only person involved who had ever been to France and used the French language in real life. The tank captain failed the exam and had to take it a second time. Well, "C'est la vie!" or perhaps more appropriately, "C'est la guerre!"

Finally, we should note that there is an increasing tendency in graduate science departments to reduce the requirement to a reading knowledge of scientific material in only *one* foreign language. In some universities, students have been given the option of substituting another course, such as one in computer science or statistics in place of the second language examination. You should inquire early about the specifics with regard to the foreign language examinations and possible options. The sooner you know the facts, the sooner you can start to prepare.

Finally, you should note that there is another important reason for getting the language requirement out of the way as soon as possible; in many universities you will not be allowed to take your preliminary doctoral oral examination until you have met the departmental foreign language requirements.

The Written Predoctoral Examination. Written predoctoral examinations are generally the major examination hurdle for the graduate student. They vary in nature from university to university, from department to department, and even from area to area within a given department. Thus we will not attempt to discuss them in detail, but instead offer some general observations on the two common types, qualifying examinations and cumulative examinations.

Qualifying Examinations. Qualifying examinations are a series of written examinations generally lasting three or four hours each. They are given at a specific time each year, usually either in the early fall or in the late spring. In some instances they are given twice a year. Each of the qualifiers covers one of the key subdisciplines in a given field. For example, a graduate student in chemistry would commonly take qualifiers in physical, organic, inorganic, and possibly analytical chemistry or biochemistry. However, one should recognize that a student's performance on the qualifier exam dealing with his particular subdiscipline is scrutinized by the faculty more carefully than his grades in other qualifiers.

After being graded by the appropriate faculty members, the results of these qualifiers are reviewed by the departmental graduate study committee, and a summary of the results and a detailed comparison of the performance of each student is presented to the faculty in a special, top-secret session. It is in this crucial meeting that the faculty decides who gets the kudos and "passes with distinction," who gets the axe and perhaps some sympathy, and who are borderline cases and must be dealt with in special ways.

A student who passes his written qualifying examinations may also be required subsequently to take a lengthy written major field examination in his specific subject area. For example, a physical chemistry graduate student who passed all of his qualifiers may be required, about a year later, to take a major field examination strictly in the field of physical chemistry.

Major field examinations range in style from closed book exams lasting some eight hours or more (with breaks at appropriate times) to week-long, open book, take-home examinations. Sometimes both an open book and a closed book part are included in one examination.

Cumulative Examinations. The historically accepted approach of written qualifiers, followed by a written major field examination, fell into disfavor among some educators during the early fifties and the era of "cumulative examinations" came in. However, before discussing "cumes," we should point out that the pedagogical pendulum swings back and forth. It is amusing to observe today that in some departments, that which was championed as great pedagogy some three to five years ago, (e.g., the cumulative exam system) is now considered old-fashioned and obsolete, and new examination schemes are being devised.

Cumulative examinations are given approximately once a month during the academic year and usually once during the summer term. They are generally scheduled for one or two hours each and are designed to test the student's knowledge of some specific subject in his or her major field. Thus, for example, a student majoring in inorganic chemistry would take cumulatives only in the field of inorganic chemistry. Some exceptions to this practice exist. Under certain circumstances, students are sometimes permitted to take a certain number of cumulatives in subjects other than their major field.

The subject of cumulative examinations in chemistry departments has been discussed in detail in two papers in the *Journal of Chemical Education,* the first by Frost and Hussey[26] of the Department of Chemistry at Northwestern University, and the second by Professor G. Ross Robertson at the University of California at Los Angeles.[27] The following description of the practice in chemistry at U.C.L.A. taken from Professor Robertson's paper is a typical example of the cumulative system:

> Cumulative examinations occur approximately monthly. Papers are marked "passed" or "failed", with percentage marks, not A, B, C, etc. No grades are changed after original judgement of papers has been rendered. If the first term of the cumulative program occurs during the student's first year of residence, it is called a "free" semester. That is, passes are credited, but failures are not charged to the candidate. In each subsequent term, successes and failures are both charged on the student's record. Seven passes, if attained at frequency consistent with regulations cited below, complete the cumulative requirement.

A single cumulative examination is supposed to be of length which a competent student can handle in one hour; but actually two hours are allowed. The subject is normally in the field (referred to in this article as "division") selected by the candidate for his whole thesis period. Occasionally an examination covers two divisions, e.g. "physical-inorganic." Flat exceptions, in which a student writes an examination outside his division, are occasionally allowed by the committee. Once per year a student may arbitrarily withhold his examination paper without penalty. Four consecutive failures, or six failures out of eight consecutive examinations, place the candidate on probation for some specified period; a letter of warning is then sent. Disqualification in the Ph.D. program may result from seven consecutive failures to pass seven in twenty attempted, or if work during a probation period is judged by the committee as unsatisfactory.

Regardless of the specific type of written predoctoral examination employed by a given department, certain common observations can be made. Generally, it is advisable for you to take these examinations as early as is both possible and prudent. Just how soon this will be will depend upon your characteristic qualities in each of the scientific disciplines. Thus, a freshman graduate student in chemistry who comes in with a good undergraduate background and who passes all the placement examinations and all graduate courses to date would normally expect to take the written qualifying examinations or start his cumulatives sometime during the second term of his first year. On the other hand, if he came in with an inadequate background and did poorly on the placement examinations, he would spend much of his first year taking remedial undergraduate courses. This normally defers his starting the qualifiers for an additional period of six months to a year.

The situation is somewhat different in some physics departments where considerably more graduate course work is required and the written examinations, even for a well-prepared entering student, are not given until the end of his second year in graduate school. Furthermore, in some cases, the student does not start his research until he passes these qualifiers.

Consequences of Failing.   A big question for the average or below-average student is what do you do if you fail one or more of the written examinations. The options depend upon the type of examination system employed. We have described in detail the U.C.L.A. system for the cumulative examinations. In the case of written qualifiers, a variety of options also exist. Generally, if a student passes two of the three qualifiers and *almost* passes the third, he may be given some additional assignment to regenerate his competence in the area of his deficiency. This may include taking that particular exam over again. On the other hand, if he fails all the examinations, he may be asked to do one of the following, depending on his course work and the faculty's overall opinion of him, including their evaluation of his sincerity and ability as a teaching assistant:

(1)   Take a terminal master's degree

(2)   Remain in school and have another go at the examinations

(3)   Transfer to another university where the overall environment, academic and personal, might be more conducive to success on the part of the student.

We cannot state too strongly the need for a detailed, frank, and immediate appraisal of yourself if you fail these written examinations. Serious and necessarily embarrassing questions must be asked and honest answers presented in order to forestall one of the common tragedies of graduate school life —becoming a "perpetual predoctoral student." Some people, for one reason or another, continue on and on, getting more and more deeply involved and deeply depressed, as they try to cram for another round of written tests, with the pressure mounting all the time. Failure in written examinations does not mean failure in life. On the contrary, we know numerous graduate students who, after "busting out," made a real go of it elsewhere. They carefully re-evaluated their interests and abilities and changed their career objectives. In most cases, they wound up being far happier and far more productive than they would have been had they retaken the exams, barely managed to skim through, and, in time (a long time), become a marginal Ph.D.

We note in passing that there is a certain type of student who secretly seems to dread getting his degree and going out in the real world to be judged by his peers. This student consciously or unconsciously, seeks to prolong his graduate education and the moment of truth. Certainly, with the possibility of being drafted to serve a cause such as the Vietnam war, we could understand a graduate student's reluctance to leave the university. On the other hand, procrastinating graduate students were commonplace long after World War II and long before the Vietnam war. In the final analysis, they stay there because the faculty as a whole are being "nice guys" and lack the guts to throw the student out of the academic womb. It is our opinion that in the long run the prolonged extension of the trial period of graduate training does the student more harm than good; still, it is a difficult decision to make. The term for Ph.D. study in the sciences in some European countries (for example, Sweden) is commonly ten years and more. However, this is not the case in the United States; an exceptionally long time to get a degree here will be on permanent record in your department, and it will continue to reappear and may cause some serious concern among your prospective future employers.

In line with this, there is one feeling common to all faculty in the natural sciences. It is that in fairness to the student and to the institution, the decisive judgment on whether or not he is to be advanced to candidacy for the Ph.D. degree should be made as early as possible in the student's career. The "catch" is that we live in an imperfect academic world populated by faculty and students who are human. It is difficult in many borderline cases to reach a decision. If you find yourself in this position, we urge you to evaluate your alternatives carefully and discuss the matter with your research director, the departmental graduate advisor, and possibly the chairman of your department; in this way, you help the faculty make an honest and realistic decision if further procrastination occurs.

The Preliminary Oral Examination: Your Doctoral Committee.   The key committee with which you will come in contact while working for your Ph.D. degree is your doctoral committee. This committee is appointed by the dean of the graduate school. It usually consists of five faculty members, three or four of whom are from your own department and one or two of whom are from related fields. Generally, your research director is a member of the committee and in many departments, he is also its chairman.

The precise time in your graduate career when your doctoral committee is constituted depends upon a number of factors and may vary from department to department and from discipline to discipline. In general, the committee is appointed at the recommendation of the departmental chairman or graduate advisor after you have passed all the written examinations (including the language exams), and it appears that you have a good chance of completing your research and the doctoral program.

However, you should remember that the appointment of your committee does not automatically guarantee that you will wind up with a doctoral degree. There are still four more challenges in your path:

(1) The preliminary doctoral oral

(2) The successful completion of research for your dissertation

(3) The writing of your dissertation

(4) The final oral examination

In practice, the first three are the guts of any doctoral program.

In the case of your preliminary oral, all of your training in undergraduate school, coupled with the preliminary written examinations and graduate course work (some six years of effort!), have led you to this point. You must stand up in front of your superiors as they question you to determine how well you understand your chosen field and how you handle yourself under a verbal barrage of questions and comments.

With regard to your Ph.D. dissertation, your committee will be the final authority in judging whether or not you have really done an acceptable piece of original research and have written it up in a concise, lucid, acceptable form. In other words, it is their responsibility to accept or reject your thesis. Clearly, your doctoral committee plays a major role in your graduate career.

Preliminary Oral Doctoral Examination. It is this particular examination that strikes terror in the hearts of many otherwise well composed graduate students. As noted above, the purpose of this particular examination is to see whether you have matured scientifically and personally to the point where you can discuss a variety of topics in your major area, can reason through, with composure, difficult and penetrating questions, and generally can conduct yourself as a mature, young scholar.

The exact form of the predoctoral examination again varies, so we will not go into detail here. There are, however, several bits of general advice on "examinationship" that we can pass on to you which are based on several decades of experience with a wide range of students.

The first point is that members of doctoral committees are usually friendly toward the student and are not "out to get him." Since they generally are on the student's side, the first rule in taking an oral examination is to be calm and collected and to think positively. One of the major problems common to many students is that they are, or become, so "uptight" when they enter the examination room and are confronted by their doctoral committee that they simply can't get their minds working and show up far worse than they really are. This is embarrassing not only to the student, but, as a matter of fact, to the faculty as well. Of course, if the student is particularly cocky and overbearing, faculty committees have been known to derive a certain amount of pleasure out of putting him through his paces and educating him a bit in the committee room. If he is very bright and composed, he can get away with being cocky and everyone winds up quite satisfied. However, if he is cocky and not so bright he may find it a humbling and unfortunate experience.

A second point to remember is that while you can prepare for the oral examination by reviewing your major field in some depth, one never knows what to expect in the way of questions from the faculty committee. Thus it is not particularly fruitful and occasionally is actually hazardous, to cram excessively for a preliminary oral examination. Very often all this extensive cramming only gets the student tied up and functioning at less than his normal efficiency when he appears before the committee. It is particularly disconcerting to have studied the complex, difficult aspects of your subject only to be somewhat shattered by questions taken straight out of the undergraduate freshman course. It has been our experience that a fair percentage of the questions asked at a doctoral oral examination could be answered on the basis of the knowledge available in good, solid undergraduate freshman and sophomore courses. This fact is often overlooked by the graduate student.

Our advice would be, then, in preparing for your preliminary oral (or master's oral) to be sure that you have a good firm understanding of the basics of your subject. Start all the way back at your undergraduate freshman course and study a good, modern text at that level. Then proceed through your subsequent key undergraduate courses, and finally hit the graduate courses and literature in your research field. To re-emphasize, rarely have we seen graduate students fail their oral on the basis of their inability to answer highly complex and difficult questions. Rather they are failed because they lack a comprehension of the fundamentals of their subject.

When you take your oral examination, it is a good practice to listen to the question posed by the faculty member and take time to think about it. If you don't understand the question, ask a faculty member if he will repeat or clarify the question. Often times problems arise when you think he is asking you one thing and actually he is asking you another, much simpler question. After you are sure you understand the question, it is good planning to answer it in simple, straightforward terms. Be sure you don't assume that the question is necessarily complicated. Quite often, all that is really wanted is a simple explanation expressed clearly in fundamental terms. If you jump straight off into a complicated explanation, you might get into undue difficulty. Stop when you're ahead. If a more detailed response is desired, work your way into the more complicated answer. In this way, if you get stuck on some particular point well into the discussion, at least the faculty will recognize that you know the fundamentals behind the question and were simply hung up on a detail. Unfortunately, a student often starts right in with complex details and gets hung up on them. The faculty members then are never sure whether or not he understood the fundamental points behind the entire question. If you don't know the answer to a question, admit it. This fact will be evident to your committee in any case.

We will repeat our advice: don't cram; do relax, but remain alert during the examination. Your committee will consider it good taste if you choose to wear a coat and tie for the occasion. It won't change the verdict of the committee, but it adds an expected dignity.

Finally, if you successfully pass your preliminary oral examination, you will be duly congratulated by your committee members, and they will then sign papers attesting to your successful performance. These are forwarded to the graduate dean who in due course notifies you that you have now been "advanced to candidacy for the Ph.D. degree."

The Doctoral Committee and Your Dissertation. Another key function of your doctoral committee is to read, criticize, and ultimately accept or reject your research dissertation. Just how much help you will get from members of your committee depends upon who is chosen, the amount of time they have available, and their particular expertise in your specific research area. It is possible that other members of your committee, in addition to your research director may have a genuine interest in some specific portion of your thesis; they may, therefore, make particularly valuable contributions to improving the content as well as the form of your thesis.

Your major informal interaction with members of your committee will come a year or two after the preliminary oral examination when you start writing your thesis. Of course, a rough draft of your thesis will be reviewed critically by your research director. Some committee members will not be interested, but others will want to see a rough draft so that they can make corrections and additions early in the game rather than being faced with a thesis presented to them in final form several days before the final oral examination. In cases like this, it seems like a *fait accompli* since it is an expensive and time consuming job to make corrections and additions to a final draft. Your best tactic is to discuss with each individual member of your committee, well in advance, whether or not he wants to see rough drafts. If so, be sure to follow his suggestions. Incidentally, when we say rough drafts, we mean typewritten copy, not hand-written copy. Remember that while you are responsible for writing only one dissertation, an individual faculty member may be on several doctoral committees in a given quarter and the careful reading of a dissertation is a time-consuming job. He shouldn't have to translate your handwriting as part of the bargain.

This brings up another point. Be sure to allow the committee members ample time to read your rough draft. Don't rush in a day or two before you want to start the final typing, hand it to the obliging faculty member, and ask for his detailed comments. If you do procrastinate to this extent (and we have known students who did), he'll either throw it right back at you or will accept the rough draft and do little or nothing substantial to it.

The Final Oral Examination.   Now we come to the last act in your career as a graduate student, the final oral examination. In most departments, this is actually a defense of your thesis rather than a searching comprehensive examination. Only in rare instances will a student who has written an acceptable thesis be failed on his final oral examination. However, students have gotten this far and still failed; this can happen if your thesis research is sloppy and poorly thought out or if you make a weak defense of your research. As far as you are concerned, if you have written a definitive research thesis and in the process have consistently checked it out with the members of your doctoral committee, you should have no qualms about going into your final oral examination.

The format of the final oral usually involves certain common elements: first, you may be asked by the chairman of your committee to discuss briefly the results and overall significance of your thesis; second, the faculty may quiz you about any aspect of the dissertation they choose. Actually, of course, the faculty is not really limited to a discussion of your dissertation alone, and in some departments, the questions may range far afield. This is up to the discretion of the committee; there are no fixed ground rules for the game.

In some departments, in place of a final oral, you are required to give a formal seminar before the entire department, students, and faculty alike. This is more in the European tradition. In this case, the student gives a seminar based on his thesis and may then be questioned on his work not only by members of his committee, but also by other members of the department faculty and, in some cases, other students.

This seems to us to be a more meaningful approach than going through the formality of a closed, final oral, because it gives the graduate student valuable experience in presenting his own work to a critical but sympathetic audience. Whether or not you make your career in teaching, industry, or government, you'll find that the more experience you can get in presenting your ideas before a large and critical audience. the better off you'll be in the long run. You will be asked to perform in this fashion with increasing frequency as you move up the professional ladder.

The Master's Thesis and Oral Examination. We have not discussed the oral examination for the master's degree and master's thesis committee. In this case, there is simply one oral examination, the final oral. In the case of a "coursework-only" master's degree, in which no research is involved, it may be a demanding examination in which you are asked questions on a variety of subjects. On the other hand, if you have taken a research master's degree, the final examination is generally oriented around your thesis research, but it can expand into any areas of your subject that your committee chooses to discuss.

The general rules outlined above for your conduct in a predoctoral oral pretty much apply to your conduct in a master's oral examination. That is, remain calm and always go back to fundamentals when preparing for the exam and when answering the questions posed by your committee.

5. *Your Graduate Research and Dissertation*

A. CHOOSING A RESEARCH AREA FOR YOUR THESIS

One of your first questions, and one which you may well have answered while still an undergraduate, is "In what sub-discipline should I do my thesis research?" In some fields the decision is made before one enters graduate school. This is often true of chemistry where most entering students know initially whether they want to go into physical, inorganic, analytical, organic, theoretical, or biochemistry. This may not be the case in other disciplines where students take courses for a year or more before deciding what specific topic interests them. In any case, there are several factors to keep in mind when you choose a research area. Are you adept at mathematics? If not, don't plan to go into highly theoretical fields such as quantum mechanics, either as a chemist or as a physicist. This may sound obvious, but it is surprising how many students of only average caliber want to do their research in high-powered theoretical fields because they sound glamorous. Not only is this risky from the success point of view, but even if you do eventually wind up with a Ph.D. degree, the career opportunities are poorer for a theoretical chemist or physicist of only average ability who possesses little understanding of experimental techniques than are those for an average Ph.D. who has, however, carried out his re-

101

search in an experimental field and has a good background in modern instruments and experimental techniques. Industry finds far more uses for the average experimentalist than for the average theoretician.

By the same token, if you suffer from a dearth of natural aptitude in the laboratory, don't pick a research problem that involves the construction and maintenance of highly complex and sophisticated apparatus.

In choosing your graduate research problem, you should think of the short-term consequences as well as your long-term career goals. Until now, a scientist has been labeled, for example, as a physical chemist, a molecular biologist, or a solid state physicist; however, the scene is changing. The dawning age of multidisciplinary research is weakening these artificial and highly limiting barriers. In the future you may take a Ph.D. degree in chemistry, spend two years in an institute for biological research, take a year's apprenticeship in an air pollution agency, and eventually wind up as an expert in some aspect of environmental health. It is the authors' conviction that this type of training based on a strong, in depth background in one particular field, followed by a branching out into widely different disciplines, is far more conducive to developing researchers who will have genuine impact in the solution of societal problems than will the traditional specialist or the total generalist.

This leads to another consideration. Do you want to do research in an area that is "pure," basic research, with no obvious direct application to the real world, or would you be happier working on a problem which has a more immediate link to society's problems, for example, a problem related to water pollution, the synthesis of insecticides, or the toxicology of atmospheric pollutants? This is a critical question and one you should consider in depth. However, remember that what is considered pure, "ivory tower" research today may eventually wind up being critical in the solution of one of our applied problems. In this regard we would be wise to heed the recent words of Professor George S. Hammond of the California Institute of Technology.

> Surely Priestly was not thinking about air breathing rockets when he was fooling around with combustion; yet, his work and that of many others helped to create the theoretical models on which rocket technology depends. I think that there is always a chance that if man searches for answers to unanswered questions, and shares the results of his search, ultimately he will have some impact on the affairs of other men.[28]

This argument is a strong one for maintaining basic research today. While the swing to applied research has been fast, it is essential that basic research does not suffer, as we shall certainly pay for such shortsightedness in the future. One other point, if you are considering a highly applied and directed research problem for your dissertation research, you may miss one of the great opportunities of your life—a problem that demands a high degree of ingenuity and challenges your mind and physical skills to the utmost. Occasionally one can realize the best of both possible worlds by working on a really exciting fundamental problem in basic science which at the same time has a direct bearing on some very practical problem of man.

Perhaps the most important factor in your choice of research area is the depth of your interest and excitement in it. You'll devote not only the three years or more of your graduate student life to the difficult tasks related to your problem, but in turn the expertise which you develop in the research area will help determine the nature of the career opportunities which will open up for you during the rest of your scientific career. Obviously you don't want to spend your lifetime in a scientific area of only marginal interest to you. Your choice of research area and research director should not be taken lightly.

B.   CHOOSING A RESEARCH DIRECTOR: THE CONTRACT BETWEEN STUDENT AND PROFESSOR

The only person, other than your spouse, who will have the greatest influence upon your success as a graduate student is your research director. The specific role played by the research director varies from discipline to discipline, but in each case he is the crucial person who helps you to choose a specific research topic, who offers advice and counseling both in your academic and personal life, and who determines when you can stop working in the lab or at the computer and start writing your thesis. His approval of your dissertation is mandatory. You and he will have a working relationship which will extend beyond your years as a graduate student and remain throughout your professional career. He is the first person generally contacted by your prospective employers. His letters of recommendation have the most clout, and his general overall opinion of you as a scientist and as a person will be a crucial factor in your career.

Because of this very close interaction, it is critical that you make the right choice of a research director. If you decide to work with a given man and subsequently find out that you either do not like the research topic or simply cannot get along with him, you would be well advised to change research directors. If you are so far along in your thesis research that this would be too time consuming, then you simply had better make the best of it. Do the best job possible and suffer in silence. This won't be the last time you will face this kind of situation. Whether you go into industry, government, or academia you will meet people who will be troublesome and who will not live up to your expectations. You might as well learn to accept this early in the game and make the best of the situation.

Learning to take direction and to get along with the boss is one of the real-life experiences you will encounter in graduate school; it is so important that later it can literally make or break you in your professional career. We do not mean to imply that you have to be a "yes man" or a "Mr. Milktoast," but you should have a responsible interaction with your research director. For example, if you are working under his direction and particularly if you are supported on one of his research grants or contracts, you should act toward him in a loyal and mature fashion. He may not be the greatest research director in the world, and he may have a variety of human frailties, but you made your choice, and you should act accordingly. Furthermore, one consequence of your having a responsible and mature attitude toward him is that this will, in most cases, engender a similar response on his part.

While you as a graduate student are under a variety of pressures, it is important for you to recognize that your research director is in the same situation. Some of his attitudes and actions may be better understood if you consider some of his pressures. From your point of view as a graduate student, you want him to be highly intelligent, filled with creative ideas, and in the laboratory with you a substantial part of each day. You want him to have an international reputation, or at least an excellent reputation with the "in" group in his particular subject, and be well recognized by federal authorities responsible for research grants and fellowships. You will receive support as a research assistant, or as a fellow on his recommendation; depend on this. You want him to be thoroughly conversant with the detailed literature in his field, to be a dedicated teacher in his graduate and undergraduate courses, to be well respected by his departmental colleagues, and at times to be a friend or "father confessor" who will listen sympathetically to your problems both in research and in the personal sphere.

From the point of view of your research director's colleagues, he is expected to be a dedicated teacher, a good research man, and a thoroughly conscientious individual when it comes to departmental, university, and public service. He is expected to pay his own way in research by generating his own grants and contracts. The university administration welcomes and encourages his serving on departmental and university committees and also on national and international advisory boards. Finally, he is expected to hit the seminar speakers' trail across the country, bringing attention to his research, his department, and his university.

Recently another voice has been heard—that of the community. The taxpayers' revolt has set in and the professor's activities in teaching, consulting, and research are being scrutinized carefully by students, alumni, politicians, and the public. They are raising the question daily, "Why isn't he devoting more of his time to teaching, and undergraduate teaching at that?"

As an additional commitment, governmental agencies at the local, state, and federal level are asking the professor to consult on pressing problems often on a no-fee or a minimal-fee basis which may not cover his expenses.

If you add up the pressures on the professor from these various directions, it is no wonder that he may have less time to spend with you than you would like. These demands have become increasingly more intense during the last decade, and it is no secret that they are generating real problems involving the professor and the university. Admittedly, he generates some of the problems himself, but they often arise from external sources as well. Most of the requests are for beneficial ends, but when the professor takes on too many of these, he is subject to criticism for not minding the shop, and justly so.

The above comments are in no way an excuse for the actions and attitudes of research directors. We cite them so that you can get a better understanding of our hangups. Remember our rule: you can't have it both ways. If you expect your research director to be deeply involved and interested in your problems, research and personal, then it is only natural that you should be concerned with his problems, academic and personal. If you expect him to be tolerant when you are in a jam and pushed for time, at the very least you should display toward him some of the very same tolerance and understanding. You don't have to do this, but by the same token, he doesn't have to perform more than the routine functions of the research director.

Let us now consider in a somewhat more specific way the person you may consider as your research director. The comments we made above concerning the involvements of a professor vary in degree, depending upon his experience. He may be (1) an assistant professor on his way up, (2) an established scientist at the associate professor level who has tenure in his department and is beginning to be well known among his peers, or (3) an internationally recognized scientist-scholar. Your choice depends upon your own particular needs. Do you feel you need a great deal of personal guidance in the laboratory? If so, consider working with an assistant professor who will probably spend more time in the lab than you will. He is likely to be close to your own age, so you will probably share a number of common experiences, both educationally and financially. On the other hand, he will generally not yet be well known in the scientific community. He may also have less in the way of financial support for your research, but this isn't necessarily the case.

At the other end of the spectrum, if you are able to work independently in the laboratory and want to be exposed to the research ideas of a recognized scientist with a large research group of graduate and postdoctoral students, then you should consider working with an established professor. A major drawback is, however, that he may simply have little or no time to spend with you in the laboratory. In some cases you may even have to make appointments with him to talk about your research.

The role of the associate professor generally falls somewhere between these two extremes. His research may be nationally and internationally recognized by his peers, but at this stage of his academic career, he may also be exposed to an increasingly heavy administrative load such as service on major departmental and university committees. However, in general he should have more time for your problems than the nationally recognized scientist with the large research machine.

You should ask yourself these questions about a prospective research director. "Is he doing exciting, significant research? "Is he productive?" "Does his research turn me on?" These are really the critical factors; if you can answer yes to these questions, then you can often overlook a wide range of personality conflicts and wind up with a splendid piece of research as well as an outstanding educational experience.

Our discussion to this point has been from the graduate student's viewpoint. Let's now turn the coin and consider the situation from the point of view of the research director. On what basis does he make the decision to accept you into his research group?

Basically, he expects his research students to be motivated by an intense desire to learn the formal aspects of the science and to tackle the unknown. Thus he expects his research students to be vitally interested in their research topics, to be abreast of the current literature, and to be dedicated workers in the laboratory. He also hopes to find in them those personal qualities of unselfishness and loyalty which promote a harmonious team spirit in his research group. Every research director knows that one bad actor who is careless in his experiments, who gripes continually, who is lazy, or who is domineering and intolerant can cause all kinds of problems, both in his own crew and in the department. In short, there is a strong mutual interaction between the research director and his graduate student, and this may lead to a lifelong friendship based on mutual respect as scientists and individuals.

The actual approach to research and the amount of research appropriate for a research dissertation varies from department to department and from professor to professor. However, one thing is common. The critical feature of the doctoral research is whether or not it presents original and significant new information which is of direct value to your scientific disciplines. One positive test of the suitability of your research is its acceptance for publication in a recognized, scholarly journal where it will be read and criticized by your peers in the outside world.

During your long hours of thesis research, keep alert and continue to think about what you are doing and why you are doing it. Plan your experiments carefully, observe the results with an open mind, and record in a bound notebook exactly what you see. Don't try to see what you and your preceptor expect to see. Theories may come and go, but good data will last forever.

It is in the interpretation of the experimental findings, particularly the unexpected findings, that you will have a chance to demonstrate your real value as a scientist. When something goes wrong with an otherwise well-conceived experiment, stop, look, and listen—Mother Nature is trying to tell you something. No one can teach you how to do this, but there are a great many common ground rules for the conduct of research that have been summarized beautifully by Professor E. Bright Wilson. Every new graduate student should read his book, *An Introduction to Scientific Research.* [29]

The actual mechanism of scientific discovery is a much more difficult area to understand, but it is a fascinating area for speculation and should be mentioned briefly. In this regard, prospective research scientists should also read the interesting little book, *The Psychology of Invention in the Mathematical Field,* by Hadamard. [30] Although Hadamard's field was mathematics and most of his examples deal with this area, most of his considerations apply to the other sciences as well.

Hadamard believes that invention or the process of scientific discovery starts in the scientist's unconscious mind through the combination of ideas. During the preparation of the scientist in a given area and during his years of continued learning, he has filed away in his memory many ideas, facts, and theories which he continues to sort through in his search for the solution to the problem he faces. Hadamard perceives this sorting process as a testing of the enormous number of idea combinations which may apply to the solution of the problem. Many of these combinations, presumably formulated in the unconscious, are devoid of interest, while the few which may be fruitful are perceived by the conscious mind. Hadamard sees the role of chance in the scientific invention process as contributing only to the rather random idea-combining process which occurs in the unconscious during this first step in the invention process. He feels that the process of invention is discernment, or choice between alternatives in the combination of significant ideas. Hadamard agrees with Poincare[31] that invention is choice and that this choice is imperatively covered by the sense of scientific beauty. The choice may occur to the scientist as a sudden illumination.

According to Hadamard, following the preparation, the period of incubation, and the illumination, the fourth stage of invention is reached. This stage is one of conscious work to verify and specify the new ideas which the scientist has developed. It is often during this stage that both the frustration and the real thrill of scientific work are encountered.

In regard to the unsuccessful attempts at the solution of scientific problems, Hadamard advises students beginning research work:

> . . . after working on a subject and seeing no further advance seems possible, to drop it and try something else, but to do so provisionally, intending to resume it after an interval of some months.

The question often arises as to who is responsible for writing up the student's doctoral research for publication. In some scientific fields the student writes the manuscript and is sole author on the publication. In other fields such as chemistry, the accepted practice is that the research director co-authors the paper with the student, who generally prepares the first draft.

Regardless of the authorship, it is very much to the advantage of both you and your research director, to write up your research for publication as soon as possible after its completion. Never again will you know so much detail about that specific topic, and this is the time to write it up. Unfortunately, in some cases the graduate student races through his dissertation, takes his final oral examination, and runs off to his first job. He gets immersed in his new position, and often times many years elapse before the dissertation work is written up, if at all. This is no great loss to science and mankind if it is a rather poor research thesis. On the other hand, if it is first-rate research, it is a real waste not to have it published and readily available to scientists throughout the world.

One other situation should be considered, that of the graduate student who accepts a job and actually leaves the university to work full-time before completing his dissertation and taking his final oral. We have seen examples of this in which real problems arose both at the university and in the new job. We strongly urge you not to follow this course even if it is given the blessing of your preceptor and the department. In such cases, students leave the university, take a job at a Ph.D.'s salary, and accept the title of "doctor." This is not only potentially embarrassing to all concerned, particularly if the student never returns to take his oral, but, in a sense, it is also highly improper. We know that toward the end of graduate school you may be in a financial bind and that an industrial salary looks most attractive. However, you would be far better advised to borrow some money and stay one hundred percent on your prime mission. Get that degree officially, then go to your new employer and put all of your effort into your new job. It will pay off in the long run.

C. PROTECTING YOUR ORIGINALITY: COPY-RIGHTS, PATENTS, AND TRADEMARKS

Original ideas are precious, as your preceptors and mentors will point out, and as history reminds us. You should be thinking, therefore, as you pursue your research, write your thesis, and present your candidacy before an examining committee, whether any of your original ideas, imagination, and creativity are inventions.

One may be idealistic, and grant his ideas, creations, and inventions to mankind. A few—you name them—persons in history have been so altruistic. Most of us, however, are egocentric enough to want to be associated with our original ideas. After all, you will have to defend and be responsible for your original work, so you and your university might as well enjoy the benefits.

The purpose of this section, then, is to alert you to copyrights, patents, and trademarks. They are granted by the United States government and give you certain exclusive rights. It is important that you are aware of these in starting your graduate work, for this is probably the first time in your life as a scientist that you will be doing something original.

First, let's take a look at a copyright. You have undoubtedly been warned in your school career about plagiarism and copying without the proper references. Major reproduction companies that use xerographic, electrofax, diazo, and other duplicating techniques, are also keen in their rights and the possible abuses of their copying machines; they usually notify their customers about what can and cannot be copied. Open almost any book (including some Bibles), and you will see a copyright statement. Copyrights are issued to protect the writings of an author from being copied. They include dramatic, musical, literary, certain artistic works, and some recording and performing rights. The key to the understanding of copyrights is that they relate to the *form of expression* rather than to the actual subject matter. Thus, a recent patent office bulletin states, "A description of a machine could be copyrighted as a writing, but this would only prevent others from copying the description—it would not prevent others from writing a description of their own or from making and using the machine."[32] If you want to get further information on copyrights, write to the Register of Copyrights, Library of Congress, Washington, D.C. 20540. Copyrights are not handled by the patent office. You may want to ask your preceptor whether your thesis, or portions of it, should be copyrighted. You should be particularly familiar with copyright regulations if you intend to write a book.

The use of the trademark is a rarely encountered event in graduate school. Trademarks are assigned to a name or symbol used in the trade of goods to indicate their source or origin. A stroll through any supermarket will reveal many trademarks.

The patent is something which you may encounter during your future career and which could arise from your graduate work. However, even more important is that the completion of graduate school will launch you into a career in which you may continue to create and invent. There are some good habits to develop in your graduate work which will alert you to the possibility of a patent.

The government grants a patent for an invention. This grant to the inventor or to his heirs or assignees gives certain exclusive rights to the invention for seventeen years throughout the United States. Now, note that a copyright protects an author's expression from being copied, a trademark prevents others from using the same name on the same goods, and a patent gives "the right to exclude others from making, using, or selling" an invention. Note that although it excludes others, it does not give the inventor the right to make, use, or sell the invention.

There are some good habits to develop which bear on patents. You should always sign your notebook and date it every day as you start to record your day's findings. Remember the origin of the apparently unique idea or suggestion. Note whether it came from someone else or from yourself. Have a unique finding witnessed by a colleague in your laboratory, and have him sign your notebook to attest to your finding. You may wish to investigate whether or not any processes you originate may be reduced to practice on an industrial scale.

The patent office emphasizes that to be patentable, an invention must be new and useful. It will grant patents to any person who "invents or discovers any new and useful process, machine, manufacture, or composition of matter, or any new and useful improvements thereof."[32]

You should ask your department chairman what your university policy is with respect to patents and what procedures are required at your university. Often the university, the research foundation of the university, or the government or industrial sponsoring agency retain all or a certain portion of the patent rights on your work. In industrial research there is no question—your idea is company property; you will get a gold star on your record and probably some financial recognition, especially if the idea forms the basis of a good money-making process.

From a consideration of the data of Table 3, you can get a feel for the fate of ideas for which patents were sought over the years. Note that the column headed "Applications Received" does not necessarily imply that the applications that year resulted in the patents granted, for there is about a three-year backlog in applications to patent granting. However, if we extrapolate, out of 95,000 applications processed, about 55,000 patents are granted. Hence the average probability of having a patent issued is roughly just under sixty percent.

An extensive patent search is necessary to substantiate that your idea is new. Fees of a few hundred dollars will probably be needed to cover the search, and there will be incidental charges when you apply for a patent. Contemplate the success statistics of Table 3, and evaluate the chance that your patent will be useful to someone before spending your money on this procedure.

TABLE 3: Comparison of the Number of Applications Received by the United States Patent Office and the Number of Patents Issued.[a]

Year	Applications Received	Patents Granted
1790	–	3
1800	–	41
1850	2,193	992
1900	41,980	26,499
1920	86,893	38,882
1930	94,203	48,322
1940	69,857	48,850
1950	74,295	47,976
1960	84,475	49,989
1964	93,170	50,392
1969	102,000	65,000

[a]Data from reference 33.

6. The Postdoctoral Fellowship

One of the most significant changes that has occurred in graduate education during the last decade has been the tremendous increase in postdoctoral instruction. The impact varies from discipline to discipline, but it certainly has been felt in the natural sciences. The "postdoc" has changed from a rather rare honor bestowed upon a few young Ph.D.'s, as was the case until about 1950, to a situation where most good Ph.D.'s could find at least one or two years of postdoctoral support. In fact, the situation during the mid-sixties became such that a year or two of postdoctoral instruction was almost a requirement for a university position. With the present squeeze on federal funds, your chances of securing a postdoctoral fellowship are somewhat less than they were a few years ago. However, if you are a good student, have done a first-rate research job, and can get strong letters of recommendation from your research director and other faculty, you still have a good chance of obtaining postdoctoral support.

Should you seek a postdoctoral fellowship? Will it be of significant value to you? If you are looking for an academic job and your academic and research records are very good, you should probably spend the additional year or two at this advanced level. Most academic vacancies will be filled from the ranks of the postdoctoral fellows. However, if you plan to go into industrial work, there may be some question as to the benefits of postdoctoral work. Ask the representatives of the companies with which you eventually hope to work about your attractiveness to the company with and without post-doctoral training. In some industrial positions the postdoctoral years could be of much value; in others it may be of very little value.

There are two main classes of postdoctoral fellowships: the so-called "open fellowships" administered on a competitive nationwide basis by such agencies as the National Science Foundation, National Institutes of Health, and the Public Health Service, and the postdoctoral research positions funded by research grants or contracts and administered by faculty in their roles as principal investigators.

There are some pertinent tax considerations involved with your position as a postdoctoral research scientist. You will actually be serving a period of postdoctoral *instruction* and as such, you are continuing your education and improving your chances for a better job. It is thus worthwhile to check out the tax status of your particular position.

Your postdoctoral research is different than your graduate research in many ways. It is your chance to devote all of your time and effort to research. There are no exams and no courses (unless you choose to take them), just the challenge of tackling a tough problem and cracking it. Your success as a postdoctoral fellow will be based on many of the same considerations as was your status as a graduate student. However, since you are free of other obligations, your research director expects you to produce more first-rate research at a faster pace and with less personal direction on his part than he would expect from a predoctoral research student. Thus, if you view a postdoctoral fellowship as simply a relaxing year or two of research involving a thirty-five to forty-hour work week, you'll be a disappointment to all concerned, unless you are a truly exceptional, highly organized individual.

You might ask the question, "Where and when should I apply for a postdoctoral fellowship?" Your best bet is to have a frank talk with your research director, at least a year before you expect to take your final oral. If he thinks highly of you, he will suggest you compete for the open fellowships, and will provide you with a list of his colleagues throughout the world who might have vacancies in postdoctoral slots. He will then suggest that you write to them directly and give his name as a reference. In some cases he may initiate the correspondence by writing directly to the professors to suggest that you are completing your Ph.D. and are a good prospect for a postdoctoral position.

Be sure to allow plenty of time between your initial letters of inquiry and the date you expect to be available. Also, when you write a letter of inquiry, it is advisable to enclose a brief summary of your background and experience, awards you have received, etc. Be sure to include reprints or preprints of your research papers that have been published or are in press. You should also include the names of at least two additional faculty members as references in addition to that of your research director. Incidentally, be sure to check with these faculty members before you put their names down as references; they will appreciate this courtesy.

Finally, remember that in recommending you for a postdoctoral fellowship, your research director is putting his reputation on the line. Don't disappoint him and yourself by doing less than your best in your postdoctoral years.

III

The Payoff: Employment in Industry, University, or Government

7. Introduction

Every Ph.D. faces the crossroads of his career as the degree-granting date approaches. During the final months of his graduate effort, in the midst of the turmoil of thesis writing, preparing for the final oral examination, moving, etc., he must answer the "big question": Will I teach or do research, and with which agency, university, industry, government, or other will I seek employment?

In large part, this decision may be made for him. His preceptor will be relatively free with advice, and pressures from his family and friends will influence his choice. Furthermore, the nature and availability of jobs in industry, university, or government will help establish the direction in which his career moves. For example, on the average in 1968 the Ph.D.'s choice of the pure research route, whether in industry, government, private laboratory, or other, gave him about a twenty percent chance of entering the areas of management or administration (note the data presented in Figure 9). Among all the Ph.D. scientists in the United States, approximately 40% worked in industry, government, and other nonacademic institutions (see Figure 10). Somewhat less than 60% were employed in educational institutions. Approximately one-half of the number employed in educational institutions were on the faculty and involved in teaching and research. The other half were employed on research grants and contracts and in administration and service positions related to the functions of the university.

As far as you personally are concerned, however, these figures may be misleading as is often the case when one tries to relate a personalized event to a grand overall average. For

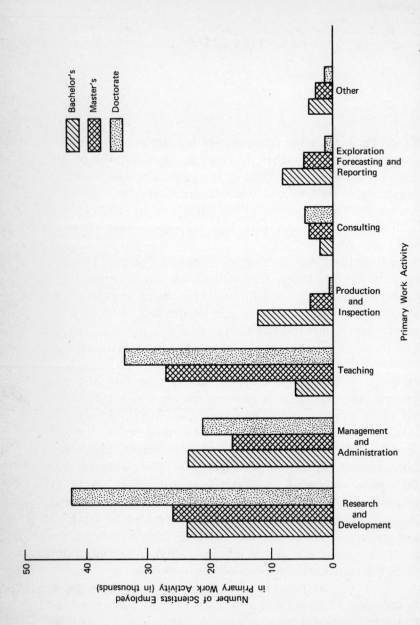

Figure 9: Primary work activity of the United States scientists for various highest degree categories, 1968. (Data from ref. 15.)

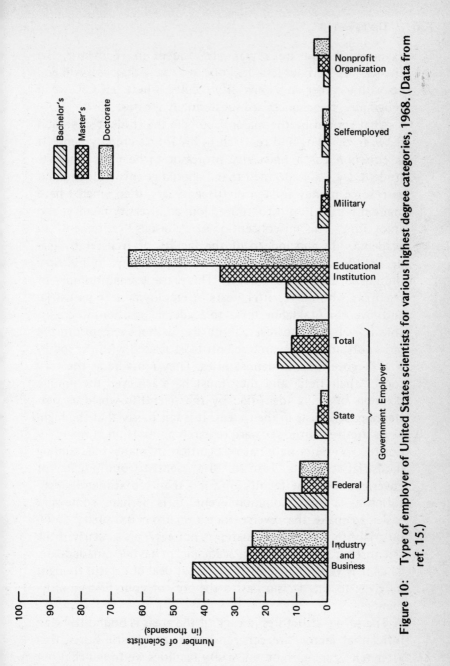

Figure 10: Type of employer of United States scientists for various highest degree categories, 1968. (Data from ref. 15.)

example, if you are a graduate student in chemistry, the chances are perhaps less than one in twenty that you will end up with a career on a university faculty, whereas if you are in geography, the chances are substantially greater.

What should be the major factors in the student's decision between teaching and research in his future employment? It is common for a university professor to hear his graduate student say, "I've decided that I should go into industry and earn some money for ten or fifteen years; then when I have made my pile, I want to 'retire,' join a university faculty, and enjoy life." This misconception of a glorious "retirement" to academic life and indeed of the facility of transfer to academic life after fifteen years of employment in industry should be eliminated quickly. There are a small number of scientists who move, after years of employment in industrial and governmental laboratories to academic positions in creditable universities; however, those are, without exception, the most outstanding research scientists associated with the industrial or governmental laboratories. They must be at the very top of their field, and they must have achieved the unique position of being identified by the scientific world as outstanding scientists in their areas. It is fair to say that the highly restrictive attitude toward research publication in many industries prevents national recognition of many outstanding industrial scientists. Transfer of a scientist from industry or government to the faculty of a less than top academic institution is a more common event. It is perhaps somewhat easier to make the reverse transition from university to industrial life, but even this step is not easy, particularly if the scientist's track record as an academician has been inadequate. Thus it is very important that a great deal of careful thought be given to the decision as to the area of your first employment.

The salary structures in each of the areas is bound to be an influential factor. We can remember, and it still hurts, that after ten years each on university faculties we found that our graduate students then leaving the university with a Ph.D. degree and going into industry, received more money in starting salary than we were receiving at that time from our universities.

This disparity in salary structure is striking. Note in Figure 11 that the average industrial salary for all full-time employed civilian scientists in the United States as of 1968 was about $17,500 per year. Government employment of Ph.D. scientists provided a median annual salary of $15,800. On the other hand, the academic year (nine months) salary of a Ph.D. scientist in educational institutions averaged $12,000. Some university professors in the sciences are able to supplement their academic year salary to some extent if they are fortunate enough to have research grants and consulting opportunities, but the total of all these is probably no more than one-third of their academic salary. Thus the typical total salary of the Ph.D. scientist in educational institutions may be as much as $16,000 per year if he is an eager, research-oriented professor. The differential of $1,500 per year between the median take-home pay of the industrial and academic scientists is appreciable but it should not be the determining factor in your decision. There are many more important issues that should help you determine your future employer.

If your choice of position is with the faculty of a university, then be very sure that you are willing to accept the obligations involved. Professor W.T. Lippincott at the Ohio State University has clearly enunciated a major problem in the American university today,[34] in indicating that the underemphasis on teaching is a critical problem in many of our universities. The university professor can be characterized easily in terms of his number of research publications and the amount of money which he has attracted to the university. Until the recent student revolution focused on the problem, university administrations often seemed to accept inadequacies in the teaching ability of its staff provided that their

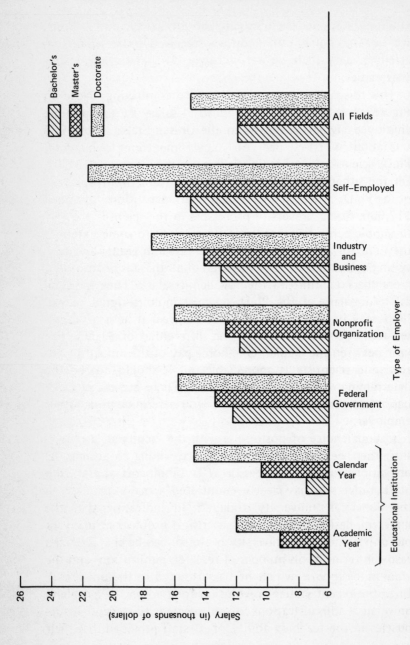

Figure 11: Comparison of the median annual salary of full-time employed civilian scientists in various types of employment, 1968. (Data from ref. 15.)

strengths in financial attracting power and research productivity were dominant. While on a number of campuses this inequity is at least being partially rectified, it is sobering to note that Hayes has recently concluded,[35] on the basis of a study of seventeen academic departments at one university, that "promotion is strongly related to measures of research activity but appears to be unrelated to teaching ability."

The dilemma has not necessarily developed because of "uninformed and evil" administrators, but rather, relates to several problems they continually face. One problem is associated with the difficulty of evaluating good teaching. Furthermore, it is very difficult to employ faculty who are both at the forefront of their research areas and who also excel in exposition in the classroom. Finally, when graduate education continues to be supported in a large part through federal grants and contracts, the very existence of the graduate program in most universities depends critically on the prowess of the faculty in the various research categories. Professor Lippincott states that, all too often, teaching is a hoped-for fringe benefit. This situation must, and will, change, but it is what we are faced with today; your decision of whether or not to accept a university position must be based upon this knowledge. Vice President Garrett of the Ohio State University put his finger on the dilemma of the teaching and research "conflict" when he stated, "No Nobel Prize has been awarded for good teaching alone, but good teaching has made possible many Nobel Laureates."[34]

There really need be no conflict between research and teaching in the university. This conflict often exists in the minds of the citizen, and is sometimes self-imposed by the professor who responds best to the stimulation of tangible research rewards. Cullis[36] suggests that research increases the confidence and sense of involvement of the teacher. He feels that the ideal teacher is, among other things, a person with an original mind who is actively participating in the development of his subject. Research provides one important way of becoming involved, and it is desirable that the number of people in the university who are engaged in research should be sufficient at least to create a well-defined "research community." He feels that the coexistence of research and teaching in the same institution demonstrates in the clearest possible way to students that their subject is a rapidly changing and developing one. In the university, what is taught today can be substantially different from what is taught only a few years in the future. Changes in our knowledge brought about by research in the intervening period force a constant revision of the curriculum.

Our major point concerning opportunities in university teaching and research is, then, that the scientist who seeks academic employment must be dedicated to his teaching as well as to his research. He is morally wrong to accept a university faculty position if his motivation is only to pursue, at university or government expense, his pet research project. He must accept, as his primary function, leadership in communication with budding scientists in addition to leadership in some particular scientific area. If he does not, he is doing a great disservice both to the students and to the entire academic community. The students of today are demanding of the university's administration and faculty an honest re-evaluation of what the educational process should be. They are reminding professors in graduate and undergraduate schools that they expect some significant and meaningful contact with their professors. They expect discussions and interchange of ideas with their professors. There is no great advantage to reading of the presence of a Nobel Laureate in the department brochure, if they never see him, talk to him, or listen to him expound on his specialty. Today the student rightfully demands that the university professor be a teacher as well as a scholar-scientist.

Every graduate student who is thinking seriously of entering university or college teaching should read the excellent report of the Rothwell Committee on Undergraduate Teaching.[37] You can better judge your capabilities for teaching and your interest in teaching after reading this report.

Now let's face your career choice with the realistic feeling that satisfaction in the university of tomorrow can only be derived through significant contributions to both teaching and research; fundamental to your decision is an evaluation of your potential both as a teacher and as a research scientist. Do you enjoy working with people and explaining ideas to your colleagues? Was your experience as a teaching assistant in the university enjoyable? Were you at ease in front of your class? Were you able to come up with an honest and educated response to that searching question that was asked in your recitation class or seminar? Did the students seek your advice and counsel on their academic problems? Was your thesis research well received? Do you have some inventive and new ideas for continuing research? If you can answer yes to these questions, then you will probably enjoy and be successful in academic life. If the answer to these questions is no or maybe, perhaps you would find your greatest satisfaction in industry, government, or other employment.

In the following chapters we will consider in great detail many of the opportunities and responsibilities which face the scientist in industry, government, and the university. Your career in any of these areas can be most exciting and rewarding. However, there are many aspects of employment in each area which are little known to the inexperienced graduate student, yet which are worth serious consideration before his or her choice is made. Our frank comments concerning the virtues and the disadvantages of the various areas may be considered by the "pure" academician or "practical" industrialist as unwarranted commentary. However, the student will soon learn that life is not all roses. Every day is not payday, and complete satisfaction in one's employment is built on many intangibles as well as on the more obvious factors.

8. Industrial Employment for the Scientist

Industry continues to be the first employment choice of the majority of graduate students in the physical sciences. Let's consider some of the benefits and problems associated with industrial employment for the scientist. We first compare and contrast industrial and academic employment and then proceed to review briefly some basic elements characteristic of industry. Finally, we discuss how to conduct a search for an industrial position.

A. THE INDUSTRIAL SCIENTIST VERSUS THE ACADEMIC SCIENTIST

Conjure up in your mind's eye a picture of the "typical" industrial scientist and of the "typical" academic scientist. What do you see? What are the dominant characteristics of each? What are the major functions of each man? Through the years, whenever we have played this game with undergraduates and graduate students in the sciences, we have gained some most interesting insights into their thinking. Generally, the students see the industrial scientist as a well-dressed, well-heeled gentleman with a deep tan; he smokes good cigars, orders extra-dry Beefeater martinis with a twist, and has a pleasant line of chatter which skirts broad areas of interest,

133

including the stock market, the seventeenth hole at the Pebble Beach Golf Club, French wines, and Florida women. On the other hand, the students see the academic scientist as a tired-looking man with round shoulders and unkempt hair, wearing a wrinkled suit splotched with chalk dust. He seems to be isolated in another world, dreaming up impractical or esoteric problems and is well remembered lecturing passionately and tirelessly to a group of complacent students.

Of course, neither of these pictures is fully justified by the facts, but there is just that dash of truth in them which makes them "accepted" by students and citizens and, alas, by much of the media. We have been taught to expect the industrial scientist to be much better off financially than his counterpart in the university. We have somehow been led to believe that the industrial scientist has much more free time than the academic scientist of the same age group and education. Perhaps both of these expectations are, on the average, true. However, don't think for a moment that all industrial scientists are rich men with nothing but free time on their hands, nor that all academicians are relatively poor and overworked. The truly successful scientist in both industry and academic life works hard. Furthermore, both industrial and university scientists usually direct research groups a good share of their time. In fact, the similarity of duties may extend even further. Today many industrial scientists teach an occasional course at a nearby campus or in the company's continuing educational program, while the academic man, who acts as an industrial consultant, commonly gets involved in industrial research.

We have noted some striking similarities between the two groups of scientists, but there are also some significant differences. Our industrial and academic colleagues usually point to one major factor which serves to maintain these differences. In our free enterprise system, industry is, and indeed must be, *profit oriented*. The university provides an educational service and is a *nonprofit* agency. This basic difference results in moulding patterns which are rather characteristic for each group of scientists.

The successful industrial scientist is a good team man, or he soon becomes one, if he is to survive. The academic scientist, on the other hand, is much more independent; he plans and executes his research and teaching on a more individual basis.

The profit motive of industry leads to another recognizable difference between scientists at national meetings. The academic scientist has only self-imposed restrictions in discussing aspects of his research effort. He may hold back on some as yet unproven points, but even these results usually enter his discussions. However, the industrial scientist must show great restraint in his communication with scientists outside of his company. He has had some phase of his research cleared for public disclosure by the upper administration, and he talks about only this portion of his work. The need for this security is evident. The directors of the company have invested a large amount of money in research and development ventures requiring years to come to fruition. To release key information prematurely may result in a loss of the competitive advantage needed to complete the final research, development, and marketing of the new material or device developed from his work.

The young industrial scientist quickly learns of additional differences between his position and that of the academician. Industrial research is an expensive operation in the eyes of the upper management. Results of industrial research must continue to point to a potential money-making product, or this line of research will be discontinued. How often the academic "father" has heard his industrially employed "son" bemoan his situation! "If I could have spent just a few more weeks on that problem, I would have had a fine piece of scientific work of which I could have been proud." On the other hand, the scientist in the university usually continues his particular study through "hell and high water," employing several generations of graduate students if he so chooses. The authors can't help but recognize, however, that academicians at times may continue research on some subject of a given field far too long to maintain the real worth of his work in proper perspective. The imagination and interest of a good research problem is lost in the search for the next bit of detail.

The academic scientist generally gains far more recognition, publically if not financially, with his scientific contributions to a given field than does the industrial scientist because of the necessary security associated with industrial research organizations.

One additional difference between the academic and the industrial scientist can be agreed upon; industry provides a much broader climate of colleagues of different background than the university. We submit that the industrial scientist will, rather quickly in his career, work with, coordinate, or direct a team drawn from the ranks of salesmen, accountants, scientists, marketing men, purchasing agents, lawyers, and even a company vice president or two. In industry you must communicate with many different professionals, and your progress will be determined by a consensus of your associates. In academic life, at least before the era of multidisciplinary, societal research, you would be judged most likely by your professional peers within your department or professional association.

B. TYPES OF COMPANIES: COMPANY SIZE AND ITS EFFECT ON THE SCIENTIST

Size plays a significant role in the style of a company, and therefore bears directly on the work habits of its scientists. Obviously, the very large companies give a certain measure of security compared to smaller companies. A large company will have more elaborate facilities than a small one (computers, instruments, long-range research, plus room for specialists such as economists and public relations men). Working in a small company requires you to wear various hats. The crossover points in going from a small to a medium to a large company are hard to define in sales dollars or staff sizes, but there are certain key questions you may ask when interviewing a company to ascertain its "style size," i.e., young, vigorous, and dynamic versus mature or conservative. We hope this section will give you some insight which will be helpful in your future considerations.

While there may be a prevailing view that the large corporations are owned by a few millionaires, it should be brought to mind that if you work for a corporation, you are responsible legally to the officers of the company who are appointed by the directors, and the latter are elected by the shareholders who own the company. Let us briefly look at some figures on shareholders and then at the size of sales of the major corporations in the United States to gain some perspective on relative sizes.

The Shareholders of Industry. Unless you plan to work for yourself, are independently wealthy, or choose to lead the life of a vagabond, you must have a boss, by definition, or owners to whom you will have to report.

The major industries are owned by many people, and these people want to see their investments prosper and grow. We doubt that the three million shareholders in A.T. & T. would appreciate a drop in their dividends or a decline in the value of their ownership over a few years' span. To survive, a private company must show an eventual profit from its operations. Therefore, the company that hires you requires that you contribute in some manner to a return on its investment. Thus, although industrial leaders are becoming more and more concerned about social benefits and returns, their basic objective is to show a profit. A few companies have chosen research projects that may not return as much in terms of dollar profits as other projects but that have great social value.

Examples can be found in the educational and environmental projects sponsored by some industries.

But who owns the major United States industries? In 1969 some twenty-two million Americans owned shares of stocks, and the New York Stock Exchange said then that there were three times the number of individual shareowners in 1969 than in 1952, with over half of the shareholders being women. You might want to ask yourself, if you choose an industrial career—whom are you really working for? For example, A.T. & T. had approximately three million shareholders in 1966; General Motors, one million three hundred and thirteen thousand; Standard Oil of New Jersey, seven hundred and twenty-eight thousand; General Electric, five hundred and fifteen thousand; General Telephone and Electronics, four hundred and sixteen thousand; Ford, four hundred and one thousand; U.S. Steel, three hundred and thirty-five thousand; RCA, three hundred and five thousand; IBM, two hundred and eighty-one thousand; and Bethlehem Steel, two hundred and forty-five thousand.

We might note here a current fascinating conflict of interest. The public at large is tremendously interested in curbing pollution, yet many of the people who cry "down with the polluters" examine the dividend checks from major industries and become infuriated if the quarterly dividends drop. It is something to think about.

The Sales of Major United States Corporations.   If you consider an industrial career after your Ph.D., you should realize that there is a good chance that you may be working for one of the major United States corporations. They have the resources to handle chemists, physicists, biologists, engineers, mathematicians, psychologists, and probably in the future, philosophers. These organizations are extremely large and their style varies quite dramatically from that of a smaller company. One can appreciate their size when, for example, one compares the total sales of the top ten corporations with the gross national product of some of the world's nations. Table 4 compares the 1969 gross national product of some selected countries with the sales of General Motors and other giants of American industry. Except for the few leading industrial countries of the world, the major United States corporations have sales comparable to many of the members of the United Nations. If you decide after your Ph.D. that you would like to become president of a major corporation, you may do well to consider the responsibilities of such large organizations.

TABLE 4: Comparison of Some 1969 Values of the Gross National Product (GNP) of Countries and the 1970 Sales of the Top United States Companies

Country	GNP[a] Billions of $(U.S.)	Top Ten U.S. Firms	Sales[b] Billions of $
U. S.	931.4	General Motors	18.7
Germany	164.5	Standard Oil	16.5
Japan	165.9	Ford Motor	15.0
France	130.7	General Electric	8.7
United Kingdom	109.4	International	
Italy	82.3	Business	
Canada	78.5	Machines	7.5
Mexico	26.7[c]	Mobil Oil	7.3
Sweden	25.6[c]	Chrysler	7.0
Australia	29.9	International	
Pakistan	13.9[c]	Tel. & Tel.	6.4
Denmark	14.0	Texaco	6.4
Argentina	17.4	Western Electric	5.9

[a]Adapted from reference 38; gross national product equals gross national expenditures.
[b]Adapted from reference 39.
[c]Year, 1968.

We have been stressing the size and style of the corporations because that is where the majority of Ph.D. candidates entering industry will find themselves. However, you may wish to choose a smaller company, where your responsibility will vary greatly from day to day or even from hour to hour, and where the risks are greater, but the potential rewards are correspondingly increased.

Research Expenditures and Annual Sales and Their Influence on Your Career Choice. We have seen that the major United States corporations have annual dollar sales that compare in magnitude with the gross national product of many countries. The fraction of these sales dollars that are returned into the research and development areas is an interesting and important figure for the potential scientist employee to know. It provides a relative measure of the value that the corporation puts in the future, in new product development, and in overall growth through new ideas. It also gives you an idea of the size of the research and development organization in some of the larger corporations, which will directly affect your programs in scope and size.

Compare in Table 5 the R & D spending of some of the major chemical corporations. Expenditures are listed for a five-year period. The number of R & D employees in 1970 and the R & D budget per employee in that year are also shown for those companies for which the data were available. This latter figure is another indication of the company's emphasis on R & D work.

Table 6 shows the percentage of sales of the major chemical companies that is reinvested into their research and development programs. It is interesting to note that the amount of money spent on research and development by the chemical industry failed to keep pace with inflation in 1967 and 1968. The editors of *Chemical and Engineering News* pointed out then that "Research and development has come into some hard times in the chemical industry. This golden goose, with its promise of future products and future profits isn't starving yet. But chemical makers have cut back quite sharply on its feed and they certainly are no longer fattening it up in the way they used to just a few years ago."[42] How prophetic they were! Today the fundamental research portion of the R & D effort is literally fighting for its life; current research efforts in almost all industries have to be directly related to product and sales.

TABLE 5:   Research and Development Spending in Some of the Major Chemical Companies, 1966-1970.

Company	R & D Spending (Millions of Dollars) 1966[a]	1967[a]	1968[a]	1969[a]	1970[b]	No. of R&D Employees in 1970[b]	Thousands of R&D Dollars per R&D Employee
Air Products	4.5	5	5	5	5.5[f]	c	–
Air Reduction	12	13	12	11	8.7	375	23.2
Allied Chemical	31	28	30	31	28.5	730	39.0
Amer. Cyanamid	43	43	43	45	46	1000	46.0
Celanese	33	39	42	48	53.4	650	82.2
Diamond Shamrock	8.6	9.1	9.3	10	11.2	c	–
Dow Chemical	70	75	87	86	96.0	4300	22.3
Du Pont	110	110	250	250[d]	258	4300	60.0
FMC	27	28	10[e]	11[e]	60.9	700	87.0
GAF	11.5	12.4	12.3	13	>13[f]	c	–
W.R. Grace	18	20	19	22	20.8	1000	20.8
Hercules	21	22	23	23	21.6	300	72.0
Monsanto	76	84	86	102	99.0	1400	70.7
Stauffer	10.2	12.2	12.5	12	13[f]	c	–
Union Carbide	77	85	83	77	78.0	2200	35.5

[a] From reference 40.
[b] From reference 41.
[c] Not available.
[d] Du Pont's figures are total R & D expenditures including product support.
[e] Chemical group only; total figures not available.
[f] Estimate from reference 40.

Industry is a complex of companies, and companies are owned by a complex of individuals who own shares so that they may receive dividends and see the value of their stock grow. Therefore, a measure of how successfully a company is being run can be gained from its growth in earnings from year to year. In this day of the quick return, rate of growth is one important criterion in buying shares in a company.

TABLE 6:   Comparison of Research and Development Spending and Gross Sales of Some Major Chemical Companies, 1970.

Company	R&D Spending, 1970[a] (Millions of $)	Gross Sales 1970[b] (Millions of $)	% of R&D to Gross Sales 1970
Air Products	5.5[c]	261	2.1
Air Reduction	8.7	470	1.9
Allied Chemical	28.5	1249	2.3
American Cyanamid	46	1158	4.0
Celanese	53.4	1037	5.2
Diamond Shamrock	11.2	556	2.0
Dow Chemical	96.0	1911	5.0
Du Pont	258	3618	7.1
FMC	60.9	1331	4.6
GAF	>13[c]	599	>2.2
W.R. Grace	20.8	1918	1.1
Hercules	21.6	799	2.7
Monsanto	99.0	1972	5.0
Stauffer	13[c]	483	2.7
Union Carbide	78	3026	2.6

[a]From reference 41.
[b]From reference 39.
[c]Estimate from reference 40.

Obviously, one means of showing high earnings is to keep R & D funds down to a minimum. Recently, R & D expenditures have been more heavily scrutinized as R & D costs rise, possibly causing short-term lower earnings for the company. Although sales continue to grow, for example, in the chemical industry, costs have experienced a parallel rate of growth. Higher sales lead to higher earnings only if costs grow at a slower pace. Short-term savings can be made by cutting down on the cost of sales and administration and on R & D expenditures. Note that we say *short-term savings,* for the temptation to show earnings by drastic reductions of R & D will show a good profit picture for a few years, but then chaos will erupt as it becomes obvious that the drastic cutback in R & D has decreased the number of new products emerging, and the competitive position of the company may be threatened. This point is very important to you and your individual career as it is indicative of the thinking of upper management and the leadership in your R & D division and will greatly affect your program planning.

Your Cost to a Corporation as a Ph.D. Scientist. A more detailed consideration of the R & D budget shows that in the next few years it will cost a corporation between $20,000 and $40,000 per Ph.D. per year. This figure includes probable starting salaries for a Ph.D. in the 1970-1975 period, plus the various overhead costs, equipment costs, and salaries of research assistants. One can see that as the Ph.D. in a corporation acquires a few assistants, his dollar budget figure could soon equal the sales of a small company. For example, a three or four-man effort on a research project can well cost a company $100,000 in R & D funds; this represents, at 5% R & D to gross sales ratio, approximately $2,000,000 in sales. Obviously, many sales dollars are required per R & D man employed. Companies will scrutinize the R & D budgets through a finer lens as the years go by and focus on what they consider the projects most likely to return their R & D investment.

C. THE PATHS OF ADVANCEMENT OF SCIENTISTS IN INDUSTRY

It is most likely that you will start your job in industry at a fundamental research level, as both you and the company will want to make use of your newly cultivated talents of research and development. However, after a few years you may want to change and proceed up the growth ladder by means other than pure research. In fact, this is the rule rather than the exception; most of the higher positions require "nonpure" researchers.

In general there are two major paths which you may follow in industry. One is the research path, the other the administrative arm; some major companies call this "the dual ladder system."

If we simply focus on the ultimate financial rewards possible at the end of either of these paths, we can say from experience that only about one out of five "pure research" Ph.D.'s will go as far as his compatriots who become involved in administrative and supervisory capacities. Incidentally, many scientists who start out in research find out that for them, not only the financial rewards but also the personal satisfaction derived from successful efforts in management, production, or sales at least equal those derived from a pure research program.

Industries sometimes perpetrate a rather deceptive inference. They continue to point to their super-scientists as the "typical" result of a climb up the research ladder. General Electric, and the scientific world for that matter, had only one Irving Langmuir. It is ridiculous to infer that the average young scientist will climb to the heights of this very special and talented Nobel Prize winner. The cold hard fact is that there are just not many top jobs for research scientists in industry and only the very exceptional scientists fill the ones which do exist.

Other career opportunities will present themselves during the first three years of your industrial job. Though this initiation period varies, one can surmise that it takes from one to three years to become acclimated to the company, its style, your new research project, and the new life that you accepted with the industrial position. During this period of time, you will see around you those who have progressed relative to their peers. You will see whether administration or research, or, in fact, an industrial career at all, is your game. We suggest that you take every opportunity available to visit your company's plant locations to discuss their established and new products and their R & D growth programs. This will give you some idea of potential growth areas.

Remember that you will be judged not by research peers so much as you will be judged by supervisors and administrators who may not have your background. You will be communicating with people in production, sales, marketing, accounting, public relations, and a variety of other people with rather specialized backgrounds as well. Therefore, your moment of truth will no longer be a thesis, a scientific paper, or a research seminar, but most likely it will depend on such things as regular program reviews, company presentations, and written interoffice memos. Keep in mind that you have a multidisciplinary audience with very broad backgrounds.

Always focus on the very practical end result of your research. Unless the promise of money-making products continues at every phase, re-evaluate your work carefully, and if no new hopes for its success can be found in a reasonable period, suggest that it be dropped. If you don't do this, someone else will do it for you.

Research groups in industry serve as a potential brain tank to solve all types of technical problems arising in every aspect of product development and manufacture. You would be wise to accept an occasional challenge from the "other" departments; solving their problems promises an immediate gold star for your industrial crown. Remember that it may take as many as seven years for the proof of your worth in the form of a final product to become evident in the usual research effort. Most industrial people, who are not directly in research, seem to have a great suspicion that "Those characters in the research and development department are carrying out little more than some form of impractical and unnecessary scientific play." A little proof of your worth now and then is worth giving to the skeptic.

D.   HOW DO YOU CONTACT THE INDUSTRIAL WORLD?

Campus Interviews.   Your first contact with industry will probably be through a scheduled interview with an industrial campus recruiter. Notices of the pending visits of industrial representatives will usually be posted in departmental offices or in the college placement office. Check with your preceptor and be sure that you have progressed to a stage in your graduate work that warrants optimism in interviewing potential employers. At this time, pick up at the placement or departmental offices the information which describes the career openings at the major companies. Your careful review of this material will help you choose which companies to interview and make the interviews themselves more straightforward, since both you and the company interviewer can then talk specifics rather than generalities.

There will most likely be one of two types of individuals to interview you: the professional personnel man or the industrial scientist, often an alumnus of your institution. In our experience, the latter person is easier to communicate with and knows best the answers to specific questions relating to scientific aspects of the job.

You will be rated on a printed form which has been carefully tailored to needs of the particular company. The ratings, as you may surmise, will deal with the outward manifestations of your character and personality such as attire, length of hair, and general appearance as well as personal traits such as your ability to communicate, your outside interests, and your ability to describe your research work.

There are a few guidelines to follow as you face your industrial interviews on campus:

(1) Be on time for your appointment. The interviewer must speak to candidates all day, and you will upset his schedule if you are late.

(2) Dress neatly but not formally. Everyone knows that the style of dress on campus, especially in the experimental natural sciences, is quite different from the typical office and industrial laboratory.

(3) Relax and be yourself. If the interviewer suggests that you visit a company location or try a particular type of work in which you are not interested, be polite but honest. Present yourself in the light which reflects your probable feelings and interests after you have graduated.

(4) Think carefully early in your interview planning so as to formulate a personal statement on your career objectives; requests for this will appear again and again. Why is your Ph.D. candidacy important for your overall career objectives?

(5) Always be ready to describe your research work, both in clear scientific terms and in terms which a nonspecialist in your area can readily understand. How does your research relate to other areas of your discipline?

(6) Be prepared to fill out a company application form. Keep a copy of the more general placement office form handy, since you may often need seemingly trivial, and often misplaced facts, such as your social security number, or the date of your marriage. If you interview four or five companies, you will soon get a flavor for the typical questions asked. You will probably be asked repeatedly questions like the following:

What do you consider to be the ideal job?

Do you like to travel?

Would you mind living in certain sections of the United States?

Do you plan to stay in basic research?

Do you like working with people?

Are you interested in sales? Marketing? Management?

Keep your statements short and sweet, and remember that part of the interview system is to see how well you express yourself paperwise, talkwise and personalitywise.

(7) Remember that although you are being interviewed, you, too, are carrying out an interview of the representative of the industry. Find out all that you can about this company's opportunities. It is not unexpected that you would ask some rather mundane questions as well as some penetrating ones. If the interviewer doesn't know the answers, he can get them for you.

What are the growth areas in the company?

What percentage of gross sales is reinvested by the company into its dollar R & D budget for fundamental research and for applied or design engineering research?

How have the budget and staff sizes been maintained over the past five years?

What is next year's research budget? If the answer is, "About the same as this year," then watch out! Either no growth or a cutback is planned.

What is the possibility of having a research technician assigned to you during the first few years in the job? Skilled technicians and laboratory assistants are difficult to get but make your research much more efficient and productive.

What are the company benefits, stock plans, etc.? We suggest that you jot these down during your interview so that you can compare them from company to company. In this day and age, company benefits can consist of 5% to 30% of your total compensation, and it is an important consideration for most people.

You can ask about your probable starting salary, but at this point the company representative has little basis for judging your worth to the company. Wait until you have further contact with the company to explore this aspect of your job.

Trips to Industry and Interviews at the Company Site.
If your qualifications and interests appear to match the
personnel needs of the company as judged by both the company's campus representative and the leaders of the research
groups seeking personnel, then you may be asked to visit the
company. If you are very fortunate you may receive the opportunity to visit several companies. Make a careful study of
the alternatives, and choose to visit no more than two or
three. A greater number of visits will only serve to confuse
your choice of future position.

Most major companies will be offering the same starting
salary, plus or minus a few percent. However, such factors as
location may be quite important to you and obviously should
be taken into account in deciding which companies to visit. It
is a waste of their time and yours if you interview companies
that, for various reasons, are not employers acceptable to you.

Your trips can probably be planned so that you can visit all
of the companies on the same general trip taken during a
slack week at the university.

Remember as you proceed from the campus interview to
the company site interview that some companies will have
highly trained personnel directors, and, in some cases,
psychologists, who will be trying to get a clearer picture of
you as an individual and of your relationship to their organization. Again, relax and be yourself. If you read the inkblots
truthfully to reflect some Freudian tendencies or hatred of
your mother, let the company worry about that. If you are
not their type, they will let you know.

Each day that you spend at a company will be packed full
of interviews, laboratory tours, and discussions. You will
probably describe your thesis research to many of those
whom you meet through the medium of a formal seminar, or
more likely, through small discussion groups.

At some point in your visit you will meet a young scientist
who has been with the company only a year or so. Here is a
golden opportunity that you don't want to miss. Ask this man

what he likes and dislikes about his first year with the company.

As you continue to talk, fill out forms, and learn about the company, remember to pace yourself for the mid-afternoon and late afternoon appointments. These are probably some of the most important, as they will give you a feel for the interest which the company has in you. Try to get a clear explanation from the last person to interview you formally what the next action will be. Is the company going to make you an offer? Are they going to consider you and let you know in a few weeks? Be specific in your questions, as it will help you if the company can be specific in its answers.

At this time, be prepared to answer the question on what you expect your starting salary to be; you should have a very good idea of what to expect from discussions with your preceptor and colleagues who have been out seeking jobs during the recent months,

When you have returned home from your interview trip, you will be asked to send the company an accounting of your expenses. Don't do this casually, and don't attempt to make money on the trip. If you have traveled to several companies on the same trip, then point this out. Share the costs of the travel between the companies in some equitable fashion which you should explain carefully. Scientists, particularly industrial scientists, are not stupid, especially when it concerns money. Honesty in your expense report is an indication of future honesty in your research reports and other business dealings with the company.

In summary, the interview, whether on campus, at the company site, in the street, or over cocktails, will be a means of rapidly summarizing you in the eyes and the thoughts of the company representatives. Make sure that the company of your choice is worthy of you and that you can be a real and identifiable asset to them.

9. *Academic Employment for the Scientist*

A. HOW DO YOU ENTER THE ACADEMIC WORLD?

Let's assume that you have the ability and the interest to become a teacher-researcher in a university. How do you make your first contact with possible employers? Of all of the areas of science, academic life is most nearly a closed shop. No good American university would think of advertising in a trade journal or to the open market that they are seeking to add a faculty member in a certain area. In the British Commonwealth, it has been the continuing custom to advertise academic openings even in the most prestigious university. However, the advertising appears to be merely a formality in some cases, and the ultimate appointment seems to reflect the same academic prejudices for which Americans are famous. Such advertising on the American scene is considered a sign of weakness. The often bewildered and always overworked chairman of the department is fearful of the hundreds of replies that such an advertisement brings. He realizes that each response requires a great deal of his very limited time for evaluation and extensive time of his faculty committee which recommends action on candidates.

Thus you probably will not hear of an opportunity in the university academic life through the open media. Your first information concerning the availability of a possible position in academic life may come from your preceptor. Obviously, it is important that he have a good opinion of your research facility and character if you expect him to think of you as an attractive candidate for such a position. He may have just returned from a national meeting and talked to some of his colleagues who told him that they are looking forward to adding a new faculty member for a specific area in their department. If they trust him as a scientist of great competence in this area, they may have asked him to recommend a candidate. This is the best possible lead you can have to a job in academic life. If your preceptor is out of the swing of academic maneuvering, you may be forced to seek help from other professors and possibly from the chairman of your department. Some chairmen of departments write letters to other chairmen rather indiscriminately, seeking leads on openings for responsible candidates. This is a very inefficient approach, but when times are hard, anything goes. Make sure your chairman knows that you are looking for a job in academic life so he can clue you in on such opportunities. Since several professors, in addition to your preceptor, will be asked to write to universities concerning your qualifications for an academic job, you must be sure that they know in considerable depth your background, teaching and research qualifications, and the significance of your graduate thesis work.

An additional source of employment information in universities is available through most national professional societies (see Table A-1 of the Appendix). In many of the societies, there is an employment office which tends to match employment opportunities with applicants, keeping both employer and prospective employee anonymous until each desires further contact. Some of the smaller institutions have employed this service in the past.

Today's academic market place is extremely competitive. For every open position in a good graduate science department, there will be literally hundreds of reasonably good applicants for the job. Some of these applicants write directly to the chairman of the department seeking a lead on possible employment. However, if your professor is so inclined, he may wish to write to his university friends concerning your availability and qualifications.

If you have no good contacts and possibilities for future academic openings, letter writing may be your best route of action. Ask your preceptor and other professors in the department to suggest some schools to which you might write. Take time to write carefully a summary of your undergraduate work, graduate work, and any employment which you may have had. Indicate any special honors received such as fellowships or recognition for your teaching ability or research promise. Be sure to explain in reasonable detail the nature of your research effort both in your graduate research and in your postdoctoral work. Hopefully, you have managed to publish this work. If you can photocopy the abstract and summaries of these publications, they will be very helpful to the chairman and a graduate faculty committee in reviewing your application. If you can afford to do so, send reprints of your publications as well. It will save the time of the chairman and faculty committees assigned to review your qualifications. Just as important is a careful statement of your goals in research and teaching. What will be your first research effort upon your arrival at the university? What is a realistic appraisal of the financial commitment which you will require to start your research? What courses do you feel most qualified to teach? What do you consider your area of greatest competence in the undergraduate instructional program? To what graduate courses would you hope to be assigned?

The entire resume need not be more than a page or two in length. It should state precisely your interests and abilities. A short personal letter should be written to each chairman with whom you correspond. The largest part of your documentation can be photocopied. However, the chairman of the departments are only human and tend to regard mimeographed or photocopied letters as third class or "trash mail." He may discard the entire information without serious consideration unless there is some personal element involved in the communication.

If your qualifications and experience match the needs of some of the academic institutions of interest to you, you'll receive an invitation to either meet the chairman or his representative at some convenient location or perhaps to visit the campus. Consider a few of the important factors that your potential employer will be watching for during your visit. Furthermore, let's consider a few of the things *you* should be watching for as you visit your potential employer.

B.   YOUR VISIT AND INTERVIEW AT THE UNIVERSITY

Before you visit any university, there is considerable planning that must be done. You will be expected to arrive at the university with a firm grasp of your thesis research and postdoctoral work. You will probably be asked to present a talk to the faculty on some phase of this work. For all information that is difficult to reproduce by hand on the blackboard, you should prepare slides that show these data in readily understandable form. Don't put too much on a slide. If you photograph an entire page or large table from your thesis, no one past the front row of the seminar will be able to decipher it. Don't overdo on the number of slides—from half a dozen to a dozen slides during an hour's presentation might be a reasonable number to present. Don't be casual about the preparation for this seminar. Most universities base a good share of their value judgment of your teaching ability on your performance at the research seminar presented to the faculty and graduate students during your visit. It is the smart student who runs through his talk before the critical eyes of his or her preceptor, spouse, fellow graduate students, or other critical yet captive audiences before embarking on the trip to the university of his potential employment. Your colleagues and your spouse can be your best constructive critics in helping you formulate the best presentation of your work.

In planning your seminar, decide on a series of basic areas which you intend to cover. You should anticipate about forty minutes for the delivery of this portion of the talk. Then include some secondary topics which are less important but which can be covered in any number to fill out the total time allotted to your seminar. Anticipate questions concerning your work. Have in mind the literature and the significance of contributions that preceded your own in this area. Make sure that you give credit to those who laid the foundation for your work. Spend the last five minutes of your talk reformulating your evidence, your arguments, and your conclusions. Spell out the significance and limitations of your findings in detail. Suggest what new areas of investigation this work leads to. Give an indication of your plans for future research in this area or in related areas.

During the visit to your potential academic home, there are a variety of factors which should be of concern to you. The university will certainly find out what they want to know about your qualifications; you have to be just as sure to answer in your own mind, questions concerning the suitability of this university to you.

Firstly, are the faculty, or a large share of them friendly, communicative, and capable? Are they alive and interested in their teaching and research activities? Is aggressive departmental politics apparent among the faculty? Plan to talk to a few of the students and determine their attitudes and capabilities. Do the present graduate students seem interesting, highly motivated, and qualified to pursue graduate study? Look closely at the research interests of the faculty. Is there a need for a faculty member in the department with your research interest? Will your contribution to the department add significantly to the impact that the department will have in the future?

Secondly, what type of research support can you expect from the department? Can they satisfy your minimum needs for equipment to initiate your research effort? What does the department see as your immediate teaching responsibilities? Does the department have adequate supporting staff to help prepare lecture demonstrations, slides, etc.? Is there a machine shop, a glassblowing shop, and a storeroom facility which are arranged for the convenience of the faculty and graduate students? Is the library well supplied with the essential journals and textbooks for teaching and research in your area of interest? Does the librarian seem to be a helpful person or one who seems to protect the books against serious use by faculty and students? Do faculty members have keys to the library so that they can enter it any time of the day or night?

Graduate programs require facilities and incur costs which are way beyond those involved in undergraduate teaching. If this is not understood by the university, your research efforts may be stymied. Find out how much money is available to faculty for supplies and for maintenance of equipment. What kind of laboratory space is planned for you? Where will your office be? What major departmental equipment will be available for your use? What kind of computer is available for use by department faculty and graduate students? How much free computer time will the university allow you? Is the computer available for use by the undergraduate students? What is the turnover time when data to be processed are submitted to the computer center? Ask a few of the graduate students about the various pieces of major equipment in the department. How available is this equipment to them? How much secretarial help can you expect?

Guidelines as to what to expect from a university as a newcomer to the faculty are somewhat different in the various fields of science. However, in the experimental sciences, both physical and biological, the new professor should be endowed with at least five to ten thousand dollars to buy basic minimal equipment for his research. He is usually expected to make application for major equipment and research support from outside agencies. He should expect that his potential office will be clean, freshly painted, and pleasant to work in. He should expect that the laboratories assigned for his work will be in good shape. At least one laboratory which will conveniently house two graduate students' research efforts in addition to his own should be provided. This should amount to 150 or 200 square feet of laboratory space per student. In the laboratory of an experimental scientist the proper safety equipment should be readily available: fire extinguishers, shower, fire blanket, well-ventilated hoods, etc.

Your teaching assignment at a major university will probably include complete responsibility for one to two major courses per quarter, adding up to some three to five courses per year. If you are teaching in a small college or junior college where graduate and undergraduate student research opportunities are nonexistent or very limited, you may be responsible for more than two courses per quarter. Be sure to establish your probable teaching assignments during your visit. If you are planning to carry out an active research program as well as present well-designed and well-prepared courses, then make sure that the number of courses assigned is realistic with these aims. Plan on spending about twenty hours per week on each course—more if it's your first time in teaching it; somewhat less if you've taught the particular course before.

During the visit, you should get some idea of the salary structure from the chairman of the department. Although he can't share with you the exact salary of various faculty members, he can indicate at what salary entering Ph.D.'s with your experience commonly start, and he may be able to tell you what the top salary in the department is at the moment. Ask him as well how often department meetings are held. How are policy decisions concerning the department made? How is your promotion or denial of tenure determined? Does the university give cost of living raises in addition to merit raises?

Of critical importance is whether or not the position available is on "hard" money or "soft" money. Hard money refers to slots for which funds are guaranteed to be available from the regular university operating budget and applies to the tenured as well as to the nontenured positions. Soft money positions are those for which all or part of the funds must be derived from some type of grant or contract external to the university and which is subject to cancellation or nonrenewal on relatively short notice. For example, the normal faculty positions in the regular departments at the University of California, Ohio State University, and probably in most reputable universities, have traditionally been hard money positions. A young assistant professor, while he has no guarantee of making tenure, is at least assured of his nine-month academic salary coming through whether or not he lands a fat research contract. During the research support boom of the 1960's, the distinction between hard and soft positions was not too critical and some universities tended to have a substantial number of their teaching faculty supported in one way or another from research grants or contracts during the academic year. That is, the professor putting in for the grant would ask for fifty percent of his salary from the research agency and fifty percent from the university. Well, the bust of the 1970's put a lot of high-flying universities in real trouble, because they couldn't match their bets; this unfortunate practice had serious effects on all concerned, but most particularly on young assistant professors.

While you are in the university community, find out which of your favorite intellectual and social activities are available. Is there a symphony orchestra or a string group sponsored by the city or the university? Are the theatre, the opera, and the museums in the city well supported by the community? What is the feeling of the community toward the university and vice versa? Is there an effective Town and Gown Society, which will work to maintain good relations between the campus community and the citizens of the city?

Find out how long it will be before you get a reply from the department. Inform the chairman of the department of your schedule of visits and how soon you can tell him of your decision if you are given an offer. Tell him frankly your impressions of the department. Without being pretentious, let him know honestly whether you would or would not like to receive an offer from them. You don't have to accept the offer on the spot if one is given then. In fact, you have an obligation to visit as a free agent the other universities or industries with which you have made such plans.

C. EVALUATE YOUR OFFERS

Let's assume that you are very fortunate and receive more than one offer from attractive universities. How are you going to compare these offers? You certainly do not want to take the highest offer without having more significant reasons for doing so than the salary structure. A very large salary may be an indication of weakness in the university or a sign of an attempt at improvement in faculty. Spend a few days reviewing your notes, observations, and the departmental brochures of the schools. Review carefully the attractiveness of the research facilities, the teaching responsibilities, the university community, and the environment of the city in which you must reside. Review the quality of the faculty as evidenced by their research publications and your contact with them. It's particularly important that you spend a considerable amount of time in the library reading the research publications of the faculty. Make sure that you have a real respect for most of your colleagues. Remember that most faculty members receive tenure, and you may be living with these scientists for a great number of years. If you do not have respect for them, you could not possibly live up to your potential contributions as a faculty member.

From a careful review of your offers, you can probably decide rather quickly that there are one or possibly two universities which stand out. It's important at this stage that you arrange a return trip to these universities. Write quickly to the department chairman and indicate that you are very interested in his offer and that (if applicable) you wish to bring your family to review the living conditions, university environment, the urban community, etc. The chairman may supply you with a limited budget to help you make this trip. Now is the time to answer those many questions which the first visit left unanswered. You have now read considerably more about that faculty since you first met them and have formulated some new notions concerning problems of growing interest which you may wish to discuss with some of the faculty members. You may wish to ask Professor Jones whether you can use his special apparatus for a couple of hours per week in your own research effort. It may be important to find out what the current text is in the course for which you will assume responsibility and how the text will be chosen for the next year. Furthermore, you may wish to sit in on a lecture or two of this course as it is now being offered in the university.

Don't waste the time of the administration and faculty of a university which stands little chance of having you as a colleague. However, if you are interested in them and they are interested in you, everyone benefits by this preacceptance revisit to your potential academic home.

In view of all these considerations, make a positive decision as soon as possible, but no later than two or three weeks after receipt of the last of your offers. Write to each of the universities which has given you offers, explaining your decision. Even that school which impressed you least deserves the courtesy of a letter thanking them for their considerable effort in hosting you during your visit. It is not out of order for you to indicate the major problem you associated with joining their faculty. They can benefit and perhaps even improve their status by acting upon your advice. Certainly, future students in that university will bless you for any improvement which you may have helped bring about.

Perhaps you have received only one offer of an academic position after the several visits that you have made. Should you accept this offer, or should you look further? Obviously, if the offer is from a major university for which you have high regard, you probably will want to accept. You certainly should revisit this school though, and, as described above, face the problems of living in the community, etc., that are important to you and your family. However, let's say that the offer is from a university of rather mediocre stature. You don't have to take a job in which you will find little enjoyment and challenge. You may consider doing further postdoctoral work and delay your decision concerning future employment until such time as a more attractive position becomes available. You should not take a position in a university which is not up to your intellectual level and offers little challenge for your future. You'll be unhappy there, and at best, it can be only a temporary home.

It is very possible, particularly today, that you will not receive any attractive offers, either as a result of a rather mediocre showing on your visits or because of the very keen competition for the position. If you find yourself in this bind, consult with your preceptor, and seek his advice as to your next course of action.

At this stage in your life, it may suddenly occur to you that competition for suitable academic positions is so keen that you will not be successful in getting an appropriate academic job. It is not too late to evaluate thoroughly research opportunities in industry and government and assume a role which you had never thought about seriously until now. If you are really successful in your industrial research, you may receive an opportunity some day to enter a university under more favorable circumstances

D.   RESPONSIBILITIES OF ACADEMIC LIFE

Obligations and Rewards in University and College Teaching.   The young scientist finds himself in an extremely peculiar position on the first day of classes in his first year at the university. He has spent four years in an undergraduate science curriculum, about four more years in graduate school learning a specialty area of science, and probably one or two years of postdoctoral work. Yet he has arrived at this day of his first class without any formal instruction on how to teach. Scientists continue to disparage courses in education as unnecessary hogwash. This is not necessarily so. Certainly there are ways that one can improve his teaching ability, but these are ways which you yourself must learn. It is sometimes said that in the real world of science today you do not have time to become an expert in subject matter and an expert in methods of presentation as well. In general, the scientist argues that teachers are born, not created. A person who is extremely knowledgeable of his subject matter and is adequate in his oral presentation is certainly preferable to a dynamic, well-organized, and inspiring lecturer who relates only prattle or outdated theories of little value to his students. However, there are a few basic techniques that the authors have learned from their successful teaching colleagues which it might be well to review.

Before you face that first class, reflect upon the attributes which your "best teachers" in the university had. Each one may have been quite different from the other. Some were inspiring lecturers; some were very quiet mannered; some used the lecture approach for the entire hour; others never lectured, but led a discussion of the subject for the entire hour. However, it's likely that there were certain things which were common to these successful teachers in your past. First, you respected this "good teacher" as a person who knew his subject matter very thoroughly. He had a degree of enthusiasm and interest in his subject which was obvious and contagious. He was able to organize his material in a logical fashion, pick out the important problem areas of the material for discussion, and ask the appropriate stimulating questions of his students. The teaching methods which each teacher employs must be built upon the teacher's own natural abilities. He does best that which comes naturally.

There are a few points which you may find helpful in the preparation of your first lecture. First, define the background of the audience to whom you will be speaking. Will these students have had biology, physical chemistry, quantum mechanics, calculus, differential equations, statistics, or other mathematical background? What prerequisite courses in the sciences have they had before coming to your class? One important secret of good communication between faculty member and the student is a recognition by the faculty member of the experience and capability of the student. It may take a bit of prodding on your part to have the student admit he has had any course prior to attending yours. Don't forget that the student considers it poor strategy to admit to any prior knowledge of the subject. He feels that you may hold him responsible for this, and he may not recall all pertinent aspects of the topic. Find out from the faculty and (by judicious inquiry) from the students, what the background of the students really is. If your subject is sufficiently advanced and complex, then your lectures should contain a review of the basic concepts needed for your advanced presentation. It is always good planning to start any presentation from first principles even though just a reference to these may be made in certain cases. The student then realizes that he is expected to know these basic principles, and if it is missing in his background, he will feel compelled to review them or to learn them for the first time.

Check out from the library or from your own supply of information, the various textbooks that you respect as the most authoritative in the area. In graduate areas where most textbooks are out of date by the time they are published, you'll want to review the literature carefully and photocopy the key articles that you think are most significant in the area. Read these carefully. Now, prepare an outline of the most important ideas which you must cover in this lecture. Select or design a few examples which illustrate in a very practical way the concepts or points which you are trying to teach. Make a list of what you consider to be the most important references for the students from the standpoint of significance and clarity. Be sure to make copies of these supplementary reading assignments for the class. Make sure that you never organize your lecture to duplicate exactly the coverage of the specific material as it is given in the textbook. To be sure, you should pick the textbook that is relevant to what you will cover, but don't forget that the student will read thoroughly and comprehend most of this material. Where he needs the help is in the delineation of specific problem areas and the elucidation of the unexplained, "it can be shown" examples of the text. Your value as a teacher is in the anticipation of the problem areas of the assignment and in the careful explanation of these to the students.

Let's say that you have prepared an outline of your lecture consistent with coverage in the period of time allotted to your class. Take this outline with you to class and refer to it if you need to do so. Don't write out your lecture. It should flow naturally and never be memorized from a prepared text. A good teacher will amplify or shorten certain of his planned coverage to fit his students' needs as they become apparent during the class.

There are some key methods of presentation which you should try to develop. Start your lecture by stating what you are going to do for that day. Indicate that there are some very interesting ideas and important features of that particular area. Perhaps the most important rule for the teacher to follow is: speak to your audience, not to the blackboard, and watch the reaction of the students. It is surprising what you can learn from this. The students probably do not realize that they reflect every emotion as they are listening and observing a lecture. Disinterest, boredom, enthusiasm, interest, disbelief, discontent—all are signaled clearly to the instructor who watches for them. The bright instructor will call on Miss Smith and ask her what's troubling her when he sees a reaction which suggests some problem. More than likely, she thinks you have made a mistake on the blackboard, and it worries her. Either your recognition of the mistake and correction of it, or a little further explanation to calm this concern will allow the student to be with you during the next thirty minutes of your lecture. Otherwise, she would be distracting others in trying to prove or disprove her contention on your presumed error.

Don't try to cover too much material in any one lecture period. What is the most important idea that you are going to convey during that period? Make sure you cover this idea well; it doesn't matter what else you may have time to accomplish during the hour. The first part of any hour is the period of best comprehension and attention by the student. In the latter part of the hour you can expect to have much greater student disinterest and boredom. It is wise planning to have some interesting examples or even some clever teaching aids to turn to during the last part of the period.

As you sort out those factors which you recognize in your favorite teachers, undoubtedly near the top of your list will be his contagious enthusiasm. For an undergraduate to encounter the blinding sparkle and effervescent enthusiasm of a Linus Pauling or a Paul Erlich is an unforgettable experience. Now this talent for a sincere, nontheatrically motivated enthusiasm is not common with all good teachers. However, lacking such physical and psychological construction, a person can exhibit pleasure and interest in his subject which will serve much the same purpose with the student. You must motivate the students to want to learn in this area. If you start your lecture by apologizing for the material to be covered, rest assured they will be in *another*, more interesting world during your presentation.

Make your students feel free to interrupt your presentation at any time with questions which are relevant to the ideas being discussed. However, there is one serious limitation upon this important teaching method. The classroom clown will continue to hound you with trivial and unrelated questions, and he must be discouraged. His first question about the obvious material or the unrelated subject is fair game, but the second one of this type should be met with some firm control measure such as, "If we need to cover that topic again, Mr. White, see me after class." When he arrives after class, open the textbook and indicate the sections he should read in detail and the problems he should work to gain some insight. He needs help, but at this point he doesn't know enough to use your extensive help constructively.

There is one common problem which plagues the professor in the sciences. We either can't write legibly or often fail to take the time to do so under the stress of the classroom situation. In this regard, note Figure 12. This isn't an attempt of Picasso or the bar bill from a Tokyo lounge, but it is the direct copy of the writings made by a famous and capable professor on the plastic tape of an overhead projector. The occasion was a recent Gordon Research Conference. Frankly, most of us in the audience probably didn't notice the fact that the writing was illegible at the time of the lecture. The lecturer had an interesting story to tell, and he told it in a fashion that held the interest of most of the group. At one point, however, one of us tried to copy the written material. To his surprise, he found that he couldn't read a word of it. Our good friend, the professor, had never used an overhead

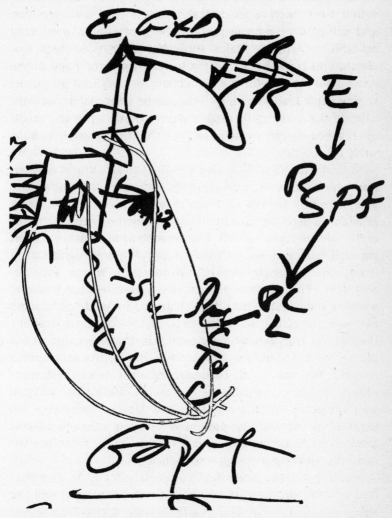

Figure 12: What does it say? A copy of a friend's lecture writings from an overhead projector tape.

projector before and had not practiced his technique with it. There can be no question that the degree of communication would have been a great deal better with a little practice and self-control on the part of the professor in producing readable notations. Make sure that after your first few classes you stand back and try to read from the back of the room your writing on the blackboard or overhead projector. If you can't read it readily, you can be sure that those who haven't the code can't read it either. Don't write too much on the board, but make sure that the things which you do write can be read.

Style in teaching is a very personal thing. You'll develop one which fits your qualifications and temperament well if you have not already done so in your career as a teaching assistant. There are various important methods applicable to each science area which the experienced teachers learn through trial and error. You can benefit most significantly from watching these methods in operation within your department. The students and faculty have a feel for knowing who are the best teachers. Plan to attend some of the lectures of these professors, sit in the back of the room, and see how they do it. They'll have some examples, some methods of explanation, and some mannerisms which will probably appeal to you. You may wish to incorporate a few of these techniques in your own lectures. Certainly, professors who are well respected by the students and faculty, and who for years have successfully presented difficult ideas in a clear fashion, have something which you as a young instructor can only develop through experience.

You'll probably never feel completely ready to give that first lecture. However, if you have spent time doing well the things outlined above, you should be ready to try your wings. If it is at all possible, take one piece of equipment to class with you in addition to your outline, text, and the list of additional reading references. Borrow from the electronics technician or the teaching aids laboratory the video tape television camera and equipment to record your lecture from the back of the room. Turn this on at the beginning of the hour and proceed with your lecture. Following the lecture and discussion period, recover the tape and playback equipment, and retire to your office for a thorough critique of your performance. You'll be amazed at what you see. You will like some of the effort, but it is highly probable that you will only now recognize that portions of your lecture were a shoddy mess. It is distressing to watch yourself and relive those embarrassing questions, that unexpected pause in your memory, or the misstatement that you are sure you could not have made. The important aspect of this critique is that you see yourself as others see you. All the little distracting idiosyncrasies of which you were not aware are there on the playback of the tape. There is no reason that you should, through careless practices, be known as the professor who picks at his nose or who clears his throat forty times during the lecture; your message is in disguise and your ideas may fail to come through when problems of this sort exist.

Although we are convinced that most scientists are basically honest and consider the several aspects of the evidence presented before arriving at a conclusion, it appears to us that many are basically insecure. Although they may evaluate carefully the soundness of some experimental finding in their research effort, they would commonly avoid evaluation of their teaching effectiveness. Don't forget that every teacher can improve. The problem in self-improvement is to discover those areas of weakness which can be improved. One method which has been used somewhat successfully in teaching is the student evaluation. It is possible to request and receive anonymous comments from your students which evaluate not only the effectiveness of the coverage of the course material but also the strengths and weaknesses they observe in your presentation. No one needs to see these comments but yourself. The fact is, however, that some of them may be meaningful. It is just as well that you learn about problems and correct them before some of your erudite colleagues observe these in your performance and find you lacking.

The style and mannerisms of a professor must be developed through experience and self-discipline. Remember, you already have many of the attributes of a good teacher or you wouldn't be in this position now. Your knowledge of the subject area is undoubtedly extremely good. You have something to tell these students that they do not know. If you've planned your lecture well, if you speak to the students and watch their reaction, if you answer their questions of importance during the presentation, and if you exhibit the natural enthusiasm which you have for your area, your lecture will be successful. The degree of this success will grow as you develop your style. But remember that few scientists can deliver a good lecture on a subject of any complexity without thorough and careful preparation. You are probably not an exception.

There are certain peculiar problems that are inherent in teaching very large classes. The young assistant professor is often given a share of the responsibility for the instruction of large undergraduate classes. In the experimental sciences, one may find that lecture demonstrations are particularly valuable to maintain student interest for the entire lecture period. A simple yet definitive experiment performed by you in front of the class is sometimes worth much more than the equivalent time spent in lecture. Don't try to do too many demonstrations or to choose ones which are only indirectly related to the subject, as you will not have time to teach your important material, and your class will resemble a three-ring circus. Most of the modern universities have supplementary staff who can arrange and design the experiments for you to present in the lecture. Put some careful thought on what might be done in the way of visual aid utilization to clarify a particular point in your discussion. There are some excellent movies which have been made in recent years to illustrate many of the basic principles in chemistry, biology, and physics. For example, it is now possible to demonstrate easily the fundamental modes of vibration of a complex molecule and even the superposition of these modes as they would appear in a vibrationally excited species. It is possible through the use of a computer to demonstrate dramatically such concepts as the electron distribution in molecules and the solution of complex, mathematical equations.

In the large class you must avoid serious distractions and yet be aware of problems you have created by virtue of your presentation. Certainly, during one lecture session you cannot expect to answer the questions of all 200 or 300 students as well as cover any significant material.

There is one technique which is useful with a large class, yet provides for beneficial question and answer periods. We have been somewhat successful in the use of "help sessions." These are agreed upon by the students and the instructor as to time and place and are designed on the spot to cover any area of the course which is of interest to the students. These sessions are very informal. Although they were developed originally to help the average or below average student with the more difficult concepts, the help session seems to be beneficial and attractive to the best students as well. There are a variety of ways in which the help session can be handled. One format which has been successful in our use is the following: a list of topics is arrived at by student suggestion at the start of the help session hour; each student then indicates, by raising his hand, which of these areas he feels is important to discuss. He can vote for as many topics as he chooses. Thus a number weighting of each of the subject areas is arrived at in the usual democratic fashion and the discussion proceeds, starting with the area of greatest concern. An extremely informal atmosphere must prevail at these sessions. They should be held in the evening or on a weekend. The senior professor must be in charge. Don't make this another recitation section meeting; don't assign it to your teaching assistant. The students must feel free to argue and question anything that is said. Out of a class of 200, perhaps only 25 or 30 students will attend a given session. It is probably good planning to hold two or three such sessions at alternative times so that at least one of them will match the free time of the student who wishes to attend. The satisfaction which is usually exhibited by both the professor and the students is gratifying to say the least. It allows the "lost" student of the large class to experience the educationally sound experience of the small discussion group.

Examinations are as much of a burden to the professor as to the students. Let's consider a few factors which are important in the preparation of examinations. Look back on your experience in your undergraduate and graduate course work. What do you recall about the examining system which was utilized in your courses? Some examinations which you took were keyed to the unusual—the exceptions—in that area. Others were designed as true and false or multiple choice tests, often of extremely limited depth. Students with minimal intellectual endowment can often find the "correct" answer to these tests more easily than the good student. There were those well conceived examinations which you remember as true learning experiences. Let these experiences guide you. You must take time to prepare your examination carefully. Test for comprehension of the material as part of the examination. Make the first couple of questions ones which are fairly straightforward to the person who has a grasp of the material. Toward the end of the test, the questions should be more challenging; make the students extrapolate what you have taught them into new conditions. At the end of the test you might provide an extra credit question that demands a great degree of sophistication and which challenges even the most intelligent and well-prepared student.

Never come into the classroom and write the final examination on the blackboard. Have it duplicated. In these days of the Xerox and other handy duplicating equipment, there is no excuse for the blackboard test. Make sure that the students can read the test, and that they can understand what you are asking. Phrase every statement in the test very carefully. A good examination requires several hours to prepare, but the time you spend in preparation of that examination will be saved in the grading time. You may wish to prove the adequacy of your examination by allowing some of your teaching or research assistants to take the examination before it is duplicated for the students. In our opinion, problems and discussion questions are much more suitable to the testing of a student's knowledge than true and false or multiple choice type examinations. One must sacrifice the ease of grading in accepting this format. In very large freshman classes in the major universities, where uniformity between the many sections of the same course is often desired, it may be necessary to prepare some form of multiple choice examination. Even in these cases, be sure to put at least one significant discussion question on the examination and grade this yourself. Through this practice you'll get a real feel for what your students know and what they don't know. If you allow the teaching assistant to share with you in the grading of this examination, as is commonly done, then be sure to allow the teaching assistants to write out their own answers for this examination and discuss them with you before grading the exam. This avoids the embarrassment of recalling the tests for regrading after the discovery of some faulty practice.

The professor should assume responsibility of being available to his students for consultation outside of class. However, this doesn't imply that the student can occupy your every free minute during the day. You'll remember that we indicated about twenty hours of your time will be devoted to activities related to your teaching responsibilities. Part of this twenty hours is a scheduled set of office hours. You must plan to be present during advertised office hours when students with special problems can contact you and discuss their problems. We have found that students are very fair in their demands upon the professor's time. Usually two or three hours per week of scheduled office hour contact with the students is sufficient to satisfy their needs. Tell the students that in cases of real emergency they can contact you in your office or laboratory.

One very important responsibility of the university professor exists which he may not fully appreciate or understand. Schmitz and Davies[43] have discussed well the responsibilities and the legal liability of the professor and the university for the safety of their students in the classroom and particularly in the laboratory. They indicate that liability for injuries sustained by students is increasing. Educational institutions can no longer take refuge in the defenses of charitable immunity and governmental immunity. Due care must be exercised by educational institutions to provide reasonably safe laboratory procedures and equipment. Proper precautions must be taken to protect the students from injury. Schools and universities are obligated to provide competent instructors who will properly instruct students and actively supervise student experiments. The chemistry professor should make sure that all of his undergraduate and graduate students wear safety glasses at *all* times in the laboratory and that they are cognizant of the hazards of the various chemicals and hazardous procedures. Every new professor in the experimental sciences should read the commentary and case histories given by Schmitz and Davies and consider seriously the desirability of procurement of personal liability insurance for protection against the unfortunate laboratory accident. It is highly probable that your university does not protect you in any way against liability claims by your students. The insurance agent who handles your home owners' policy or other insurance policies, probably can put in a rider on your policy to cover this situation at very little additional expense.

We have mentioned a few factors which we have found important in teaching in the university, both at graduate and undergraduate levels. It is entirely possible that you could be an excellent teacher and still not follow the few suggestions which we have outlined; if you were a Nobel Prize winner or had some special status which the students respect, they may tolerate you in spite of serious inadequacies as a teacher. However, until you win that prize, you'd better practice using every possible aid which will add to your effectiveness as a teacher. If you work hard on your lectures to insure both accuracy and clarity of the material, the students will respect your effort, and you're on your way to being one of their "good" teachers.

Obligations and Rewards in University Research. The motivation for active research by the young faculty member is very great. He has usually entered university life at least partially to fulfill some burning desire to investigate some interesting research problems. The young professor of today may work as long as forty hours per week in the library and the laboratory with his graduate students. The initiation of his research program is an important and time consuming business. He must remember to keep a reasonable balance between the time allotted to his undergraduate and graduate classroom teaching responsibilities on the one hand and to his graduate research and teaching responsibilities on the other. This balance between the two major university activities will become more and more important in the newly structured university now evolving. Student and community pressures will force a realistic partitioning of the time spent on teaching activities. In some state legislatures there have been vigorous attempts to force by law university professors to "teach" for twenty hours each week. Of course, all professors who are still breathing teach this many hours a week now if one includes in the count all of his teaching activities. Such misguided action points to the complete misconception of the average person of the enormity of the professor's obligations in the university. There is little realization that most professors now spend about forty hours per week in some very important teaching activity. They usually put in at least twenty hours on their classroom teaching responsibilities and course preparation, but during another twenty hours per week they teach graduate students and advanced undergraduate students the highly intricate art of scientific research. In the opinion of the authors, if one legislates a time-clock approach to education in the universities, they will attract undesirable types who will put in the twenty hours of classroom instruction required by the legislature and then depart. Also impressive to the citizen and legislator should be the fact that the successful science professor must be a businessman as well as teacher-researcher, who provides the university, his department, and himself with governmental, industrial, and private funds procured through his own efforts and abilities. That significant portion of his funds which the university captures under the "overhead" category is usually more than sufficient to repay the university for the entire salary of the professor. The funds brought to the university usually pay all or most of the costs of the stipends to the professor's students and buy much of his research equipment and supplies.

Frankly, the university professor does have an excellent case to make to the citizen and to the legislator, but he must improve the communication with these people. We remember how very successful the late Dr. E.W.R. Steacie was as a scientist-diplomat at the National Research Council (Canada). He would walk smartly into our laboratory some mornings unannounced, flanked by a covey of impeccably dressed and very distinguished-looking gentlemen who were members of the Canadian Parliament. "I would like you gentlemen to meet a few of our postdoctoral fellows," he would say. "Calvert, here, is from the University of California, Los Angeles. He will take a minute from his work to tell you a bit about the nature of his experiments here at the National Research Council."

The comments of Calvert and others probably were not too understandable and likely didn't help much in securing the approval of an adequate budget for research at N.R.C. the following year; however, the open attitude of Dr. Steacie and his direct communication with the legislators made them realize something of the spirit and hopes of the laboratory. It was undoubtedly a most important factor in the very great success of Dr. Steacie in building and establishing this outstanding Canadian research organization.

The average citizen and particularly the legislator, has a great distrust of the academic scientist; this is largely brought about by ourselves. We must communicate honestly with these people. We certainly have nothing to hide and a lot to gain by doing so.

We have discussed the importance of budgeting sufficient time for fulfilling your teaching responsibilities. It is just as important to your success as a young professor that you initiate, with all dispatch, your research effort at the university. Although your graduate students will soon carry a large share of the burden associated with the routine chores of building and maintaining equipment, you must get things going with your own efforts. You must start planning your research immediately and collecting data soon. Graduate students won't be attracted to a young professor who already gives an indication of mental or physical retirement. During the term before you appear at the university, send to the department chairman or to the appropriate finance officer, your list of needed equipment and supplies for which funding was approved in your earlier negotiations. This will allow a period of several months for orders to be placed and special equipment to arrive. If you wait to do such planning and ordering until you appear at the university, you may be a year or so getting to a good starting point in your research.

Place schedules on the doors of your office and laboratory which spell out your teaching and research time schedule. Make sure you stick by this schedule and that at least twenty hours per week are budgeted for the research activity. Committee work, consulting work, and any extracurricular work should be built around these research activities and your teaching—not into them. The appropriate department secretaries and the chairman of your department should know your schedule so that they can help you avoid conflicts in it.

As you initiate your research through the necessary, complete library review of the pertinent background literature, be sure to extend the courtesy of a brief note to the established scientists who are now working or who plan to work in your chosen area. Indicate your plan to pursue the problem of mutual interest. It is thoughtful to suggest that if this plan conflicts with or duplicates any programs that they have in mind, or have started, that you will pursue some other aspect of the problem. This kind of courtesy is too often neglected.

Those of you who are familiar with Nobel Laureate Watson't brief and delightful book, *The Double Helix,*[44] will recall the fierce competitive spirit at the time of the development of the double helix concept for the molecular structure of DNA. The secretive, independent research of the several English and American research groups is mentioned many times. We expect such secrecy from businessmen who must protect their financial position. However, scientific discoveries are based usually upon the contributions of a great number of people. Obviously, no one has a real priority on any given area. International, fierce competition to accomplish the same goal, without communication, is unfortunate. History has a way of placing credits under the proper names, regardless of the personal claims of individuals.

The graduate schools in the university today are financed largely through government and industrial funds. Figure 13 shows the extent of federal support to scientists in universities and colleges during the past several years. Of the 3.4 billion dollars committed in 1968, 2.3 billion were devoted to the academic science programs.

Your chance for success in the procurement of a portion of federal funds for the pursuit of your research effort can be anticipated somewhat from the data shown in Table 7. This shows the federal support received by scientists in the

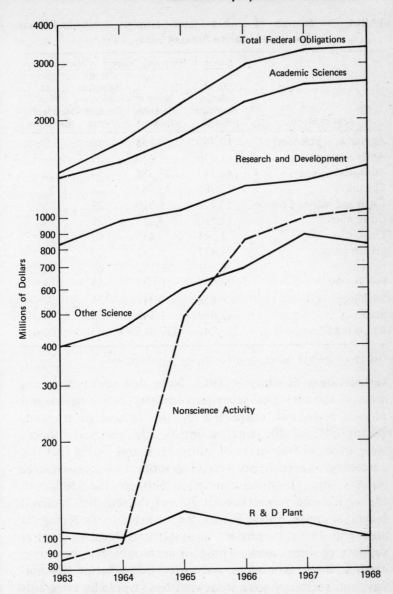

Figure 13:   Federal obligations to universities and colleges by type of program, 1963-1968. (Data from ref. 20.)

TABLE 7: Number of United States Scientists Receiving Federal Support in Various Areas of Study, 1968.[a]

Area of Study	Scientists Receiving Support in Various Areas			
	Total Number Scientists Polled	Number Receiving Support	% of Scientists Supported in Each Area	% of Total Support for Each Area
Agricultural Sciences	12,740	8,858	70	7
Anthropology	1,219	476	39	–
Biological Sciences	46,183	27,356	59	21
Chemistry	93,788	25,967	28	20
Earth and Marine Sciences	23,746	6,910	29	5
Economics	11,510	4,353	38	3
Linguistics	1,541	450	29	–
Mathematics	24,477	8,757	36	7
Physics	32,491	20,190	62	16
Psychology	23,077	10,024	43	8
Sociology	6,638	2,311	35	2
Statistics	2,639	1,545	58	1
ALL FIELDS	297,942	127,415	43	100.0

[a]Data from the NSF report, *American Science Manpower, 1968.*[15]

various areas of study in 1968. Note that scientists in the areas of the biological sciences, chemistry, mathematics, and physics were well supported by the federal government. About 64% of the total scientists who received support were in these four areas of study. It is interesting that the percentage of scientists receiving support in a given area reflects some keen discrimination between the areas.   In the agriculture sciences,about 70% of the scientists received federal support. About 60% of the scientists in the biological area and those in physics and statistics received federal support of their work. Those in anthropology, chemistry, earth sciences, economics, linguistics, mathematics, psychology, and sociology were somewhat less favored by the granting programs. These areas received from 30% to 50% support for their scientists. The number of scientists supported in various federal government programs as shown in Figure 14 is also an indication of the financial popularity of the various fields. Programs related to agriculture, atomic energy, defense, education, health, natural resources, and space, supported a large number of scientists. As you might anticipate, the data suggest that the largest fraction of those receiving support have the doctorate degree. While this employment picture has changed somewhat since 1968, the relative numbers shown are probably still a good measure of the situation.

Grants are awarded to scientists with interests in all varieties of pure research in the sciences and the competition for these awards is fierce indeed. The National Science Foundation, United States Public Health Service, National Institutes of Health, the Atomic Energy Commission, and various other government and industrial granting groups accept applications for support of programs relating to the specialty areas of their major concern. In the appendix of this book we have drawn on the more complete tables of the *Annual Register of Grant Support*[45] and other information to show the major sources of funds for research in the sciences (see Table A-5). A short description of the type of research which these agencies favor is also given. Reference to the details of the original compendium may be helpful to those just starting their research careers, as would be a visit to your university vice president or dean of research. They may have up-to-date and complete lists of granting agencies and the latest scuttlebutt on where the action is in terms of areas favored for research funding.

"Grantsmanship,"—The Art of Writing Research Proposals. The ultimate approval of your proposed research grant request for funding depends on your ability to show both the uniqueness and the significance of your work to your area of science; in addition, the relevance of your research proposal to the solution of some larger problem of na-

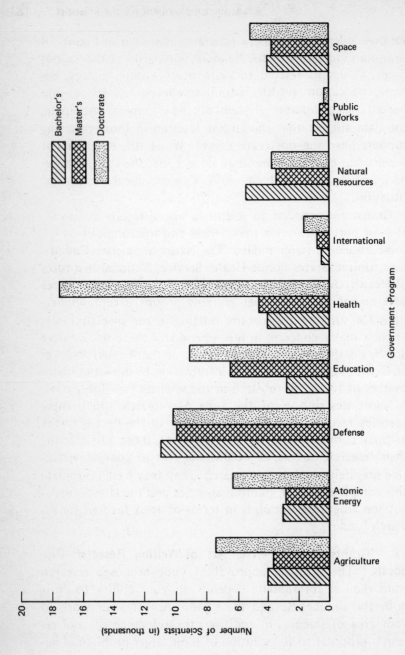

Figure 14: Comparison of number of United States scientists receiving federal support for various government programs listed by highest academic degree, 1968. (Data from ref. 15.)

tional concern may be a major criterion of the review panel today. "Grantsmanship" is an art which professors develop quickly. If they don't, they're liable to die on the academic vine; at best they will not be able to reach their full potential as a scientist. Let's review a few of the fundamentals involved in writing a successful research application.

First, be sure that your idea for a research proposal is unique and has a real chance of providing new information. During your graduate and postdoctoral years of research you have had some good ideas for future work which you should now evaluate carefully.

The young scientist's choice of research problem will be influenced strongly by his previous areas of specialization. He should give some very careful thought to the alternatives before choosing his first research problem. As we noted earlier, every young faculty man should read the book by E. Bright Wilson, Jr., *An Introduction to Scientific Research.*[29] Professor Wilson gives a very helpful and readable discussion of every aspect of research which the young faculty man and graduate student must face. Pay special heed to his statement on the consideration of the choice of a research problem: "Many scientists owe their greatness not to their skill in solving problems, but to their wisdom in choosing them . . ."

Among the important points which he suggests that the young scientist consider are the following, which we have embellished with some of our own thoughts on the subject:

(1) The problem should interest the investigator strongly. Particularly when the going is tough, you need a deep interest in the work, or you will give up before making a real attempt at solving the problem.

(2) Usually it is desirable to have new ideas for research before undertaking a problem, especially in a field which has been extensively investigated before. It is almost always worthwhile to explore a region which is really new. More ex-

citing, unexpected results can generally be anticipated under these circumstances. However, as Professor Wilson suggests, hitherto untouched fields are not easy to find.

(3) When really new virgin territory is not open to the new scientist, then it is usually best to undertake experiments which are designed to test well thought out hypotheses.

(4) It is reasonable to ask not only what connection a given problem has to other branches of science, but also what connection it has to the problems of our society. It is important that every scientific research effort undertaken be selected because it is likely to tell something about a wide area, rather than a very limited field.

(5) Under normal circumstances make sure that your research is unclassified. The authors' experience and views reflect Professor Wilson's feeling on this subject. He feels the greatest difficulties, and consequently the greatest losses in efficiency, occur when secrecy, either military or industrial, is involved. Science, particularly academic science, simply does not flourish under such circumstances. We feel that unless the country is involved in a veritable "fight for its life," scientists in universities can contribute more to their country by actively pursuing unrestricted research which opens new areas to all and which will improve the physical and intellectual environment of all humanity.

(6) Be sure to plan your experiments so that costs are kept to a reasonable level. Don't spend the university's or the government's money foolishly. Frugality in science is again becoming a necessity as well as a virtue. The simplest and the most economical experiment which tests your hypothesis adequately without loss in the necessary accuracy of the results will be most respected by the scientific world.

(7) Be sure to put honest and realistic boundary conditions on the scope of work you propose. Two of the authors have critically reviewed and written detailed reports on literally hundreds of research proposals over the last two decades. One of the most common faults which we encountered was

that the principal investigator proposed programs that were far beyond his capacity to complete within his time scale, budget limitations, and in some cases, abilities. In short, remember the old duck hunting adage: "Don't flock shoot; aim at one duck at a time, and you may have something in the pot for dinner."

(8) Dr. Wilson poses this question for the scientist to face before undertaking some possible research problem: "Why should I, among all of the scientists of the world, be the one to do the job?" If you haven't just the right theoretical or experimental experience, don't possess the necessary unique equipment, or the problem doesn't interest you so strongly that you are willing to invest the time and effort to develop these special assets, then it is unlikely that anything very startling will ensue.

There is a final sobering comment from Professor Wilson that we feel each potential faculty member should read carefully. His answer should help him decide on his career direction: "A research worker in pure science who does not have at all times more problems he would like to solve than he has time and means to investigate probably is in the wrong business."

Once your careful review and planning effort has pointed the way to your first research effort, plan to spend several days in the library documenting the past related work. Don't forget that it is likely that some of the very best scientists in your research area will review your proposal. They will know the literature well and will give a poorer rating to your proposal if proper credit is not given to the research upon which your proposal rests.

The actual format of your research proposal is often dictated by the agency to which you are applying. Regardless of the format of the proposal, make sure that you state clearly the objectives of your work and the methods by which your research will be carried out. Indicate any problem areas which you anticipate and alternative plans which you will use if

these problems develop. Show clearly the nature of the conclusions which may possibly come from your work and the
significance of the potential findings to your area and other
areas of science.

Be realistic in the proposed budget for your research. It is
common to seek support for one or two graduate students'
stipends. Make sure that the request is in line with the stipends given to other research assistants and fellows in your
department.

We'll be honest with you. One of the most important fringe
benefits that accompanies the award of a research grant from
a major agency is the fact that you'll be allowed to supplement your nine-month academic salary with several additional
months of summer salary. During the summer months you'll
devote full time to your research efforts so that you'll get
double green stamps—a shot in the arm for your research
and an extra shot or two in your wine cellar. Most universities
and agencies fix the amount you can be paid in the summer
so the rate per month you receive is identical to that for the
academic year. For example, if your nine-month academic
salary is $9,000, you would be permitted to earn an addition-
al $1,000 per month for two or sometimes three months, de-
pending on the policies of the university, granting agencies,
and your spouse. However, we recommend against a full
three month summer stipend. Take some of those vacations
when you're young. Nobody can take them for you. You'll
do a better job all the way around when you return.

The new professor in science will find that his most difficult fund raising task is the procurement of major research
equipment on research grant requests. Research sponsored by
the Defense Department agencies have been somewhat freer
in their allotments for major research equipment in research
grants or contracts. However, certain of these agencies usually
earmark all equipment procured for their sponsored research
to return to them after completion of the research effort. The
"small" equipment requests, up to $10,000, stand a favor-

able chance of approval by most granting agencies, if the equipment is not already available at the university at which the work is done. Awards for larger equipment, say from $50,000 to $150,000, usually must be obtained on major equipment grant proposals funded by the National Science Foundation, Public Health Service, or special state appropriations. A plus benefit in moving into a new science building is the fact that in equipping it there is generally the opportunity to add one or more large and expensive instruments to the departmental roster.

All granting agencies look favorably on "matching fund" requests for major items in which the university or department budget may allow a partial funding of some expensive items. It is a good investment for the university to get a needed item of major equipment for one-half price. In addition, the granting agency gains some confidence in the real value of its investment to the university; it will probably be much more favorably disposed toward support of your request when you promise matching funds.

It is probably obvious to you that you must write clearly and spell and punctuate carefully. In preparing your manuscript make sure that the document is typed carefully and proofread thoroughly for errors in preparation. If your proposal looks bad and reads poorly, it will be rated considerably lower than the scientific content alone would warrant.

You may submit your research proposal to more than one research-granting agency. However, if this is done, you must note on each application the alternative agencies to which the proposal has been submitted.

Until recently some limited financial support was available from industry and private individuals. However, the recent recession in business has quite naturally been reflected in the extent of support. Many of the larger companies give fellowships and unrestricted grant money directly to a good department without stipulating the area of interest to be supported by the fellowship or the grant. Support of this type, while relatively small in terms of the total extra-mural funds coming into the department, has a value to the faculty and students far greater than might appear on the surface. One thing every departmental chairman needs is his own "kitty" which he can use for all types of contingencies; these may range from sending a deserving young faculty member to a meeting to the purchase of a special keyboard typewriter which would not normally be funded by the state.

In most universities, there is a small university research budget which faculty members draw on for pressing research needs. Often a university or departmental faculty committee reviews applications for grants from this fund. Usually not more than $1,000 or $2,000 per man can be made available from this very limited but important resource.

The wise young professor has alternative research plans which are not financially demanding and which he can immediately pursue while awaiting the word on his research proposals.

In summary, get busy on your own research well before you arrive to start your new job. When you do come on the scene, don't get so carried away that you spend more than your designated time period on this activity but accept this responsibility as conscientiously as you do your teaching responsibility. Remember that one important criterion of the award of tenure is that you have demonstrated that you can pursue well-conceived, new, and important research on your own. Until your research has resulted in a publication, there is no tangible evidence of your capabilities as a research scholar, at least to the scientific world.

Graduate Students and Research.   What obligation does the professor have towards his graduate students and their thesis research? It is a rare graduate student who comes to his preceptor with a well-conceived and imaginative research problem of his own. Even when this happens, it is often impossible for the student to get financial support to carry out his research under the direction of his chosen preceptor. Since the professor's funds have been designated for a specific research effort, he must show progress in this if subsequent renewals are to be expected. In most cases, the research preceptor delineates several possible problem areas which the potential graduate student may choose to investigate. The preceptor has an obligation to pick carefully the problem areas which are solvable within the budgetary limitations of his research group and within the time period consistent with normal graduate study (three to five years). Professors differ in their opinions as to the obligations, if any, which exist for the research preceptor in the direction of the graduate student's thesis work. In our opinion, the young professor must give a high degree of close supervision to the detailed, day-by-day research effort of the graduate student, although he should neither dominate the work nor give the impression of this close supervision to the students. The senior professor, of necessity, will spend much less time with his students in the laboratory, but this should be made up by close contact of the graduate student with one or more postdoctoral students on his research team. The point of the close supervision is to help the student in his effort before he has wasted a month or year on some unsolvable, unimportant aspect of his problem. The graduate student must demonstrate his independence, and you must encourage this, but he is still a student and can learn a few things from the style of the pros. Make sure he does.

Many young preceptors get so caught up in their research that they neglect to pass on to their young wards the background of the problem which they have chosen. Professor E. Bright Wilson has suggested that every young faculty man should explain carefully to each student how his particular research problem arose, why it is important, and what will be done with the results. If we and every professor whom we have known had practiced this policy, there would have been many problems which the professor would not have assigned and many others which never would have been accepted by the graduate student.

Be available for help and consultation when major problems arise. Overcome the great temptation to step in and run the student's experiment or help him interpret it as he first collects his data. The student should get the first opportunity to collect and treat his data and formulate conclusions based on his own reasoning. The teaching role of the preceptor in graduate research enters most strongly in his discussion and criticism of the student's evaluation of his own work.

Some professors feel that the research of the master's degree candidate should receive more input from the professor, and the more serious time limitation on this research tends to support this view. In every case, however, the student should indeed be the prime individual responsible for his thesis research.

The preceptor should read very carefully and evaluate independently the interpretation of the student's data as presented in the thesis. Obviously, the professor should question any points which are without firm foundation or which lack rigor. In the long run though, it is the student's thesis. He must write it, and he must defend it.

In the final oral examination of his thesis work, the student must stand on his own feet in the defense and presentation of his thesis. The preceptor should not give the oral presentation for the student. You will find it most difficult to sit quietly by during his oral examination and see him miss some crucial point in his argument. If the professor intervenes excessively in the final oral, which happens occasionally, the examination may disintegrate into a discussion between the preceptor and the committee. This is the student's day. Let him enjoy the sunshine or shiver in the rain, if it begins to fall.

The typical Ph.D. student has a high vapor pressure and tends to evaporate from the scene after his thesis is awarded. Subsequent demands on the student in his first full-time job and the complications of personal resettlement all force a delay in the preparation of articles for publication which are based on the thesis research. Thus, it is very important for the preceptor to encourage the graduate student to write up his work in publishable form before receipt of his degree. It is very good experience for the graduate student and helps him prepare for his final oral. It also allows the preceptor at least a head start in the final preparation of the paper for publication.

Views concerning the desirability of joint authorship by the preceptor and the graduate student are mixed. In practice, in most physical and biological sciences the student's thesis work is published jointly with the preceptor as co-author. After all, the research problem was probably the preceptor's idea, and if the relationship between student and preceptor is not unusual, the preceptor has managed to infiltrate the student's interpretation with several of his own original ideas. The final decision concerning joint authorship or single authorship should be made through consultation between preceptor and student. The student often benefits greatly from having his name linked with the senior scientist with whom he has worked. Even in postdoctoral research where independence of the researcher is maximized, joint authorship with the preceptor is the common route in the physical and biological sciences.

Responsibilities for Committee and Service Work in the University. Very often the inexperienced professor comes to the university with the misconception that his teaching and research duties constitute his total responsibility to the university. This is hardly the case, however, as academic faculty are a very democratic lot. They insist that academic decisions, no matter how trivial, must be made by majority agreement on recommendations put forth by the appropriate select committee. As a consequence, a professor is drawn into a veritable jungle of committee responsibilities. During his first year he may serve, for example, on the departmental curriculum committee to help redesign the undergraduate program; he may be appointed to the Phi Beta Kappa membership committee which searches the academic records of the registrar for the names of students with sufficiently high scholastic abilities and proper breadth in subject matter to qualify for nomination; he may serve on from two to six graduate written and oral examination committees; he will probably act as advisor to a number of undergraduate students and undergraduate student committees. He may even be elected by the faculty to such important assignments as the athletic council, and in this capacity he may serve on one or two subcommittees involved in the investigation of student athlete misconduct or revised methods of athletic ticket distribution.

Committees run the entire gamut from student-motivated to university-motivated missions, investigations, and fact-finding bodies. They are a definite part of the academic system and must be tolerated if not enjoyed by faculty members. However, in our opinion, every faculty member should protect himself against involvement in more than one major committee assignment at the department level, one at the college level, and one at the university level. If this is not done, he will find that in a very short time the great majority of the time allotted to his teaching and research duties will have been usurped through committee involvement.

All young scientists are involved rather quickly in their careers in requests from journal editors to act as referees for a variety of journal articles and research proposals to various government and professional societies and agencies. After his first significant publication in an area, a young professor will probably be sent an article or research proposal for review at least once every few months. When he becomes an established and well-recognized scientist he may get five or ten requests of this sort every month. There is no compensation for this service, yet in some cases it may require as much as half a day of your time to accomplish the study and evaluation of a single comprehensive article if you are completely fair to the authors and honest with the editor of the journal. This is not the case for the really good articles or the really bad ones; the time consuming ones are those in which you're not sure if the author is a genius or a nut. Professors probably will continue to tolerate this invasion into their already limited free time for several reasons. First, someone else has to review *your* publications, and turnabout is fair play. Second, articles and proposal reviews provide the chance to see a preview of new work long before publication (as much as one year). Finally, it is somewhat flattering to the professor to be asked to judge the quality of an erudite colleague's contribution to his field. However, when you accept the responsibility for review, do the job thoroughly. If you just haven't time for this, send it back to the editor immediately. Neither the author nor the editor wants shallow comments or correction of his trivial spelling or grammatical errors. That's the editor's job; don't do it for him.

Every professor, certainly those in the "relevant" research fields, should accept his share of lectures for groups such as the P.T.A., the school board, and committees of the city, state, and national governments. On the average, such groups seek the involvement of an established professor as much as one evening a week; while this may be very time-consuming, your informal view is probably helpful on many issues on which school, civic, and government groups must formulate policy and develop new laws.

As you see, it isn't just the grade school and high school teacher who is given assignments of questionable challenge. The university professor has his little tasks which chew away at least 20% of his available useful time. Limit your contribution to those areas of community and university service which interest you most and for which your effort is most uniquely useful to all parties concerned. Don't forget that your scientific career depends primarily upon your prowess as a teacher and a scientific researcher.

Consulting for Outside Interests While in the University.
There is perhaps no more controversial subject related to the
responsibilities of the university professor than his role as a
consultant for outside interests. In nearly every university
there is either a formal written faculty rule or an informal
gentlemen's agreement that one day per week of the faculty
member's time may be spent on outside consulting. In principle, in addition to these permissable fifty-two days per
year, the professor is free to consult during all vacation periods and weekends during the regular year. Actually, very few
if any, professors take advantage of this extent of involvement
in the consulting practice. However, it is very attractive to the
young professor to be recognized by some important industry
or governmental agency as an expert in some particular area.
To be invited to sign a consulting agreement with a well-
known, multimillion dollar company and to have them seek
your expert advice are flattering experiences. Few professors
refuse at least one such involvement.

On the favorable side of consulting involvements is the
tangible reward the professor receives for his services. His
consulting fee is agreed upon in consultation with the company officials. What kind of fee should you charge for such
services? If you want to do a particular consulting job for the
practical experience and the very special knowledge which
it appears *you* will gain, then accept a fee as low as is consistent with the use of your time. For a young professor, around
$100 per day should be the minimum. You may not be
particularly enthusiastic about some consulting opportunity
which will arise; it may require extensive travel or considerable library work in preparation for the consulting trip. However you may feel that you can contribute significantly to a
solution of the problem and the supplementary income is
needed for some pressing family matter or new extravagance
you have developed. Then a consulting fee of several times
this minimum figure per day would not be out of line. The
company can always refuse your offer or renegotiate a more

reasonable fee if it can't accept your request. If a company seeks your help, then it should expect to pay you at least at the same rate of pay as that received by the scientists with whom you are consulting. Whatever you are paid, plan to work hard on the assignments given to you. They are seeking an expert's advice; you had better be one, or they will look elsewhere next time.

There are several other advantages to limited consulting work. The faculty member learns some very practical and inventive ideas from a modern research-oriented company. Although some of these may be of a restricted nature, many things you learn will be available for your continual use and can be passed on to your students who are always eager for an authoritative slant on the real world of industry. The academic consultant with a reputable large industry will probably learn as much from this practical experience as do the scientists with whom he consults.

Very often the involvement of the company with the faculty member is arranged through the suggestions of alumni or former graduate students of your university who are now employed by the company. The suggestion of your participation in a consulting arrangement may even come from members of your state legislature who have been approached by company officials or at the recommendation of the university administration—including the deans and the president. Universities recognize that the salary level of their scientific faculty is inconsistent with the professor's counterpart in industry, and they may attempt to compensate for this inequity through the fringe benefits of consulting opportunities.

The source of problems related to faculty consultants arises largely from the possibility of the professor's consulting effort interfering with his teaching and research obligations. It is really a matter of personal prejudice as to which view is taken. The authors feel that the use of limited consulting time by the faculty is extremely valuable in that it allows him to be more knowledgeable of the problems of industry and

industry's requirements for Ph.D. scientists, the major employer of the scientists he trains.

The university professor must be extremely careful in ar-
ranging his consulting agreements so that he avoids possible
conflicts of interest. Industry operates like a secret government agency in some respects. Its security must be protected by both employer and consultant alike. When a professor consults in the same area for two competing industries,
he is asking for trouble. It is very difficult to compartmental-
ize your mind and not utilize directly or indirectly the knowledge obtained from one company for the benefit of the competitive company. Every professor who does consulting should
be very sure that the companies with whom he works are
completely knowledgeable of the other consulting arrangements and the fields of interest which these encompass. If the
professor at the time of the consulting visit sees an apparent
conflict of interest developing, he should point this out immediately to the management. It is easy for the company to
relieve the consultant of responsibilities in the area of possible conflict.

There is one type of consulting in which most academic
scientists eventually become involved. This concerns service
on governmental review panels and evaluation committees.
Your pay for such services is nonnegotiable; it is fixed by the
government and is usually quite modest. It may not, in fact,
even cover your expenses. You will review, on your own time,
many scientific proposals and potential government documents, perhaps for several days before the actual meeting of
experts. Your recommendations are then sought during a
central meeting of consulting experts who gather from
around the country for a one to three-day period; you receive the per diem and government rate consulting compensation for this meeting period only.

Although the hours are long and the time consumed may
seriously cut into your university obligations, university
administrators and citizens alike seem to accept the role of

the university professor in government consulting opportunities. Such review panels are responsible for the allocation of large sums of research and other monies earmarked for universities and other research organizations. The university professor is considered the most nearly "pure," uncommitted, independent agent who is scientifically competent to judge the quality of applicants for government grants. In principle, they have neither the axe to grind nor the personal involvement which is characteristic of the scientist in private business and industry. It is probably necessary that this kind of consulting arrangement be continued. The academic scientist will accept it as a service to his country and a duty and responsibility in which he must share.

The inevitable problem of possible overextension of the professor and possible conflicts of interest through his various consulting arrangements will continue to crop up to the apparent chagrin of the university administration, faculty, industry, and government alike. There appears to us to be an obvious solution to the apparent problem. The professor, together with the university administration, representatives of government (both legislative and administrative), and industry, could by joint consultation arrive at some equitable distribution of the consulting time of each professor concerned. The professor should not be subjected to the harassment which ultimately occurs from the present loose agreements between the various parties bidding for his time. There are only 168 hours in a week. Counting 56 of these hours for the professor's rest and rehabilitation, only 112 hours per week are left, including some little time off for good behavior. We feel sure that the professor would be happy to have the parties who bid for his time suggest how he might best partition it. Certainly, it is "dirty pool" for industry and government to tie up a professor by contract and then argue that he is spending too little time with his students. Make sure that, in any case, your university administration approves, in writing, of your consulting arrangements. Remember to keep your perspective clear and accept only as many consulting assignments as you can handle well within your tight teaching and research schedule.

Academic Freedom and Tenure in the University.   One of the most important heritages of the university is that of the job security promised to the tenured faculty members of the university. Obviously, academic freedom and academic tenure are not intended to protect a professor against prosecution for criminal acts. They protect him against the threat of firing as a result of political, social, or other pressures which he may stir up by virtue of his controversial or unpopular position expressed in the pursuit of his profession or in his legal actions as a private citizen. As one might expect, the social scientist and the humanist have attracted more attention in this regard than the natural scientist and engineer. Their studies commonly come closer to the nerve center of the populace and often seriously disturb a large body of citizens. However, today's scientists involved with a relevant societal problem such as environmental pollution sometimes stir up a hornets nest.

There is no need here to expound on the great importance of preserving tenure in academic life. In our opinion some of our colleagues, particularly during the last several years, have taken serious and, in some cases, almost fatal liberties with the security that comes with their tenure. We deplore this. Nevertheless, on balance, we feel that the positive effects of tenure handled responsibly far outweigh the irresponsible minority. Tenure certainly is as important to the academician and the society as a whole as is the congressional immunity of the government representatives of the people within the halls of Congress. Of course, the professor is not protected against libel suits and must live within the law of the average citizen. This is as it should be. However, the tenured professor has the security of position which allows him to make a close re-evaluation of the existing practices and theories which may require change. Obviously, it is important for the scientists to continue to defend and champion this tradition as it represents the true spirit of a university. Only through the thorough and open discussion and evaluation of ideas and facts can we continue to improve our democratic way of life. The university professor and his students must continue to play a leading role in the search for the understanding and the solution to our many problems.

Remember that academic freedom is not a license to exploit or violate the law. It implies a responsibility to act within the law and to allow the opponent of your view as fair a hearing as your own.

The award of academic tenure in your post as a young professor will be made no later than seven years after your first academic appointment as an assistant professor. Normally you will receive tenure before this time if you and your efforts have been well received by your colleagues. The faculty never takes lightly their considerations concerning the tenure of a young colleague. If he is not outstanding (by the local standards) in either his teaching or his research and good, or at least acceptable, in the other areas, he will be asked to leave the university after some designated short period allowed for his relocation. Don't assume that the award of your tenure is an automatic event—it is far from that. Your colleagues will spend countless hours of careful discussion and study of your work before they reach their decision.

There is one aspect of academic tenure which at times seems to act against the best interests of the university and the building of strength in the faculty. If, after receiving tenure, the professor should decide to retire from the active pursuit of new knowledge in his area, or his fascination with and his efforts toward his teaching drop off seriously, he can't be fired or replaced readily. Only if he shows evidence of violent misconduct and is convicted can he be removed. However, this problem is not as serious as it appears to be at first sight. The professor whose efforts become seriously inadequate will be discouraged in staying at the university by his colleagues; his salary may be frozen until there is evidence of his old spirit, or he may be reassigned to certain necessary routine chores not directly associated with the students or the classroom.

The potential young scientist in academic life should keep this point in mind: don't worry about tenure. If you are capable and hard-working, you will be rewarded by your colleagues. It is the scientist with borderline capabilities or the one who works very inefficiently that will be dismissed. If you feel that you fit into one of these classes, then don't enter the academic life. You'll be much happier and more secure in your future if you avoid the ordeal of consideration for tenure.

10. Government Employment for the Scientist

Opportunities for the employment of scientists in the research laboratories and administrative agencies of the federal, state, and local governments are many. Lindveit[45] points out that the role of scientists in the United States government is as old as the nation itself. The Constitution charges Congress with the responsibility for promoting science for national defense and for developing standards of weights and measures. The federal government has clear responsibility for development, testing, and standardization in many areas. In addition to the development of military weapons, responsibility exists for the control of the food and drug traffic, control of air and water pollution, etc.

The government is better equipped than any other agency to support such vast activities as research in atomic energy and space exploration. These activities are of such high cost and low immediate commercial value that private research groups are not attracted to them. The large and successful agricultural research program supported for years by the United States government probably could not have been accomplished as effectively through farming groups or individuals. In 1960 the Department of Agriculture was called the largest single research organization in the world.[45] Today scientific research on a large scale is done in a great multitude of government departments and agencies.

201

In the report, *American Science Manpower, 1966,*[16b] it was reported that 11% of all the Ph.D. scientists of the United States were employed by the federal, state, or local governments. The largest share of these government scientists, about 79%, worked for the federal government. Among United States scientists whose highest degree is the master's degree, an even higher percentage, about 15%, were employed in the government service; about 68% of this group of scientists worked for the federal government.

The distribution of scientists employed by the federal government among the various disciplines is shown in Figure 15. The percentage of all the Ph.D. scientists in the United States working for the federal government in 1968 in each discipline is indicated. Interest and opportunities for agricultural scientists were the highest of all service areas. In fact, about 38% of all Ph.D. agriculturalists in the United States worked for the federal government in 1968.

Scientists in government find a variety of opportunities for employment. There are a great number of national laboratories which hire scientists. In addition, there are federally funded research and development centers which are administered by the universities and colleges. The relative economic importance of the best supported members of the latter group in 1968 are shown in Figure 16. Some shifts have occurred since then. In Table A-6 of the Appendix, a complete list of these centers is shown. There are a number of other government-supported research centers in universities which have merged with the administering university.

The distribution of scientists in government in 1968 between the various work activities is illustrated in Figure 17. By far, the largest share of the scientists were either in research and development work (about 41%), or in management and administration (about 36%). Detailed data on work activities of scientists in various areas of science are available in Table A-3 of the Appendix.

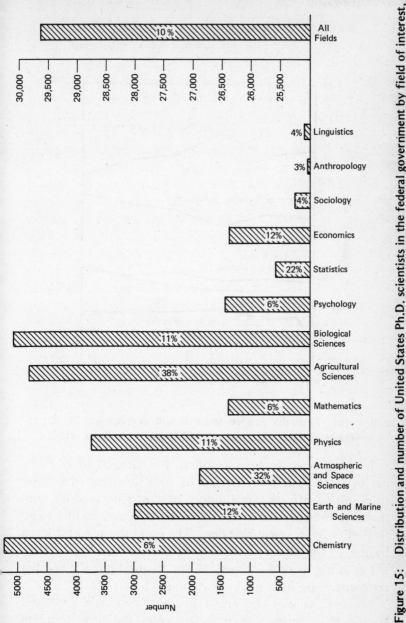

Figure 15: Distribution and number of United States Ph.D. scientists in the federal government by field of interest, 1968; the number shown on each bar represents the percentage of all U.S. Ph.D. scientists in the given area who are working for the federal government. (Data from ref. 15.)

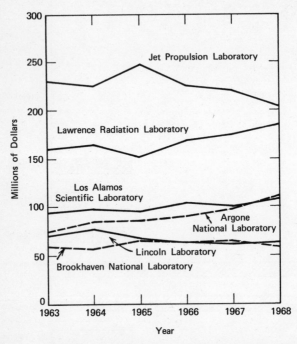

Figure 16: Federally funded research and development centers receiving the largest obligations, 1963-1968. (Data from ref. 20.)

In its attempt to hire scientists, the national government has been plagued for years by its own financing of competitive hiring efforts. Its support of cost-plus-fixed-fee contracts for industry allows the industrial employer to buy more flexibility in its scientific talent. The government is restricted by law to the salary which it can offer the new Ph.D. scientist entering its ranks. Laws are not changed quickly and the competitive position of the government is often lost.

However, salaries of scientists in government have improved significantly during the past ten years and now compete

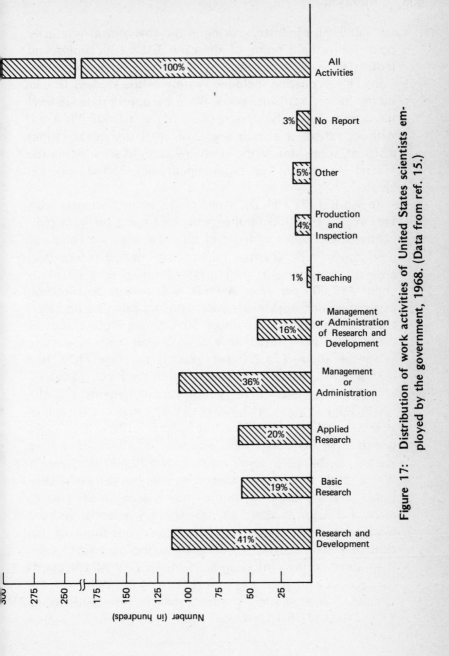

Figure 17: Distribution of work activities of United States scientists employed by the government, 1968. (Data from ref. 15.)

favorably with industry. Hiring in the government is usually done following a rating of the candidate's educational and industrial work experience by the Civil Service Commission. This evaluation includes a rating of the student largely by his former academic peers. When the appropriate GS-level has been assigned, the starting salary of the individual is fixed. Although there is a small degree of flexibility in the ratings assigned, some idea of the starting salaries of scientists in the federal government can be obtained from the following examples.

In April 1971 a Ph.D. in one of the natural sciences with two years of postdoctoral experience, some significant publications, and other evidence of his prowess as a mature and productive Ph.D. scientist might have entered federal government employment with a GS-13 rating at a salary of about $18,000 per year. A Ph.D. with neither postdoctoral experience nor work experience who was rated by his references as being from the upper 50% among Ph.D. graduates could have been hired at a GS-12 level with a starting salary of about $15,200 per year. If the new Ph.D. had been judged as being in the lower 50% of the Ph.D. graduates, he might have entered the government employment at the GS-11 level at about $12,800 per year. A master's student in science with no experience but judged to be in the upper one-third of his class by his academic references may have started at the GS-9 level with about $10,600 per year; if the master's student was classed as being in the lower two-thirds of his class, then he may have started in the government as a GS-7 at about $8,700. The B.S. scientist without work experience but from the upper one-third of his class may have entered government at the same GS-7 level.

In some of the critical agencies of the government, scientists can look forward to possible future advancement to the so-called "super-grade" positions which now pay up to $37,624 at the GS-18 level.

In 1968, the median annual salary of the Ph.D. scientist in the federal government ($15,800) was well above that for the Ph.D. scientist in the universities, $12,000 for the academic year and $14,800 for the calendar year. Although government salaries were significantly lower than the median annual salary paid in industry and business ($17,500), they were comparable to that of the nonprofit organization ($16,000). However, this is no longer necessarily true today. Salaries in many government organizations are competitive to those in industry.

Scientists see some very attractive features to employment by the federal government. Among these are the excellent laboratory facilities commonly available to government scientists. In many cases, these facilities are the very best in the world, and in some cases the particular piece of equipment which they have available is the only one of its kind. Furthermore, the government scientist is often free to do basic research in his area and to publish these results quickly. In contrast to the industrial scientist, the government scientist is usually not inhibited by company doctrine or company security. Of course, there are some government scientists who work on sensitive matters concerned with national security. They must accept the unusual role of a scientist without hope of recognition for his work by his colleagues outside the agency, at least during the immediate years of his work.

The fringe benefits of government employment are excellent. There are liberal sick leave and vacation periods and early retirement programs.

The government scientist is, however, not without his problems. Perhaps his most nagging problem is a rather intangible one. Unfair though it is, there seems to be a general tendency to deprecate both government work and government workers. For example, in a rather thorough survey to establish the image of the federal employee,[46] nonfederal employees were asked to rate their own jobs on a scale from one to ten; the higher the score, the more favorable was the rating. The same employees were then asked, "Suppose your work or occupation stayed the same, but you worked for the federal government—that is, the United States government—how much better or worse would that be?" Almost all groups rated the government work lower. The natural scientists, social scientists, and engineers in education showed a strong negative reaction to changing to an equivalent federal position; on the average, these groups of scientists rated work with the federal government below that of their present work by 1.8, 1.7, and 1.5 points, respectively, on the ten-point scale. Groups in business and industry rated the government positions as being even less attractive to them than their present positions. Executives, natural scientists, social scientists, and engineers in these areas rated the analogous federal job down 2.6, 2.1, 2.7, and 2.5 points, respectively, on the ten-point scale.

Federal employees in the sciences were asked this question in reverse. They rated their present federal job compared to the equivalent job outside the government. In this case, the natural scientists, social scientists, and engineers in the government rated the suggested change as only slightly unfavorable, down 0.5, 0.3, and 0.1 points, respectively. The implication is clear that, at least in 1964, scientists rated work in government as less attractive than that in the university or in industry. The federal government has been well aware of this problem and some of the reasons for it. Recently, successful efforts have been made to improve the financial and professional status of its scientists' positions.

There is at least one other problem area experienced somewhat uniquely by the government scientist. We are all familiar with the common complaint that the government is being buried in its own red tape. The government scientist may experience administrative delays and the effects of political manipulation more often than the scientists in industry or the university. The governmental system of checks and balances hovers over the government scientist like a huge cloud which is ready to dampen his spirits if the sudden switch in research direction, so often necessary in productive research, is attempted. It is by comparison easy to switch courses in research when an industrial research director or a university professor decides to do so in his research program.

In spite of these problems confronting research scientists in government, academicians often look with envy on their excellent facilities and the demonstrated excellence and productivity of their efforts. Certainly, it would pay the new Ph.D. graduate to thoroughly investigate career opportunities for scientists in his area in government service.

11. *Employment of Scientists in Research Institutes; Other Nonprofit Organizations*

In many ways, opportunities for employment in a research institute are similar to those found in industrial research, but fewer jobs are available. Thus in 1966 less than 4% of all the Ph.D. scientists in the United States worked in research institutes. Of United States scientists employed by nonprofit organizations, over one-half are involved in management or administration. A list of the major nonprofit research organizations and research institutes in the United States in 1968 is shown in Table A-8 of the Appendix.

In general, the nonprofit organization has a salary structure somewhat between that of industry and the federal government. For example, Ph.D. scientists received a median annual salary in 1968 of $16,000 in the nonprofit organizations, $17,500 in industry, and $15,800 in the federal government.

There is one common complaint of the scientist employed in a research institute. He is continually pressed to develop a new research proposal and apply for funds which the institute desperately needs to maintain his salaried position.

211

Since most of the support for private research institutions comes from federal and industrial sponsors, he finds himself developing his expertise as a vendor of his wares. He must act as an innovator in the design of research in which he has little or no experience but which satisfies the expectations of the agency which has sent out the Request for Proposal (RFP). This practice is in contrast with that of large industry which usually allows only a small portion of its budget to be derived from government sources. The very small business or industry is often as dependent on the availability of government funds as is the research institute. Within the authors' limited experience, it appears that in recent years the research institute has attempted to diversify its support base and hence avoid serious hiring and firing crises which tend to result from fluctuations brought on by governmental periods of feast and famine. Unfortunately, some of these efforts have not been notably successful. The general trend of employment in these organizations is certainly down at the time of this writing, partly because industry is now competing with the nonprofit organizations for available government funds which, in the past, were of such a relatively "small" size that industry did not consider them worth bidding for. Need we say more? The research contract and grant game is an extremely competitive business.

There are several significant differences between scientists employed in research institutes and those employed by major industries. Firstly, the scientist working in a major industrial laboratory would appear to have a more stable job situation than his counterpart in the research institute (barring mergers, phase-outs of divisions, etc.). Secondly, the industrial scientist meets the needs of his own company, whereas the scientist working for a research institute has to satisfy the varied needs of continually changing clients. However, within that framework, the scientist in the research institute may have more freedom in carrying out his research program than does the industrial scientist.

In any case, if a research institute exists in a suitable geographic area and if you are inclined toward this type of work, you would be wise to investigate the opportunities for employment. Both the so-called "pure" and "applied" research areas are represented in the research institutes as well as in industry, probably no more in one than the other.

12. The Self-Employed Scientist

If you are a capable and daring soul and have a source of immediate capital, you may wish to try it on your own. Certainly in the long run the most financially rewarding opportunities available to the scientist fall in the self-employment category. You may start a consulting firm or a small company which demands the talents of a scientist. The risks are great, but so are the rewards to the successful scientist-entrepreneur. In the 1968 survey of United States scientists, it was observed that the self-employed Ph.D. scientist had a median annual salary of $21,600. This compares with $17,500 median annual salary for scientists in industry and business, $16,000 in the nonprofit organizations, $15,800 in the federal government, and $14,800 for the calendar year in education.

If you have been well steeped in a family heritage of success in business, if you have great ability both as a scientist and a businessman, if you have great confidence in yourself, and if sufficient capital is available to you to allow an adventure, then you will find an interesting and perhaps a rewarding opportunity as a self-employed scientist. However, remember that the business world is no place for the inexperienced, insecure, incompetent, or lazy scientist.

13. The Unique Situation of the Woman in Science

Although nature always seems to provide about equal numbers of males and females, women in science are relatively few. For example in 1971, Terman, in discussing the percentage of recipients of the B.S. who successfully complete their Ph.D., considers data applying only to men on the basis that "the number of women who carry their studies to the doctoral level in science and engineering is so small as to be statistically unimportant."[10]

The research careers of women in science often have been much shorter than those of the men. In the past, marriage and responsibilities of growing families have taken a large toll of the women in science. In the report, *American Science Manpower, 1966*[16 b] only 8% of the employed scientists (all degree categories) and only 7% of the Ph.D. scientists in the United States were women. The largest number of women (any degree) were employed in the areas of chemistry (25%), psychology (21%), the biological sciences (16%), and mathematics (12%). Of the women scientists with doctor's degrees, the largest numbers were employed in the fields of psychology (33%), the biological sciences (23%), and chemistry (18%). About one-half of the women scientists were employed in educational institutions. One-third of the women scientists were primarily engaged in research and development. About one-fourth were engaged in teaching.

217

There is a striking disparity between the median annual salaries of men and women in science today. In the 1966 survey the median annual salary of full-time employed women scientists in the United States was only $9,000. This is compared with a median salary of $12,000 when *both* male and female scientists were included. The unfavorable salary comparison continues today when one looks at the individual areas of employment. See Table 8 for the comparison of recent median annual salaries of men and women in chemistry. The discrepancy between salaries for men and women occurs at all levels of educational and professional experience. It has been estimated by an American Chemical Society salary survey taken in 1970 that at the B.S. level with five to nine years of experience, a woman chemist will earn about 78% of the salary of a male with comparable qualifications. At the Ph.D. level, again with five to nine years of experience, a woman chemist may expect to earn about 73% of the corresponding male's salary. The discrepancy between salary levels seems to increase with years of experience; a woman in chemistry with a B.S. and twenty years of experience is expected to earn about 69% of the salary of her corresponding male colleague.

The reason for the disparity in salary may be found at least partially in the type of employment which women in science undertake. Figure 18 shows, for example, that women chemists tend more toward the lower paying teaching positions rather than to management or administration. However, such different career emphases may be due to discrimination in career opportunities and advancement. For example, 26% of all women chemists in 1968 were employed by industry, which simultaneously employed 60% of all men chemists. The situation in the federal government was more encouraging; 6.8% of all women chemists were employed by the government, while only 5.5% of all male chemists were so employed.

TABLE 8:   Comparison of Median Annual Salaries for Men and Women Chemists for the Various Highest Degrees Obtained and Years of Service[a]

| | Chemists' Salaries by Sex:[b] | | | | | | | |
| Years | B.S. | | M.S. | | Ph.D. | | Distribution % | |
	Men	Women	Men	Women	Men	Women	Men	Women
<1	9.1	9.0	11.2	na[c]	12.1	na[c]	89.9	10.1
2-4	10.5	9.3	11.7	10.3	15.0	11.0	89.6	10.4
5-9	12.4	11.1	13.2	11.3	16.8	14.0	90.2	9.8
10-14	14.6	11.7	15.4	12.7	19.0	14.5	91.4	8.6
15-19	16.0	13.2	17.0	12.0	20.7	17.0	92.1	7.9
20-24	17.0	14.2	17.8	15.0	22.5	16.4	92.5	7.5
25-29	18.0	15.3	18.9	13.2	23.7	16.0	92.7	7.3
30-34	19.0	na	18.6	na	24.0	18.0	93.0	7.0
35-39	18.6	na	18.5	na	23.0	na	93.1	6.9
40+	18.0	na	16.7	na	22.9	na	93.1	6.9
Overall	15.0	11.2	16.0	12.0	18.5	14.1	93.1	6.9

[a]From a survey made in 1971; see reference 12.
[b]Thousands of dollars.
[c]na = not available.

There are many arguments as to the cause of this discrimination. A common one is that the usually short tenure of the woman in her chosen employment militates against an equal salary treatment. The argument is based on the premise that several years are spent in training a new scientist, and that in the case of the woman scientist, she is likely to raise a family, or at least retire from active employment after a very short period of time on the job. There is also the problem of possible job relocation; this is often more difficult for a woman with a family.

Opportunities for women in administration are very limited in science. The male scientist usually rejects direction from the female scientist. He may accept this at home, but not at work. In addition, it is our feeling that most women do not like to take orders from another woman. These, and other

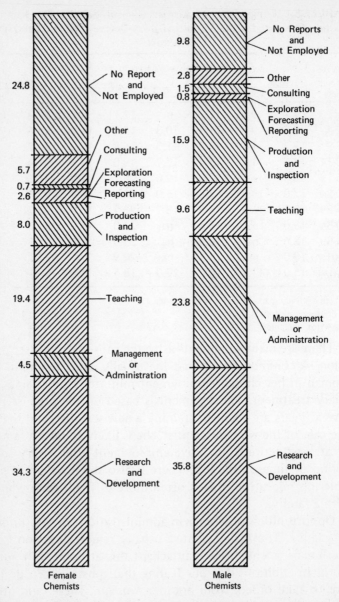

Figure 18: Distribution of male and female chemists in various types of employment. (Reproduced from ref. 48.)

factors tend to keep women from attaining the higher paying positions in science administration.

In the past, it has been almost unheard of that a woman would be elected to the faculty of a major university in the United States. There are, of course, a few notable exceptions to this practice, for example, Professor Maria Mayer, Professor Marjorie Caserio, Professor Mary Amdur, and a few others. However, the statistics on women in academia are again appalling. For example, according to a 1971 report,[49] there are *no* women in about 60% of the chemistry faculties in American universities and colleges. Women comprise only 3.1% of all faculty members in chemistry at these institutions. On the other hand, in 1969-1970, 17.8% of all undergraduates and 14.2% of all graduates in chemistry were women. Although such discrepancies may be due partially to unrecognized factors, they certainly imply that some discriminatory hiring policies exist in universities today.

In these days of increased efforts to obtain equal opportunity for the black people, the brown people, and the other minority groups, it is time that all employers look carefully at their practice of having different standards for male and female employees of equal talent. Women today are not the transients of several years ago. They intend to have scientific careers which are of the usual duration of their male counterparts. They fully intend to share household responsibilities, other than childbirth, with their husbands. Women, as well as men, have a real need for a feeling of fulfillment. Housework and families no longer satisfy this need in most women. Industry today seems to be recognizing this trend and the disparity between starting salaries of men and women has become much less evident in some instances.

From the time the girl in high school decides to major in the sciences, until the time she receives her Ph.D. degree, and appears at the market place to accept her job, she is given little indication of the preferential male treatment to come. It is only fair that the unpublicized discrimination which has been practiced be eliminated. We suggest that the woman in science ask her potential employer to show her the record of his industry, governmental agency, or educational institution. It would seem to us that the feminine charm of the woman scientist should more than compensate for the little ego damage which her success might bring to her male colleagues.

14. Summary: Career Alternatives; The Continuing Obligations of the Scientist

If you accept a career in science, you must also accept the obligations of the scientist. He is expected to remain objective and base his conclusions on a completely honest evaluation of the scientific facts. In this process he must keep a completely moral conscience that is sensitive to the real world's problems. Scientists are, after all, human beings; they are subject to the same weaknesses and virtues in their character as are lawyers, medical doctors, businessmen, and plumbers. However, the scientist has a very special role to play in the society of today, and he should feel a special obligation to be completely honest in the practice of his science. His scientific evaluation of problems which relate directly or indirectly to the welfare of society are given special weight by the community. He should weigh carefully the facts in every case in which his company or his community are involved. He should insure that his scientific conclusions are based upon the best scientific judgment which he can make. Obviously, scientists don't always agree on the interpretation of the evidence even when there has been an honest evaluation by all parties. As

223

long as this disagreement is an honest disagreement based on the differences in the interpretation of the evidence, it can serve as a most constructive influence in the case at hand. It points to the need for further study before final conclusions or laws based on these interpretations can be formulated.

What will be your reaction when one day your industrial, academic, or government superiors ask you to make a "scientific" case for *their* particular view on a matter of public concern? You are not worthy of the title "scientist" if you do not evaluate the scientific facts honestly and let the chips fall where they may. If the company position has been formulated on either correct or incorrect scientific reasoning, don't be afraid to tell your superiors your honest view. They will respect you for it, although they might not choose to use your conclusion in their public disclosures.

In a recent discussion of the social responsibilities of the engineer, Professor Benjamin Linsky has described some interesting examples of scientific dishonesty that represents an all too typical event in today's world.[50] In one case Linsky described how an engineer, the resident manager of a large iron foundry, skillfully fought a proposed tight air pollution control law by contending that his industry could not meet such restrictions because there was no control equipment known to be able to do the clean-up job demanded. When asked later by Linsky how he could tell such lies, his response was, "Ben, engineering is engineering, and business is business. I was battling for the stockholders." Linsky added the interesting note that when the air pollution control regulation ultimately was passed the same engineer set a very tight schedule for stages of compliance, including engineering procurement, fabrication, erection, and adjustment. In a very short time he had operating, the largest, truly cleaned up foundry cupola then in existence. Obviously there was no scientific or engineering problem related to the required control of the foundry, although he had so stated in the official public hearing.

Scientists and engineers who intentionally mislead the public, the judiciary, or other responsible groups to protect their company, industry, university, or governmental agency, ultimately ruin their own image as well as that of their organization. A company president or the head of a federal agency who seeks the help of his scientific staff should know the truth; tell it to him. If *he* wishes to distort the truth to gain some temporary economic or political advantage, don't let your good name be associated with this action. If a dishonest position is taken, object strongly to the stand. You may wish to consider seriously transferring from this job at your first opportunity as a significant protest. Conversely, you run the risk of your superiors dissociating you from the project. We know of two such cases that happened to friends of ours who are distinguished and forthright scientists. This action is inexcusable in science.

Industry today needs competent scientific leadership as much as any other influence. Most of the upper administrations in industry are now accepting a much healthier view of their responsibilities to protect the citizen as well as to sell to him. In 1969, Paul F. Chenea, research vice president of General Motors Corporation, expressed a view which shows promise of industrial concern over its responsibilities:[51]

> . . . Let me close these few thoughts of mine with a few words on one of the most perplexing and exasperating parts of the management of science and technology for the public good. I speak of our wholly unsatisfactory understanding and analysis of the economics or value of such efforts. Without real and quantitative values we are at a loss to measure either the progress or the worth of what we do, much less to make the critical trade-offs between the alternative courses of action available to us. We are hardly able to assess the pros and cons of a given course of action, to determine if the net effect is positive or negative. In the real world of limited re-

sources and time we must learn to do this and do it properly.

Consider the question of the intelligent distributing of the billions of dollars available to reduce air pollution, water pollution, effectively dispose of solid waste, reduce crime, eliminate illiteracy, eradicate cancer and other crippling diseases, reduce the ravages of mental disorders, beautify our environment, and I could go on. What are the payoffs to the general public of a dollar spent on one and not the other? It is ironical that if I spend a quarter to have my shoes shined, it shows up in a direct way in the gross national product and adds to the economist's evaluation of our increase in wealth.

But progress in air pollution or a new cancer cure has a much more intangible effect on the GNP. We need a new quantitative way of measuring the value of clean air, aesthetic surroundings, good health, and peace of mind. It must be quantitative and it must have dollar equivalents if it is to compete with our other demands for the use of our resources measured by dollars. We see the results of our ignorance in a big way in every unsatisfactory federal budget, and at GM we see it in the smaller but also critical decisions on component design in our products, such as in making the trade-off between structural integrity and driver visibility in an automobile. Clearly, all of us must learn to think in a more hardheaded, rational way about such matters of general concern.

Personally, I am confident that we are entering a period that will see man solve many of his age-old problems, through his social institutions of government, industry, and education. Once the nature of our problems becomes more clear, as it seems to be becoming now, the talent and know-how are available to cope effectively with the problems. We need but set the priorities. The challenge is for every one of us.

Professor Kenneth Pitzer has noted the critical need for a changing role of the scientist today.[52]

> There is now both a reaction—a more critical questioning of support for science by leaders of government and industry, and a rebellion—an out-right attack by some students and writers on science because in their view it allows machines to dominate people. Furthermore, the dangers and difficulties arising from new technologies, ranging from possible nuclear war to major pollution of water and air, are forcing us to abandon the laissez-faire viewpoint that the natural result of scientific discoveries will be desirable improvements in our conditions of life. A new approach is urgently needed. We must adopt a more active role in (1) justifying specific areas of research deserving increased support, (2) developing a better pattern for federal support of graduate education, and, (3) judging the desirability of possible new technologies on a broad humanistic basis. Each of us must accept his obligations, either as a scientist or as a citizen.

Obviously, we have to accept our real obligation as scientists and as citizens to help formulate the priorities for our industry, our communities, and our country. Let us do this with the same integrity that our practice of science demands.

As one weighs the satisfaction, the rewards, the challenges, and the opportunities in the future career of the bright new Ph.D. graduate against the many problems which he faces, the balance pan on which we have stacked the many plus features far outweighs the little cluster of negative ones on the other pan. There is no question that there are real problems which face the graduate student in the sciences today and which complicate his life. We have had a brief look at many of these. The new generation of graduate students in the sciences has a keen missionary-like zeal and spirit which will help him climb out of the many little ruts which have been carved into the landscape by our "establishment" generation. We are confident that he will climb out, if he is concerned enough to attempt it. It is our hope that the considerations which we have made will not dampen, but will enliven the hopes and aspirations of the bright young undergraduate who anticipates a career in science.

We have made a brief tour through the world of the Ph.D. scientist employed in industry, the university, and in government, and we have considered many of the problems and opportunities associated with his alternative positions. The present graduate student in the sciences will find that his career in any of these areas can be an exciting and interesting one, but he must pick and choose his career area carefully to match his interests and abilities. If he is to live up to his potential in science, he must continue to learn and apply his knowledge carefully to the problems he faces. The search for the scientific truth is as fascinating a game as there is. Although you have recognized some serious problems associated with the scientist's life in each of the alternative areas of employment, most of you will find more pleasurable experiences in your scientific careers than unpleasant ones. If you take time to think, to plan, and to continue your study as you practice your trade, both your enthusiasm for science and your satisfaction in science will continue to grow.

As the computer continues to spit out the "best" mathematical or scientific solution to our problems, let's make sure that this solution is not antagonistic to the welfare of our society and the best interests of mankind. Be a scientist in the true sense of the word, but include the less tangible human factor. Your life will not only be gratifying to you and your loved ones, but it will be useful to mankind as a whole.

Appendix

TABLE A-1: Addresses of the National Societies Associated with Various Science Areas from Which Career Opportunity Material can be Obtained.[a]

1. *American Academy of Microbiology, Inc.,* 900 Market St., Wilmington, Del. 19801.

2. *American Anthropological Association,* 1530 P St., Washington, D.C. 20005.

3. *American Association for the Advancement of Science,* 1515 Massachusetts Ave., N.W., Washington, D.C. 20005.

4. *American Association of Petroleum Geologists,* P.O. Box 979, Tulsa, Okla. 74101.

5. *American Association of Physical Anthropologists,* Secretary-Treasurer, Dr. Edward Fry, Dept. of Anthropology, Southern Methodist University, Dallas, Texas 75222.

6. *American Astronomical Society,* Secretary, L.W. Frederick, Leander McCormick Observatory, P.O. Box 3818, University Station, Charlottesville, Va. 22903.

7. *American Ceramic Society, Inc.,* 4055 N. High St., Columbus, Ohio 43214.

8. *American Chemical Society,* 1155 16th St., N.W., Washington, D.C. 20036.

9. *American Crystallographic Association,* Secretary, Mrs. Ethel E. Snider, 335 East 45 Street, New York, N.Y. 10017.

10. *American Economic Association, Inc.,* 629 Noyes St., Evanston, Ill. 60201.

11. *American Entomological Society,* Academy of Natural Sciences of Philadelphia, 1900 Race St., Philadelphia, Pa. 19103.

12. *American Geological Institute,* 1444 N St., N.W., Washington, D.C. 20005.

[a]For a more complete listing of the national societies and their missions see *Scientific and Technical Societies of the United States,* reference 18.

TABLE A-1 *(continued)*

13. *American Geophysical Union,* 2100 Pennsylvania Ave., N.W., Washington, D.C. 20036.

14. *American Institute of Aeronautics,* 1290 Avenue of the Americas, New York, N.Y. 10019.

15. *American Institute of Biological Sciences,* 3900 Wisconsin Ave., N.W., Washington, D.C. 20016.

16. *American Institute of Chemical Engineers,* 345 E. 47th St., New York, N.Y. 10017.

17. *The American Institute of Chemists,* 60 E. 42nd St., New York, N.Y. 10017.

18. *American Institute of Industrial Engineers,* 345 E. 47th St., New York, N.Y. 10017.

19. *American Institute of Mining, Metallurgical, and Petroleum Engineers, Inc.,* 345 E. 47th St., New York, N.Y. 10017.

20. *American Institute of Physics,* 335 E. 45th St., New York, N.Y. 10017.

21. *American Institute of Professional Geologists,* 345 South Union Street, Denver, Colo. 80228.

22. *American Mathematical Society,* P.O. Box 6248, Providence, R.I. 02904.

23. *American Medical Association,* 535 N. Dearborn St., Chicago, Ill. 60610.

24. *American Meteorological Society,* 45 Beacon St., Boston, Mass. 02108.

25. *American Nuclear Society, Inc.,* 244 E. Ogden Ave., Hinsdale, Ill. 60521.

26. *American Physical Society,* 335 E. 45th St., New York, N.Y. 10017.

27. *American Psychological Association,* 1200 17th St., N.W., Washington, D.C. 20036.

TABLE A-1 *(continued)*

28. *American Society for Cell Biology,* Secretary, Montrose J. Moses, Box 2982, Duke University, Medical Center, Durham, N.C. 27706.

29. *American Society for Engineering Education,* Executive Secretary, W. Leighton Collins, 2100 Pennsylvania Ave., N.W., Washington, D.C. 20037.

30. *American Society for Metals,* Metals Park, Ohio 44073.

31. *American Society for Microbiology,* 115 Huron View Blvd., Ann Arbor, Mich. 48103.

32. *American Society of Biological Chemists, Inc.,* 9650 Rockville Pike, Bethesda, Md. 20014.

33. *American Society of Civil Engineers,* 345 E. 47th St., New York, N.Y. 10017.

34. *The American Society of Mechanical Engineers,* United Engineering Center, 345 E. 47th St., New York, N.Y. 10017.

35. *American Society of Sanitary Engineering,* 228 Standard Building, Cleveland, Ohio 44113.

36. *American Society of Zoologists,* Secretary, George Sprugel, Jr., Illinois Natural History Survey, 179 Natural Resources Building, Urbana, Ill. 61801.

37. *American Sociological Association,* 1001 Connecticut Ave., N.W., Washington, D.C. 20036.

38. *American Statistical Association,* 810 18th St., N.W., Washington, D.C. 20006.

39. *American Welding Society,* 345 E. 47th St., New York, N.Y. 10017.

40. *Archaeological Institute of America,* 100 Washington Square E., New York, N.Y. 10003.

41. *Botanical Society of America, Inc.,* Secretary, Dr. Barbara F. Palser, Rutgers, New Brunswick, N. J. 08903.

TABLE A-1 *(continued)*

42. *Ecological Society of America,* Secretary, Dr. Frank McCormick, Department of Botany, University of North Carolina, Chapel Hill, N.C. 27514.

43. *Electron Microscopy Society of America,* Secretary, Alden V. Loud, Pathology, College of Physicians and Surgeons, Columbia University, New York, N.Y. 10032.

44. *Engineering Foundation,* 345 E. 47th St., New York, N.Y. 10017.

45. *Engineers' Council for Professional Development, Inc.,* 345 E. 47th St., New York, N.Y. 10017.

46. *Engineers Joint Council, Inc.,* 345 E. 47th St., New York, N.Y. 10017.

47. *Federation of American Societies for Experimental Biology,* 9650 Rockville Pike, Bethesda, Md. 20014.

48. *Geochemical Society,* Secretary, E.C.T. Chao, U.S. Geological Survey, Washington, D.C. 20006.

49. *The Geological Society of America, Inc.,* 231 E. 46th St., New York, N.Y. 10017.

50. *Geoscience Information Society,* American Geological Institute, 1444 N St., N.W., Washington, D.C. 20005.

51. *Health Physics Society, Inc.,* 194 Pilgrim Rd., Boston, Mass. 02215.

52. *The Institute of Electrical and Electronics Engineers, Inc.,* United Engineering Center, 345 E. 47th St., New York, N.Y. 10017.

53. *Institute of Environmental Sciences,* 940 E. Northwest Highway, Mt. Prospect, Ill. 60056.

54. *Manufacturing Chemists' Association, Inc.,* 1825 Connecticut Ave., N.W., Washington, D.C. 20009.

55. *Mathematical Association of America,* SUNY at Buffalo, Buffalo, N.Y. 14214.

TABLE A-1 *(continued)*

56. *The Metallurgical Society of American Institute of Mining, Metallurgical, and Petroleum Engineers,* 345 E. 47th St., New York, N.Y. 10017.

57. *Mineralogical Society of America,* Executive Secretary, Ralph J. Holmes, Columbia University, New York, N.Y. 10027.

58. *Mycological Society of America,* Secretary-Treasurer, Alma W. Barksdale, The New York Botanical Garden, Bronx, New York, N.Y. 10458.

59. *National Association of Corrosion Engineers,* 2400 W. Loop S., Houston, Tex. 77027.

60. *National Society of Professional Engineers,* 2029 K St., N.W., Washington, D.C. 20006.

61. *Optical Society of America, Inc.,* 2100 Pennsylvania Ave., N.W., Washington, D.C. 20037.

62. *Scientific Research Society of America,* Director, Donald B. Prentice, 51 Prospect St., New Haven, Conn. 06511.

63. *Society for American Archaeology,* Secretary, Dr. R.E.W. Adams, Department of Anthropology, 200 Ford Hall, University of Minnesota, Minneapolis, Minn. 55455.

64. *Society for Applied Anthropology,* Lafferty Hall, University of Kentucky, Lexington, Ky. 40506.

65. *Society for Applied Spectroscopy,* Secretary, A.F. Rekus, P.O. Box 9803, Baltimore, Md. 21204.

66. *Society for Industrial and Applied Mathematics,* 33 S. 17th St., Philadelphia, Pa. 19103.

67. *The Society for Industrial Microbiology,* 2000 P St., N.W., Washington, D.C. 20036.

68. *Society of Aerospace Material and Process Engineers,* P.O. Box 613, Azusa, Calif. 91702.

69. *Society of American Foresters,* 1010 16th St., N.W., Washington, D.C. 20036.

TABLE A-1 *(continued)*

70. *Society of Mining Engineers of the American Institute of Mining, Metallurgical, and Petroleum Engineers, Inc.,* 345 E. 47th St., New York, N.Y. 10017.

71. *Society of Photographic Scientists and Engineers,* 1330 Massachusetts Ave., N.W., Washington, D.C. 20005.

72. *Society of Plastics Engineers,* 65 Prospect St., Stamford, Conn. 06902.

73. *Soil Science Society of America, Inc.,* 677 S. Segoe Rd., Madison, Wis. 53711.

74. *Technical Association of the Pulp and Paper Industry,* 360 Lexington Ave., New York, N.Y. 10017.

75. *Water Pollution Control Federation,* 3900 Wisconsin Ave., N.W., Washington, D.C. 20016.

TABLE A-2: Comparison of median annual salaries of full-time employed civilian scientists by field, type of employer, and highest degree, 1968.[a]

Scientific and Technical Field and Type of Employer	Total	Highest Degree					
		Doctorate	Professional Medical	Master's	Bachelor's	Less Than Bachelor's Degree	No Report of Degree
ALL FIELDS	13,200	15,000	20,000	12,000	12,000	14,000	12,400
Educational Institutions							
Academic	11,000	12,000	14,300	9,200	7,200	—	11,000
Calendar	13,500	14,800	20,000	10,400	7,500	—	10,900
Federal Government	13,500	15,800	20,900	13,400	12,200	13,500	12,000
Other Government	11,200	14,500	20,000	11,000	9,700	—	10,000
Nonprofit Organizations	14,700	16,000	20,000	12,700	11,700	—	13,000
Industry and Business	14,700	17,500	21,000	14,100	13,000	14,600	13,000
Self-employed	18,000	21,600	30,000	16,000	15,000	—	15,000
Other	12,600	15,000	14,800	12,000	11,500	—	11,000
No Report	14,000	15,700	20,000	12,000	12,000	—	—
AGRICULTURAL SCIENCES	11,000	14,400	—	10,900	10,000	—	9,200
Educational Institutions							
Academic	10,500	11,700	—	9,900	—	—	—
Calendar	13,200	14,500	—	11,100	10,500	—	—
Federal Government	10,900	14,400	—	11,500	10,300	—	8,600
Other Government	9,300	13,700	—	9,500	9,100	—	—
Nonprofit Organizations	12,000	15,500	—	12,000	10,000	—	—
Industry and Business	10,800	15,000	—	11,400	10,000	—	—
Self-employed	12,000	—	—	15,000	11,500	—	—
Other	11,700	—	—	—	—	—	—
No Report	11,200	—	—	—	—	—	—

ANTHROPOLOGY	12,700	12,800	—	11,500	—	—	—
Educational Institutions							
Academic	12,000	12,000	—	—	—	—	—
Calendar	13,500	13,500	—	—	—	—	—
Federal Government	16,400	16,400	—	—	—	—	—
Other Government	—	—	—	—	—	—	—
Nonprofit Organizations	—	—	—	—	—	—	—
Industry and Business	—	—	—	—	—	—	—
Self-employed	12,500	12,500	—	—	—	—	—
Other	—	—	—	—	—	—	—
No Report	—	—	—	—	—	—	—
ATMOSPHERIC AND SPACE SCIENCES	13,400	16,100	—	13,700	13,000	13,000	12,000
Educational Institutions							
Academic	12,000	13,600	—	9,900	—	—	—
Calendar	12,800	15,500	—	11,100	10,200	—	12,000
Federal Government	13,400	18,000	—	14,000	13,200	—	12,000
Other Government	10,900	—	—	—	10,500	—	—
Nonprofit Organizations	14,600	—	—	15,900	12,000	—	—
Industry and Business	13,700	20,000	—	14,500	13,000	—	11,800
Self-employed	—	—	—	—	—	—	—
Other	—	—	—	—	—	—	—
No Report	—	—	—	—	—	—	—

237

TABLE A-2 (continued)

Scientific and Technical Field and Type of Employer	Total	Highest Degree					
		Doctorate	Professional Medical	Master's	Bachelor's	Less Than Bachelor's Degree	No Report of Degree
BIOLOGICAL SCIENCES	13,000	14,200	20,000	10,000	9,600	14,000	11,000
Educational Institutions							
Academic	10,500	11,600	14,500	9,000	7,200	—	—
Calendar	14,900	15,000	20,000	9,000	7,400	—	10,800
Federal Government	13,500	14,500	20,900	11,700	11,000	—	—
Other Government	11,400	14,200	20,000	10,300	9,500	—	—
Nonprofit Organizations	15,000	15,000	20,000	10,000	9,000	—	—
Industry and Business	15,000	17,000	21,300	12,500	11,000	—	13,000
Self-employed	20,000	20,000	30,000	15,000	14,000	—	—
Other	11,500	13,700	—	8,500	8,400	—	—
No Report	15,000	17,000	20,000	11,400	10,900	—	—
CHEMISTRY	13,500	15,600	12,000	13,000	12,000	13,800	12,000
Educational Institutions							
Academic	10,500	11,500	—	9,000	6,100	—	—
Calendar	11,000	13,500	18,000	8,500	3,900	—	—
Federal Government	13,500	15,800	—	13,800	12,600	—	12,000
Other Government	10,800	14,000	—	11,200	10,000	—	—
Nonprofit Organizations	13,200	16,000	6,200	12,300	10,000	—	—
Industry and Business	14,400	17,000	—	14,000	12,500	13,800	12,200
Self-employed	17,000	20,000	—	17,500	15,000	—	—
Other	12,000	15,000	—	12,000	11,000	—	—
No Report	13,800	15,300	—	13,700	12,500	—	—

COMPUTER SCIENCES	14,100	18,100	—	14,400	13,800	—	13,500
Educational Institutions							
Academic	12,000	13,500	—	9,500	11,400	—	—
Calendar	12,800	18,000	—	12,000	13,500	—	—
Federal Government	13,700	—	—	14,400	12,700	—	13,500
Other Government	12,700	—	—	—	14,200	—	—
Nonprofit Organizations	15,100	22,000	—	15,900	14,000	—	—
Industry and Business	14,400	20,000	—	14,500	—	—	13,500
Self-employed	—	—	—	—	12,000	—	—
Other	13,300	—	—	—	—	—	—
No Report	—	—	—	—	—	—	—
EARTH AND MARINE SCIENCES	12,900	14,000	—	12,000	13,000	14,500	12,000
Educational Institutions							
Academic	10,700	12,000	—	9,000	7,500	—	—
Calendar	12,400	14,700	—	9,800	8,000	—	—
Federal Government	13,400	15,300	—	13,000	12,800	—	—
Other Government	11,000	13,000	—	11,000	10,700	—	—
Nonprofit Organizations	13,000	14,900	—	12,800	11,200	—	—
Industry and Business	13,500	16,100	—	13,000	13,300	14,000	12,500
Self-employed	15,000	20,000	—	15,000	15,000	—	—
Other	12,300	12,300	—	—	14,000	—	—
No Report	12,600	—	—	—	—	—	—

TABLE A-2 (continued)

Scientific and Technical Field and Type of Employer	Total	Highest Degree				Less Than Bachelor's Degree	No Report of Degree
		Doctorate	Professional Medical	Master's	Bachelor's		
ECONOMICS	15,000	15,800	—	12,600	14,500	—	15,200
Educational Institutions							
Academic	12,400	13,500		10,000	10,100		
Calendar	15,700	16,800		12,000	12,000		
Federal Government	17,000	19,000		15,800	16,400		
Other Government	16,000	19,000		14,400	13,200		
Nonprofit Organizations	18,000	20,500		16,000	15,600		
Industry and Business	18,000	23,800		16,000	16,400		
Self-employed	20,000	—		20,000	—		
Other	16,000	—		—	—		
No Report	14,000	—		—	—		
LINGUISTICS	11,500	12,200	—	9,000	9,000	—	
Educational Institutions							
Academic	11,200	12,000		8,800	—		
Calendar	12,000	13,000		9,500	—		
Federal Government	13,500	—		—	—		
Other Government	—	—		—	—		
Nonprofit Organizations	7,800	10,900		7,200	—		
Industry and Business	16,000	—		—	—		
Self-employed	—	—		—	—		
Other	—	—		—	—		
No Report	—	—		—	—		

MATHEMATICS	13,000	14,000	—	11,400	15,000	—	15,000
Educational Institutions							
Academic	10,200	12,000	—	8,900	7,400	—	—
Calendar	12,000	15,000	—	10,000	9,500	—	—
Federal Government	15,300	19,500	—	15,000	14,900	—	—
Other Government	13,100	15,000	—	12,300	13,500	—	—
Nonprofit Organizations	18,000	20,000	—	17,100	17,200	—	—
Industry and Business	16,800	19,600	—	16,200	16,300	—	16,400
Self-employed	21,000	—	—	20,000	22,000	—	—
Other	14,000	18,000	—	12,000	14,600	—	—
No Report	13,200	—	—	12,000	—	—	—
PHYSICS	14,000	15,900	—	12,600	12,600	—	14,000
Educational Institutions							
Academic	11,000	12,500	—	9,400	7,600	—	—
Calendar	12,000	13,400	—	10,500	8,500	—	—
Federal Government	14,500	17,400	—	14,000	13,400	—	—
Other Government	11,300	14,000	—	—	—	—	—
Nonprofit Organizations	16,800	18,000	—	14,800	13,800	—	—
Industry and Business	16,200	19,000	—	15,000	13,300	—	15,600
Self-employed	18,500	20,000	—	—	17,000	—	—
Other	7,500	—	—	—	—	—	—
No Report	14,600	—	—	—	—	—	—

TABLE A-2 (continued)

Scientific and Technical Field and Type of Employer	Total	Highest Degree				Less Than Bachelor's Degree	No Report of Degree
		Doctorate	Professional Medical	Master's	Bachelor's		
PSYCHOLOGY	13,200	14,500	—	11,500	11,800	—	—
Educational Institutions							
Academic	11,500	12,000	—	10,500	10,000	—	—
Calendar	14,000	15,000	—	12,000	11,000	—	—
Federal Government	15,500	15,800	—	14,000	—	—	—
Other Government	12,800	14,300	—	11,000	11,500	—	—
Nonprofit Organizations	13,500	15,000	—	10,800	13,000	—	—
Industry and Business	16,800	19,000	—	14,500	—	—	—
Self-employed	21,000	23,000	—	17,000	—	—	—
Other	13,500	16,000	—	12,000	—	—	—
No Report	14,800	15,000	—	—	—	—	—
SOCIOLOGY	12,000	13,500	—	9,300	9,000	—	—
Educational Institutions							
Academic	11,000	12,400	—	8,700	8,000	—	—
Calendar	13,500	15,000	—	10,000	9,000	—	—
Federal Government	15,800	18,300	—	13,500	11,000	—	—
Other Government	11,200	15,000	—	10,800	9,000	—	—
Nonprofit Organizations	14,500	16,600	—	11,800	12,000	—	—
Industry and Business	15,000	25,000	—	14,000	—	—	—
Self-employed	15,700	—	—	—	—	—	—
Other	13,000	—	—	—	—	—	—
No Report	14,000	—	—	—	—	—	—

STATISTICS	14,900	16,000	—	14,000	14,200	—	—
Educational Institutions							
Academic	12,500	13,000	—	10,600	—	—	—
Calendar	14,800	16,200	—	11,000	—	—	—
Federal Government	16,200	20,200	—	15,800	15,600	—	—
Other Government	12,500	—	—	12,800	11,400	—	—
Nonprofit Organizations	14,800	19,000	—	13,200	13,700	—	—
Industry and Business	15,300	19,200	—	15,000	13,300	—	—
Self-employed	—	—	—	—	—	—	—
Other	—	—	—	—	—	—	—
No Report	—	—	—	—	—	—	—

Note: All median salaries were computed only for full-time employed civilian scientists. No median was computed for groups with fewer than 25 registrants reporting salary.

[a]Source: National Register of Scientific and Technical Personnel, 1968.[15]

TABLE A-3: Comparison of the Number of United States Scientists by Field, Primary Work Activity, and Type of Employer (1968).[a]

Scientific and Technical Field and Primary Work Activity	Total	Type of Employer									
		Educational Institutions	Federal Government	Other Government	Nonprofit Organizations	Industry and Business	Self-Employed	Military	Other	Not Employed	No Report of Type of Employer
ALL FIELDS	297,942	117,746	29,666	10,031	11,204	95,776	6,462	7,155	1,729	12,707	5,466
Research and Development (A)	96,036	38,668	12,249	2,588	4,970	34,271	472	1,492	556	——	770
Basic Research	46,177	28,818	5,664	1,005	2,315	6,675	132	739	309	——	520
Applied Research	38,841	9,447	6,060	1,494	2,425	18,034	284	671	201	——	225
Management or Administration (B)	62,870	10,278	10,680	4,044	2,921	30,910	792	2,506	437	——	302
Management or Administration of Research and Development	28,568	3,680	4,668	1,175	1,517	16,321	209	688	171	——	139
Teaching	62,087	60,230	294	291	218	254	59	366	167	——	208
Production and Inspection	16,847	250	1,087	548	209	14,057	332	205	92	——	67
Consulting	12,334	2,181	866	955	1,642	3,222	2,952	249	124	——	143
Exploration, Forecasting, and Reporting	14,365	791	2,333	630	456	7,637	1,210	1,164	99	——	45
Other	8,416	1,854	1,362	657	425	2,861	272	751	161	——	73
Not Employed	12,707									12,707	
No Report	12,280	3,494	795	318	363	2,564	373	422	93	——	3,858

AGRICULTURAL SCIENCES	12,740	2,933	4,785	2,104	148	2,016	250	184	68	175	77
Research and Development (A)	2,984	1,335	971	361	22	243	9	16	14	—	13
Basic Research	784	383	266	103	3	13	2	5	5	—	4
Applied Research	2,195	952	702	258	18	229	7	11	9	—	9
Management or Administration (B)	6,987	393	3,216	1,475	89	1,513	165	81	28	—	27
Management or Administration of Research and Development	1,328	219	414	399	31	223	18	7	11	—	6
Teaching	1,000	902	31	26	6	14	2	8	8	—	3
Production and Inspection	82	2	25	15	—	38	1	1	—	—	—
Consulting	48	1	13	9	1	14	10	—	—	—	—
Exploration, Forecasting, and Reporting	216	14	143	26	5	19	3	5	—	—	1
Other	859	178	289	145	21	129	34	46	14	—	3
Not Employed	175	—	—	—	—	—	—	—	—	175	—
No Report	389	108	97	47	4	46	26	27	4	—	30
ANTHROPOLOGY	1,219	986	34	14	25	11	12	—	77	44	16
Research and Development (A)	258	183	16	9	9	3	4	—	33	—	1
Basic Research	222	163	11	6	6	2	1	—	32	—	1
Applied Research	36	20	5	3	3	1	3	—	1	—	—
Management or Administration (B)	130	75	11	3	13	6	1	—	19	—	2
Management or Administration of Research and Development	72	31	8	3	10	5	—	—	13	—	2
Teaching	683	678	—	1	2	—	—	—	2	—	—
Production and Inspection	—	—	—	—	—	—	—	—	—	—	—
Consulting	8	1	—	—	1	1	4	—	1	—	—
Exploration, Forecasting, and Reporting	32	9	4	1	—	—	2	—	15	—	1
Other	4	2	—	—	—	—	—	—	2	—	—
Not Employed	44	—	—	—	—	—	—	—	—	44	—
No Report	60	38	3	—	—	1	1	—	5	—	12

TABLE A-3 (continued)

Scientific and Technical Field and Primary Work Activity	Total	Type of Employer									No Report of Type of Employer
		Educational Institutions	Federal Government	Other Government	Non-profit Organizations	Industry and Business	Self-Employed	Military	Other	Not Employed	
ATMOSPHERIC AND SPACE SCIENCES	5,745	757	1,857	72	114	537	36	2,184	26	107	55
Research and Development (A)	1,079	407	357	23	68	124	3	83	8	—	6
Basic Research	497	285	127	11	23	20	—	25	3	—	3
Applied Research	581	122	230	12	45	104	3	57	5	—	3
Management or Administration (B)	1,510	60	524	21	27	143	5	718	6	—	6
Management or Administration of Research and Development	389	39	168	6	21	68	2	83	—	—	2
Teaching	293	225	10	2	—	8	—	47	—	—	1
Production and Inspection	66	—	19	4	—	21	4	17	1	—	—
Consulting	89	2	22	—	2	18	12	32	—	—	1
Exploration, Forecasting, and Reporting	1,970	14	755	14	11	165	8	995	4	—	4
Other	406	24	119	6	3	32	4	213	4	—	1
Not Employed	107	—	—	—	—	—	—	—	—	107	—
No Report	225	25	51	2	3	26	—	79	3	—	36

BIOLOGICAL SCIENCES	46,183	27,141	5,080	2,020	2,893	4,521	838	1,227	225	1,268	940
Research and Development (A)	18,897	11,158	2,706	697	1,440	1,844	69	598	110	—	275
Basic Research	13,194	8,761	1,640	390	1,053	626	23	401	90	—	210
Applied Research	5,690	2,393	1,064	307	386	1,213	45	197	20	—	65
Management or Administration (B)	8,087	2,223	1,720	834	581	2,083	133	362	67	—	84
Management or Administration of Research and Development	3,870	965	853	241	262	1,251	34	194	25	—	45
Teaching	12,484	12,100	75	59	93	14	12	30	30	—	71
Production and Inspection	107	8	17	9	3	65	1	—	2	—	2
Consulting	2,021	337	111	149	556	134	542	126	13	—	53
Exploration, Forecasting, and Reporting	299	70	81	29	24	70	14	6	2	—	3
Other	1,176	399	226	163	73	187	26	59	26	—	17
Not Employed	1,268	—	—	—	—	—	—	—	—	1,268	—
No Report	1,844	846	144	80	123	124	41	46	5	—	435

CHEMISTRY	93,788	20,510	5,247	1,221	2,121	53,291	1,069	1,442	539	6,180	2,168
Research and Development (A)	33,492	8,507	2,530	283	978	20,347	91	313	169	—	274
Basic Research	14,281	7,610	1,320	151	555	4,172	25	166	87	—	195
Applied Research	11,819	832	1,009	112	368	9,234	45	103	51	—	65
Management or Administration (B)	20,908	1,144	1,369	305	534	16,671	196	491	113	—	85
Management or Administration of Research and Development	11,498	368	889	63	296	9,625	57	113	46	—	41
Teaching	9,762	9,440	45	31	30	56	3	96	34	—	27
Production and Inspection	14,318	185	794	415	180	12,270	163	171	83	—	57
Consulting	1,315	53	46	28	43	697	402	15	18	—	13
Exploration, Forecasting, and Reporting	823	47	105	18	149	443	24	21	15	—	1
Other	2,726	474	211	87	139	1,415	108	197	71	—	24
Not Employed	6,180	—	—	—	—	—	—	—	—	6,180	—
No Report	4,264	660	147	54	68	1,392	82	138	36	—	1,687

TABLE A-3 (continued)

Scientific and Technical Field and Primary Work Activity	Total	Type of Employer								Not Employed	No Report of Type of Employer
		Educational Institutions	Federal Government	Other Government	Non-profit Organizations	Industry and Business	Self-employed	Military	Other		
COMPUTER SCIENCES	6,972	921	516	102	475	4,513	45	141	62	147	50
Research and Development (A)	2,661	337	189	30	248	1,779	7	31	27	—	13
Basic Research	159	81	16	1	16	37	1	3	2	—	2
Applied Research	1,496	183	125	22	160	956	4	17	19	—	10
Management or Administration (B)	1,555	183	132	23	95	1,040	5	56	12	—	9
Management or Administration of Research and Development	825	83	72	8	52	579	2	19	5	—	5
Teaching	212	172	5	—	—	30	—	4	1	—	—
Production and Inspection	88	6	7	2	11	60	—	1	1	—	1
Consulting	440	23	8	6	25	349	26	1	1	—	—
Exploration, Forecasting, and Reporting	1,231	132	115	35	66	830	5	30	15	—	3
Other	427	38	38	3	24	306	2	12	3	—	1
Not Employed	147									147	
No Report	211	30	22	3	6	119	—	6	2	—	23

EARTH AND MARINE SCIENCES	23,746	5,890	2,982	1,064	249	9,809	2,019	373	92	882	386
Research and Development (A)	3,737	1,196	1,269	238	114	833	31	35	29	—	12
Basic Research	2,075	973	668	126	69	167	16	23	26	—	7
Applied Research	1,652	222	579	111	45	661	14	12	3	—	5
Management or Administration (B)	3,935	402	735	255	74	2,141	145	147	25	—	11
Management or Administration of Research and Development	1,223	155	374	87	30	496	34	27	15	—	5
Teaching	4,034	3,948	10	10	3	22	2	27	7	—	5
Production and Inspection	1,554	15	147	90	2	1,146	142	2	4	—	6
Consulting	734	4	21	21	6	218	459	3	—	—	2
Exploration, Forecasting, and Reporting	7,134	70	581	336	37	4,969	1,079	27	19	—	16
Other	618	61	154	84	8	203	24	78	5	—	1
Not Employed	882	—	—	—	—	—	—	—	—	882	—
No Report	1,118	194	85	30	5	277	137	54	3	—	333

ECONOMICS	11,510	6,681	1,417	517	505	1,636	186	97	41	315	115
Research and Development (A)	2,377	1,128	498	205	241	244	25	12	11	—	13
Basic Research	655	440	89	45	46	20	8	1	1	—	5
Applied Research	1,609	668	375	142	183	201	14	10	8	—	8
Management or Administration (B)	2,630	823	605	198	164	746	34	34	15	—	11
Management or Administration of Research and Development	1,075	246	323	120	87	277	6	6	5	—	5
Teaching	4,496	4,410	18	8	8	8	5	25	3	—	11
Production and Inspection	173	16	12	4	5	125	9	2	—	—	—
Consulting	356	24	33	12	23	175	81	—	5	—	3
Exploration, Forecasting, and Reporting	515	49	141	59	26	219	12	5	3	—	1
Other	267	67	70	16	17	74	9	10	3	—	1
Not Employed	315	—	—	—	—	—	—	—	—	315	—
No Report	381	164	40	15	21	45	11	9	1	—	75

TABLE A-3 (continued)

Scientific and Technical Field and Primary Work Activity	Total	Type of Employer									
		Educational Institutions	Federal Government	Other Government	Nonprofit Organizations	Industry and Business	Self-employed	Military	Other	Not Employed	No Report of Type of Employer
LINGUISTICS	1,541	1,121	58	15	118	41	10	4	15	110	49
Research and Development (A)	246	155	12	1	54	11	4	—	4	—	5
Basic Research	160	114	4	1	28	6	2	—	2	—	3
Applied Research	86	41	8	—	26	5	2	—	2	—	2
Management or Administration (B)	164	98	22	2	24	13	—	1	1	—	3
Management or Administration of Research and Development	44	18	4	1	14	6	—	—	—	—	1
Teaching	812	780	9	5	—	1	1	1	7	—	8
Production and Inspection	—										
Consulting	18	3	1	1	6	4	1	—	2	—	—
Exploration, Forecasting, and Reporting	62	25	5	3	20	5	4	—	—	—	—
Other	20	4	2	1	8	3	—	1	—	—	1
Not Employed	110	—	—	—	—	—	—	—	—	110	—
No Report	104	56	7	2	6	4	—	1	1	—	32

	24,477	12,837	1,354	308	681	7,289	222	481	219	786	300
MATHEMATICS											
Research and Development (A)	5,147	1,987	553	54	329	2,049	22	74	47	—	32
Basic Research	2,014	1,598	98	24	74	168	7	15	15	—	15
Applied Research	2,556	357	409	19	222	1,448	9	50	28	—	14
Management or Administration (B)	5,122	852	462	98	227	3,155	23	221	63	—	21
Management or Administration of Research and Development	2,145	186	275	32	158	1,385	13	61	25	—	10
Teaching	9,491	9,172	46	62	9	59	9	55	45	—	34
Production and Inspection	184	5	19	5	6	136	3	8	1	—	1
Consulting	1,065	52	34	21	24	780	113	3	26	—	12
Exploration, Forecasting, and Reporting	926	113	125	30	38	543	25	33	11	—	8
Other	745	222	69	25	27	311	11	62	13	—	5
Not Employed	786	—	—	—	—	—	—	—	—	786	—
No Report	1,011	434	46	13	21	256	16	25	13	—	187
PHYSICS	32,491	15,522	3,717	86	882	9,436	249	603	41	1,132	823
Research and Development (A)	16,380	7,072	2,423	35	564	5,938	70	189	23	—	66
Basic Research	8,939	5,985	1,189	23	239	1,355	24	58	19	—	47
Applied Research	5,832	957	1,086	12	305	3,304	32	119	3	—	14
Management or Administration (B)	5,123	1,048	959	26	216	2,542	43	273	8	—	8
Management or Administration of Research and Development	3,679	539	823	7	183	1,965	24	130	2	—	6
Teaching	6,899	6,789	16	3	9	24	4	39	5	—	10
Production and Inspection	183	9	16	1	1	146	7	3	—	—	—
Consulting	363	28	27	2	14	191	96	2	—	—	3
Exploration, Forecasting, and Reporting	577	120	125	3	34	259	12	23	1	—	—
Other	336	62	67	12	16	119	6	49	1	—	4
Not Employed	1,132	—	—	—	—	—	—	—	—	1,132	—
No Report	1,498	394	84	4	28	217	11	25	3	—	732

TABLE A-3 (continued)

Scientific and Technical Field and Primary Work Activity	Total	Type of Employer									
		Educational Institutions	Federal Government	Other Government	Nonprofit Organizations	Industry and Business	Self-employed	Military	Other	Not Employed	No Report of Type of Employer
PSYCHOLOGY	23,677	12,810	1,443	1,977	2,318	1,747	1,402	256	176	744	204
Research and Development (A)	5,979	3,580	455	507	619	516	99	114	55	—	34
Basic Research	1,722	1,242	158	73	127	57	5	36	12	—	12
Applied Research	4,034	2,271	280	403	461	394	86	77	42	—	20
Management or Administration (B)	4,424	2,019	427	596	622	617	24	57	44	—	18
Management or Administration of Research and Development	1,471	523	230	117	230	309	9	33	13	—	7
Teaching	5,346	5,159	12	67	43	15	16	10	8	—	16
Production and Inspection	7	3	—	1	—	—	2	—	—	—	1
Consulting	5,510	1,566	479	685	921	518	1,178	60	51	—	52
Exploration, Forecasting, and Reporting	91	42	9	10	7	11	8	1	2	—	1
Other	382	147	25	63	53	43	32	6	10	—	3
Not Employed	744	—	—	—	—	—	—	—	—	744	—
No Report	594	294	36	48	53	27	43	8	6	—	79

SOCIOLOGY	6,638	4,827	240	232	343	121	53	32	60	533	197
Research and Development (A)	1,437	1,003	91	82	148	46	24	8	18	—	17
Basic Research	893	733	39	33	44	8	13	2	11	—	10
Applied Research	544	270	52	49	104	38	11	6	7	—	7
Management or Administration (B)	884	455	108	84	137	56	8	13	17	—	6
Management or Administration of Research and Development	405	170	69	45	76	32	3	5	5	—	—
Teaching	3,139	3,073	7	11	14	2	4	4	12	—	12
Production and Inspection	—	—	—	—	—	—	—	—	—	—	—
Consulting	33	12	—	6	6	—	2	—	1	—	—
Exploration, Forecasting, and Reporting	77	27	11	11	10	7	7	1	2	—	1
Other	210	126	12	30	16	4	6	3	4	—	9
Not Employed	533	—	—	—	—	—	—	—	—	533	—
No Report	325	131	5	8	12	6	2	3	6	—	152

STATISTICS	2,639	889	588	149	132	692	21	36	24	71	37
Research and Development (A)	743	204	149	36	70	263	2	9	4	—	6
Basic Research	169	105	26	8	9	16	—	1	1	—	3
Applied Research	542	97	117	28	61	224	2	7	3	—	3
Management or Administration (B)	534	72	208	48	29	151	3	11	8	—	4
Management or Administration of Research and Development	284	30	111	24	19	87	3	5	3	—	2
Teaching	482	471	3	3	—	—	—	—	1	—	4
Production and Inspection	85	1	31	2	1	50	—	—	—	—	—
Consulting	269	67	57	10	7	110	9	6	3	—	—
Exploration, Forecasting, and Reporting	286	34	90	40	17	83	5	9	5	—	3
Other	71	12	30	6	3	17	—	1	1	—	1
Not Employed	71	—	—	—	—	—	—	—	—	71	—
No Report	98	28	20	4	5	18	2	—	2	—	19

Note: (A) Includes development or design. (B) includes management or administration of other than research and development.
aSource: National Register of Scientific and Technical Personnel, 1968.[15]

TABLE A-4: Some Sources for American Scientists; Graduate Student Fellowships (*G*), Postdoctoral and Faculty Fellowships (*PD*).[a]

1. *The Alcoa Foundation*, 1501 Alcoa Bldg., Pittsburgh, Pa. 15219; *G, PD*.

2. *American Association of University Women Educational Foundation*, 2401 Virginia Ave., N.W., Washington, D.C. 20037; *PD* (women only).

3. *American Cancer Society, Inc.*, Research Department, 219 E. 42nd St., New York, N.Y. 10017; *PD*.

4. *American Congress on Surveying and Mapping*, 430 Woodward Bldg., 733 15th St., N.W., Washington, D.C. 20005; advanced study in geodesy and surveying; *G*.

5. *American Gas Association, Inc.*, 605 Third Ave., New York, N.Y. 10016; *G*.

6. *American Heart Association*, Director of Research, 44 E. 23rd St., New York, N.Y. 10010; *PD*.

7. *American Philosophical Society*, 104 S. Fifth St., Philadelphia, Pa. 19106; *PD*.

8. *American Public Works Association Education Foundation*, 1313 E. 60th St., Chicago, Ill. 60637; *G*.

9. *American-Scandinavian Foundation*, 127 E. 73rd St., New York, N.Y. 10021; *G, PD* (study to be carried out in one of the Scandinavian countries).

10. *American Society of Civil Engineers*, United Engineering Center, 345 E. 47th St., New York, N.Y. 10017; *G*.

11. *American Society for Engineering Education*, Suite 838, 2100 Pennsylvania Ave., N.W., Washington, D.C. 20037; *G*.

12. *Atomic Energy Commission*, University Participation Office or Fellowship Office, Oak Ridge Associated Universities, Oak Ridge, Tenn. 37830; *G, PD* (study can be

[a]This information was taken in part from the more complete information on fellowship support summarized in *Annual Register of Grant Support, 1969.*[21]

TABLE A-4 *(continued)*

carried out at an Atomic Energy Commission Laboratory; studies in health physics, nuclear science, and engineering can be carried out at selected universities).

13. *Austrian Institute,* 11 E. 52nd St., New York, N.Y. 10022; *G* (study to be carried out in Austria).

14. *Automotive Safety Foundation,* 200 Ring Bldg., Washington, D.C. 20036; *G.*

15. *Belgian American Educational Foundation, Inc.,* 420 Lexington Ave., New York, N.Y. 10017; *PD* (study to be carried out at a Belgian University).

16. *Boston Sea Rovers,* 58 Neponset Ave., Dorchester, Mass. 02122; *G* (research in oceanography and related areas).

17. *The Childs, Jane Coffin, Memorial Fund for Medical Research,* Office of the Director, 333 Cedar St., New Haven, Conn. 06510; *PD* (research related to cancer).

18. *The Dana, Charles A., Foundation, Inc.,* Rm. 7, Smith Bldg., Greenwich, Conn. 06830; *G, PD.*

19. *The Danforth Foundation,* 222 S. Central Ave., St. Louis, Mo. 63105; *G, PD.*

20. *Department of Defense,* Office of Scientific Personnel, Rm. 603, or Fellowship Office, National Research Council, 2101 Constitution Ave., N.W., Washington, D.C. 20418; *PD* (research conducted at Air Force Office of Aerospace Research Laboratories, U.S. Army Natick Laboratories, or elsewhere).

21. *Department of the Interior,* Director, Bureau of Commercial Fisheries, *Fish and Wildlife Service,* Washington, D.C. 20240; *G* (research related to fishery sciences).

22. *Department of State, Fulbright-Haun Program for Senior Scholars,* Committee on International Exchange of Persons, Conference Board of Associated Research Councils, 2101 Constitution Ave., N.W., Washington, D.C. 20418; *PD.*

TABLE A-4 *(continued)*

23. *Electrical Women's Round Table,* National Julian Kiene Fellowship Committee, The Hoover Company, North Canton, Ohio 44720; *G* (restricted to women in appropriate fields).

24. *Environmental Protection Agency,* (a) *Office of Air Programs,* P.O. Box 12055, Research Triangle Park, N.C. 27711. *G, PD* (research in the sciences and engineering related to the control of air pollution). (b) *Office of Water Programs,* 1750 K St., Washington, D.C. 20460; *G, PD* (research related to the control of water pollution).

25. *Ford Foundation,* 320 E. 43rd St., New York, N.Y. 10017; *G* (predoctoral fellowship for Black students).

26. *The Gloeckner, Fred C., Foundation,* 15 E. 26th St., New York, N.Y., 10010; *G* (research in floriculture, plant physiology, etc.).

27. *The Grass Foundation,* 77 Reservoir Rd., Quincy, Mass. 02169; *G, PD* (summer fellowships for research at Marine Biological Laboratories in Woods Hole, Mass.).

28. *Guggenheim, John Simon, Memorial Foundation,* 90 Park Ave., New York, N.Y., 10016; *PD.*

29. *Henry, Charles and Julia, Fellowships,* Office of Secretary of Yale University, New Haven, Conn. 06520, or Office of Secretary to the Corporation, Harvard University, Cambridge, Mass. 02138; *G* (study to be carried out at Oxford or Cambridge University only).

30. *Institute of Electrical and Electronics Engineers,* Fortesque Fellowship, United Engineering Center, 345 E. 47th St., New York, N.Y. 10017; *G* (research in electrical engineering).

31. *Institute of Food Technologists,* Suite 2120, 221 N. LaSalle St., Chicago, Ill. 60601; *G* (advanced research in food technology).

TABLE A-4 *(continued)*

32. *International Lead Zinc Research Organization, Inc.*, Executive Vice President, 292 Madison Ave., New York, N.Y. 10017; *G, PD* (research related to lead and zinc compounds).

33. *International Research and Exchange Board*, 444 Madison Ave., New York, N.Y. 10022; *G, PD* (study to be made in the Soviet Union, Bulgaria, Czechoslovakia, Hungary, or Eastern Europe).

34. *International Shade Tree Conference*, Executive Director, 1827 Neil Ave., Columbus, Ohio 43210; *G* (research related to arboriculture).

35. *Kappa Kappa Gamma Fraternity*, 530 E. Town St., Columbus, Ohio 43216; *G* (award to women graduate students only).

36. *Kosciuszko Foundation*, 15 E. 65th St., New York, N.Y. 10021; *G, PD* (award to Americans of Polish descent only).

37. *The Lalor Foundation*, Director, 4400 Lancaster Pike, Wilmington, Del. 19805; *PD* (research in reproductive physiology and related areas).

38. *Leukemia Society of America, Inc.*, Executive Director, 211 E. 43rd St., New York, N.Y. 10017; *PD* (research restricted to leukemia and related fields).

39. *Link Foundation*, Suite 301, Airline Bldg., 80 E. 42nd St., New York, N.Y. 10017; *G* (research in aerospace science and oceanography).

40. *Merck Company Foundation*, Lincoln Ave., Rahway, N.J. 07065; *G, PD.*

41. *National Aeronautics and Space Administration* (NASA); *G:* NASA, Office of Grants and Research Contracts, Code SC, Washington, D.C. 20546; *PD:* Office of Scientific Personnel, JH 606, National Research Council, 2101 Constitution Ave., N.W., Washington, D.C. 20418 (research at NASA operated laboratories).

TABLE A-4 *(continued)*

42. *National Football Foundation,* 137 Church St., New Brunswick, N.J. 08901; *G* (awards to college football players of outstanding scholarship only).

43. *National Kidney Foundation,* 315 Park Ave. South, New York, N.Y. 10010; *PD* (research on kidney function and disease).

44. *National Science Foundation,* Fellowship Section, Division of Graduate Education in Science, Washington, D.C. 20550; *G, PD;* also, Traineeship Program, Division of Graduate Education in Science, NSF, same address.

45. *National Wildlife Federation,* Executive Director, 1412 Sixteenth St., N.W., Washington, D.C. 20036; *G* (research in various aspects of conservation).

46. *Netherland-America Foundation, Inc.* 10 Rockefeller Plaza, Rm. 1110, New York, N.Y. 10020; *G* (study to be made in the Netherlands).

47. *North Atlantic Treaty Organization (NATO),* Committee on International Exchange of Persons, Conference Board of Associated Research Councils, 2101 Constitution Ave., N.W., Washington, D.C. 20418, or Fellowship Section, Division of Graduate Education in the Sciences, NSF, Washington, D.C. 20550; *PD* (research to be carried out at one or more of the member countries).

48. *Office of Education*
(a) *Division of Graduate Programs, Bureau of Higher Education,* Washington, D.C. 20202; *G* (graduate study support for students who plan to teach in institutions of higher learning).
(b) *Division of Foreign Studies, Institute of International Studies,* Washington, D.C. 20202; *G* (study abroad for graduate students who plan to teach in institutions of higher learning).

TABLE A-4 *(continued)*

49. *Organization of American States* (OAS), Technical Secretariat, Pan American Union, Washington, D.C. 20006; *G, PD* (study in any OAS member country other than one of home residence).

50. *Paint Research Institute,* Research Director, Kent State University, Kent, Ohio 44240; *G* (research in areas of interest to paint scientists).

51. *Petroleum Research Fund,* American Chemical Society, 1155 Sixteenth St., N.W., Washington, D.C. 20036; *G, PD.*

52. *Pittsburgh Plate Glass Foundation,* One Gateway Center, Pittsburgh, Pa., 15222; *G, PD.*

53. *The Population Council,* Biomedical Division, The Rockefeller University, York Avenue and 66th St., New York, N.Y. 10021; *PD* (research in various aspects of reproductive biology and fertility control).

54. *Prestressed Concrete Institute,* 205 W. Wacker Dr., Chicago, Ill., 60606; *G* (research related to prestressed concrete).

55. *Public Health Service*
(a) Career Development Review Branch, Division of Research Grants, *National Institutes of Health,* P.H.S., Bethesda, Md. 20014; *G, PD* (all areas of science and engineering related broadly to health problems).
(b) *Division of Allied Health Manpower, Bureau of Health Manpower,* Public Health Service, Arlington, Va., 22203; *G.*
(c) University Grant and Training Services, *National Center for Radiological Health,* 12720 Twinbrook Parkway, Rockville, Md. 20852; *G.*

56. *The Ralston Purina Company,* Awards Committee, Public Relations Department, Checkerboard Square, St. Louis, Mo. 63199; *G* (research in nutrition and physiology as related to animal, dairy, and poultry science).

TABLE A-4 *(continued)*

57. *The Rockefeller Foundation*, 111 W. 50th St., New York, N.Y. 10020; *PD* (awarded chiefly to candidates outside the United States.

58. *The Rotary Foundation*, Rotary International, 1600 Ridge Ave., Evanston, Ill. 60201; *G* (for support of graduate study abroad).

59. *Royal Norwegian Council for Scientific and Industrial Research*, Gaustadaleen 30, Oslo 3, Norway; *PD* (study to be carried out in Norway).

60. *Runyon, Damon, Memorial Fund for Cancer Research, Inc.*, Research Secretary, 33 W. 56th St., New York, N.Y. 10019; *PD* (cancer related research).

61. *Sigma Delta Epsilon*, Fellowship Board, Department of Biological Sciences, Wellesley College, Wellesley, Mass. 02181; *G, PD* (award limited to women applicants).

62. *Sloan, Alfred P., Foundation*, Program for Basic Research in the Physical Sciences, 630 Fifth Ave., New York, N.Y. 10020; *PD*.

63. *Smithsonian Institute*, Office of Education and Training, Rm. 130, Washington, D.C. 20560; *G;* Office of Scientific Personnel, JH 606, National Research Council, Washington, D.C. 20418; *PD*.

64. *The Southern Fellowships Fund*, 795 Peachtree St., N.E., Suite 484, Atlanta, Ga. 30308; *G, PD* (support for prospective teachers for colleges with predominantly Black student body).

65. *United Cerebral Palsy Research and Education Foundation*, Director of Research, 321 W. 44th St., New York, N.Y. 10036; *G* (area pertinent to cerebral palsy); *PD* (brain research).

66. *Von Humboldt, Alexander, Foundation*, 532 Bad Godesberg, Schillerstrasse, 12, West Germany; *PD* (study to be made in Germany).

TABLE A-4 *(continued)*

67. *Whitney, Helen Hay, Foundation,* 22 E. 65th St., New York, N.Y. 10021; *PD* (research on rheumatic fever, heart disease).

68. *Whitney, John Hay, Foundation,* 111 W. 50th St., New York, N.Y. 10020; *G* (restricted to the Black, Spanish-American, American Indian, and other specified United States minority groups).

69. *Wildlife Management Institute,* Dr. L.R. Jahn, Vice President, 709 Wire Bldg., Washington, D.C. 20005; *G* (research in wildlife management and related areas of biology).

70. *Woodrow Wilson National Fellowship Foundation,* 32 Nassau St., Princeton, N.J. 08540; *G.*

TABLE A-5:   Some Sources of Research Support Available to Science Faculty of American Universities.[a]

1. *The Alcoa Foundation,* 1501 Alcoa Bldg., Pittsburgh, Pa. 15219; research grants, matching grants, aids to education; grants to promote educational, charitable, civic, cultural, and religious pursuits within the United States and its possessions.

2. *American Cancer Society, Inc.,* The Research Department, 219 E. 42nd St., New York, N.Y. 10017; research grants in areas related to cancer; elucidation of the cause and course of cancer and development of prevention and cure methods.

3. *American Heart Association,* 44 E. 23rd St., New York, N.Y. 10010; research in areas related to cardiovascular function and disease and related fundamental problems.

4. *Atomic Energy Commission,* Headquarters, Washington, D.C. 20545; basic research and development related to nuclear energy; physical and biological sciences and engineering; practical utilization of nuclear energy.

5. *Department of Agriculture,* Chief, Forest Service, Washington, D.C. 20250; scientific and engineering areas related to basic forestry research.

6. *Department of Commerce,* Director, Office of Economic Research, Economic Development Administration, Washington, D.C. 20230; research related to economic development, urban problems, etc.

7. *Department of Defense*
    (a) *Advanced Research Projects Agency,* Washington, D.C. 20301; research pertinent to national defense but not peculiar to one military service.
    (b) *Air Force Office of Scientific Research,* Washington, D.C. 20333; research related to air force interests and planning objectives.

[a]This information was taken in large part from the more complete information on grant support summarized in *Annual Register of Grant Support, 1969.*[21]

TABLE A-5 *(continued)*

(c) *Army Research Office,* Department of the Army, Washington, D.C. 20310; research in areas of interest to the army in sciences and engineering.

(d) *Director of Defense Research and Engineering,* The Pentagon, Washington, D.C. 20301; research related to defense interests; support to help develop new academic centers of excellence in science and technology (Project Themis).

(e) *Office of Naval Research,* Main Navy Building 18th St. and Constitution Ave., N.W., Washington, D.C. 20360; research in areas of interest to navy in the sciences and engineering.

8. *Department of Health, Education, and Welfare*
(a) *Public Health Service, Division of Research Grants,* Bethesda, Md. 20014; research in medical, biological, engineering, physical, and behavioral sciences.
(b) *Environmental Protection Agency*

   (1) *Office of Air Programs,* P.O. Box 12055, Research Triangle Park, N. C. 27711; research in the sciences and engineering related to the control of air pollution.

   (2) *Office of Air Programs,* 1750 K Street, Washington, D. C. 20460; research in the sciences and engineering related to the control of water pollution.

9. *Department of the Interior*
(a) *Director, Bureau of Mines,* Washington, D.C. 20240; research related to the problems of interest to the Bureau of Mines in the sciences and engineering.
(b) *Director, Office of Saline Water,* Department of the Interior, Washington, D.C. 20240; research in the physical and biological sciences related to saline water conversion.
(c) *Training Grants Branch, Office of Water Programs,* Environmental Protection Agency, Research Triangle

TABLE A-5 *(continued)*

Park, N.C. 27711; research in sciences and engineering related to causes, control, and prevention of water pollution.

10. *The Dana, Charles A., Foundation, Inc.,* Rm. 7, Smith Bldg., Greenwich, Conn. 06830; research in areas of education, health, and welfare; effort to strengthen and improve quality of education, especially higher education.

11. *Fleischmann, Max C., Foundation,* P.O. Box 1871, Reno, Nev. 89505; research in education, hospitals, medical areas, parks, recreation, etc.; endeavors for the benefit of mankind.

12. *Ford Foundation,* 320 E. 43rd St., New York, N.Y. 10017; national affairs, education, research in the identification and solution of problems of national and international importance.

13. *The Hancock, Luke B., Foundation,* P.O. Box 149, Reno, Nev. 89501; research in a variety of areas involving the physical and life sciences, engineering, etc.

14. *The Merck Company Foundation,* Lincoln Ave., Rahway, N.J. 07065; research in education, social welfare, health, and related sciences.

15. *National Aeronautics and Space Administration,* Office of Grants and Research Contracts, Code SC, Washington, D.C. 20546; research related to space technology in the sciences and engineering.

16. *National Geographic Society,* Committee for Research and Exploration, Washington, D.C. 20036; basic research in anthropology, archaeology, astronomy, biology, botany, geology, entomology, zoology, etc.; support of research related to geography.

17. *National Science Foundation*
    (a) *Institutional Grants Program,* NSF, Washington,

TABLE A-5 *(continued)*

D.C. 20550; research in the sciences and engineering; assistance to universities in the development and maintenance of strong, well-balanced programs in research and education in the sciences.

(b) *Basic Research Grants.* Address the appropriate Division; Biological and Medical Sciences; Engineering; Environmental Sciences; Mathematical and Physical Sciences; Social Sciences; Office of Computing Activities; basic research in science, engineering, and mathematics; see 17(a) above.

(c) *University Science Development Section,* NSF, Washington, D.C. 20550; grants for institutions of higher education to strengthen their research and education progress in the sciences and engineering; increase the number of centers of excellence in science research and education.

18. *Petroleum Research Fund,* American Chemical Society, 1155 16th St., N.W., Washington, D.C. 20036; research related to the petroleum field; starter grants for young faculty and unrestricted grants for established scientists.

19. *Research Corporation,* 405 Lexington Ave., New York, N.Y. 10017; basic research in the sciences and engineering.

20. *The Rockefeller Foundation,* 111 W. 50th St., New York, N.Y. 10020; research and experimentation in agriculture, social and life sciences, public health, and medical education, etc.; research applications to human needs and interests.

21. *Shell Companies Foundation, Inc.,* 50 W. 50th St., New York, N.Y. 10020; research in sciences and engineering; support for graduate education.

22. *Sloan, Alfred P., Foundation,* 630 Fifth Ave., New York, N.Y. 10020; mathematics, physical sciences, engineering, problems of domestic needs and uses.

TABLE A-6: Federally Funded Research and Development Centers Administered by Universities and Colleges, (1963-1967).[a]

Location and Name	Federal Obligations (Thousands of Dollars)					Sponsoring Agency	Administered by
	1963	1964	1965	1966	1967		
TOTAL	$814,082	$862,353	$895,287	$917,631	$907,549		
Arizona:							
Kitt Peak National Observatory[b]	3,750	4,400	6,915	5,791	5,485	NSF	Association of Universities for Research in Astronomy, Inc.
Cerro Tololo Inter-American Observatory (Chile).[b]	1,100	1,100	1,465	1,471	1,713	NSF	Association of Universities for Research in Astronomy, Inc.
California:							
Jet Propulsion Laboratory[c]	230,168	226,194	245,094	230,091	222,169	NASA	California Institute of Technology
Stanford Linear Accelerator Center	16,193	24,122	43,943	50,969	30,891	AEC	Stanford University
Lawrence Radiation Laboratory	162,854	169,424	156,254	169,870	174,661	AEC	University of California
Center for Research and Development in Higher Education	—	—	—	—	849	HEW(OE)	University of California
Center for the Study of the Evaluation of Instructional Programs	—	—	—	—	534	HEW(OE)	University of California
Stanford Center for Research and Development in Teaching	—	—	—	—	797	HEW(OE)	Stanford University

Location / Laboratory						Funding Agency	University
Colorado: National Center for Atmospheric Research[b]	6,019	10,036	8,941	11,791	16,576	NSF	University Corporation for Atmospheric Research
District of Columbia: Center for Research in Social systems	947	934	1,843	1,808	1,936	DOD(Army)	American University
Georgia: Research and Development Center in Educational Stimulation	—	—	—	—	732	HEW(OE)	University of Georgia
Illinois: Argonne National Laboratory[d]	74,947	84,507	86,329	87,255	97,262	AEC	University of Chicago and Argonne Universities Association
Iowa: Ames Laboratory	6,549	7,360	8,464	9,089	9,371	AEC	Iowa State University of Science and Technology
Maryland: Applied Physics Laboratory	42,096	49,124	54,097	52,491	47,172	DOD(Navy)	Johns Hopkins University
Massachusetts: Cambridge Electron Accelerator	5,946 / 2,632	5,717 / 3,424	5,851 / 3,792	6,130 / 3,517	6,786 / 3,596	AEC	Harvard University / Massachusetts Institute of Technology
Lincoln Laboratory	70,606	78,764	68,683	64,060	66,989	DOD(Air Force)	Massachusetts Institute of Technology
Center for Research and Development in Educational Differences[e]	—	—	—	1,112	1,165	HEW(OE)	Harvard University

TABLE A-6 (continued)

Location and Name	Federal Obligations (Thousands of Dollars)					Sponsoring Agency	Administered by
	1963	1964	1965	1966	1967		
New Jersey:							
Plasma Physics Laboratory	7,542	8,268	6,997	6,556	6,572	AEC	Princeton University
Princeton-Pennsylvania Accelerator	6,224	5,500	7,521	8,825	7,971	AEC	Princeton University / University of Pennsylvania
	881	1,790	1,982	1,801	1,775		
New Mexico:							
Los Alamos Scientific Laboratory	93,020	97,680	94,636	103,311	102,213	AEC	University of California
New York:							
Brookhaven National Laboratory[b]	59,180	58,619	63,564	64,407	64,160	AEC	Associated Universities, Inc.
Hudson Laboratory	3,780	3,939	4,195	4,673	4,708	DOD(Navy)	Columbia University
Oregon:							
Center for the Advanced Study of Educational Administration	—	509	534	663	676	HEW(OE)	University of Oregon
Pennsylvania:							
Ordnance Research Laboratory	3,763	4,827	7,025	9,597	8,120	DOD(Navy)	Pennsylvania State University
Learning Research and Development Center	—	—	754	642	1,309	HEW(OE)	University of Pittsburgh
Tennessee:							
Oak Ridge Associated Universities[b]	4,291	5,059	5,695	6,168	5,620	AEC	Oak Ridge Associated Universities

Texas:							
Research and Development Center in Teacher Education	—	—	—	—	763	HEW(OE)	University of Texas
Virginia:							
Human Resources Research Office	2,794	3,081	3,382	2,752	2,853	DOD(Army)	George Washington University
Space Radiation Effects Laboratory	—	—	—	729	1,815	NASA	College of William and Mary
Washington:							
Applied Physics Laboratory	3,200	2,275	2,178	5,145	2,836	DOD(Navy)	University of Washington
West Virginia:							
National Radio Astronomy Observatory[b]	4,550	4,600	3,380	4,719	5,062	NSF	Associated Universities, Inc.
Wisconsin:							
Army Mathematics Research Center	1,050	1,100	1,273	1,390	1,378	DOD(Army)	University of Wisconsin
Center for Research and Development for Learning and Re-Education	—	—	500	808	1,034	HEW(OE)	University of Wisconsin

[a] Data from reference 53.
[b] One of six administered by university consortia.
[c] Includes amounts subcontracted principally to industrial firms for performance as follows: 1963, $107 million; 1964, $145 million; 1965, $163 million; 1966, $141 million; 1967, $119 million.
[d] Administered by both university and consortium.
[e] Discontinued July 1, 1967.

TABLE A-7: Comparison of the Number of United States Scientists by Field, Type of Employer, and Highest Degree, 1968.[a]

Scientific and Technical Field and Type of Employer	Total	Highest Degree				Less Than Bachelor's Degree	No Report of Degree
		Doctorate	Professional Medical	Master's	Bachelor's		
ALL FIELDS	297,942	111,206	7,455	86,717	89,141	353	3,070
Educational Institutions	117,746	64,624	3,893	34,928	13,790	8	503
Federal Government	29,666	8,461	443	8,208	12,174	51	329
Other Government	10,031	2,300	310	3,403	3,913	17	88
Nonprofit Organizations	11,204	4,937	1,093	3,113	1,976	7	78
Industry and Business	95,776	24,099	390	25,983	43,729	214	1,361
Self-employed	6,462	1,945	524	1,480	2,386	36	91
Military	7,155	949	523	2,186	3,211	1	285
Other Employers	1,729	549	36	579	517	5	43
Not Employed	12,707	2,503	38	4,671	5,278	13	204
No Report	5,466	839	205	2,166	2,167	1	88
AGRICULTURAL SCIENCES	12,740	2,332	3	3,417	6,880	13	95
Educational Institutions	2,933	1,558	1	1,030	333	—	11
Federal Government	4,785	414	—	1,093	3,244	6	28
Other Government	2,104	67	—	509	1,504	4	20
Nonprofit Organizations	148	40	—	47	60	—	1
Industry and Business	2,016	197	2	499	1,291	2	25
Self-employed	250	12	—	71	163	1	3
Military	184	7	—	49	126	—	3
Other Employers	68	12	—	22	33	—	1
Not Employed	175	12	—	72	89	—	2
No Report	77	13	—	25	37	—	2

ANTHROPOLOGY	1,219	1,158	7	33	16	2	3
Educational Institutions	986	955	4	20	4	—	3
Federal Government	34	30	2	—	2	—	—
Other Government	14	14	—	—	—	—	—
Nonprofit Organizations	25	24	—	—	1	—	—
Industry and Business	11	10	—	—	1	—	—
Self-employed	12	9	—	1	2	—	—
Military	—	—	—	—	—	—	—
Other Employers	77	66	—	9	1	1	—
Not Employed	44	34	1	3	5	1	—
No Report	16	16	—	—	—	—	—
ATMOSPHERIC AND SPACE SCIENCES	5,745	514	—	1,555	3,168	39	469
Educational Institutions	757	292	—	277	173	1	14
Federal Government	1,857	123	—	463	1,130	21	120
Other Government	72	3	—	17	48	1	3
Nonprofit Organizations	114	23	—	57	31	—	3
Industry and Business	537	44	—	165	264	9	55
Self-employed	36	2	—	11	16	3	4
Military	2,184	21	—	494	1,410	1	258
Other Employers	26	1	—	6	15	1	3
Not Employed	107	2	—	40	56	2	7
No Report	55	3	—	25	25	—	2

TABLE A-7 (continued)

Scientific and Technical Field and Type of Employer	Total	Highest Degree				Less Than Bachelor's Degree	No Report of Degree
		Doctorate	Professional Medical	Master's	Bachelor's		
BIOLOGICAL SCIENCES	46,183	22,344	7,185	10,064	6,363	31	196
Educational Institutions	27,141	15,001	3,819	5,926	2,304	3	88
Federal Government	5,080	2,393	424	1,085	1,152	10	16
Other Government	2,020	535	300	513	650	3	19
Nonprofit Organizations	2,893	1,230	1,043	300	304	4	12
Industry and Business	4,521	2,113	367	920	1,080	8	33
Self-employed	838	118	483	77	149	2	9
Military	1,227	339	499	227	157	—	5
Other Employers	255	102	28	69	48	1	7
Not Employed	1,268	273	28	620	344	—	3
No Report	940	240	194	327	175	—	4
CHEMISTRY	93,788	28,973	211	20,121	43,127	160	1,196
Educational Institutions	20,510	9,895	55	4,579	5,886	2	93
Federal Government	5,247	1,438	9	1,142	2,588	5	65
Other Government	1,221	193	8	264	726	5	25
Nonprofit Organizations	2,121	835	44	487	739	—	16
Industry and Business	53,291	14,473	12	11,154	26,777	130	745
Self-employed	1,069	303	36	227	470	9	24
Military	1,442	207	23	281	919	—	12
Other Employers	539	135	5	125	263	—	11
Not Employed	6,180	1,262	9	1,319	3,423	8	159
No Report	2,168	232	10	543	1,336	1	46

	6,972	469	1	2,736	3,513	3	250
COMPUTER SCIENCES							
Educational Institutions	921	209	1	405	272	—	34
Federal Government	516	15	—	178	297	1	25
Other Government	102	6	—	26	67	—	3
Nonprofit Organizations	475	34	—	158	267	—	16
Industry and Business	4,513	188	—	1,760	2,402	2	161
Self-employed	45	1	—	18	23	—	3
Military	141	6	—	86	48	—	1
Other Employers	62	2	—	23	34	—	3
Not Employed	147	5	—	57	85	—	—
No Report	50	3	—	25	18	—	4

	23,746	4,956	1	7,651	10,893	59	186
EARTH AND MARINE SCIENCES							
Educational Institutions	5,890	2,906	—	1,940	1,021	—	23
Federal Government	2,982	668	—	926	1,372	2	14
Other Government	1,064	128	—	356	572	2	6
Nonprofit Organizations	249	108	—	82	56	1	2
Industry and Business	9,809	865	1	3,219	5,596	33	95
Self-employed	2,019	143	—	497	1,333	19	27
Military	373	21	—	132	217	—	3
Other Employers	92	28	—	30	33	—	1
Not Employed	882	66	—	308	495	2	11
No Report	386	23	—	161	198	—	4

TABLE A-7 (continued)

Scientific and Technical Field and Type of Employer	Total	Highest Degree					No Report of Degree
		Doctorate	Professional Medical	Master's	Bachelor's	Less Than Bachelor's Degree	
ECONOMICS	11,510	6,112	2	4,306	1,027	8	55
Educational Institutions	6,681	4,568	1	1,852	237	—	23
Federal Government	1,417	489	—	676	242	1	9
Other Government	517	208	—	226	80	—	3
Nonprofit Organizations	505	251	—	206	46	1	1
Industry and Business	1,636	405	1	881	332	6	11
Self-employed	186	67	—	79	35	—	5
Military	97	9	—	75	13	—	—
Other Employers	41	11	—	26	4	—	—
Not Employed	315	76	—	208	28	—	3
No Report	115	28	—	77	10	—	—
LINGUISTICS	1,541	955	2	413	134	1	36
Educational Institutions	1,121	822	—	236	43	—	20
Federal Government	58	23	1	22	8	—	4
Other Government	15	6	—	8	1	—	—
Nonprofit Organizations	118	38	1	40	35	1	3
Industry and Business	41	20	—	14	7	—	—
Self-employed	10	3	—	4	2	—	1
Military	4	2	—	—	2	—	—
Other Employers	15	6	—	7	2	—	—
Not Employed	110	21	—	61	24	—	4
No Report	49	14	—	21	10	—	4

MATHEMATICS	24,477	6,929	3	12,094	5,147	29	275
Educational Institutions	12,837	5,363	1	6,607	821	2	43
Federal Government	1,354	196	—	618	517	3	20
Other Government	308	63	—	150	92	2	1
Nonprofit Organizations	681	177	—	314	179	—	11
Industry and Business	7,289	864	1	3,163	3,078	19	164
Self-employed	222	33	—	86	96	1	6
Military	481	52	—	315	111	—	3
Other Employers	219	33	—	115	58	2	11
Not Employed	786	96	—	532	153	—	5
No Report	300	52	1	194	42	—	11
PHYSICS	32,491	14,311	7	10,776	7,239	5	153
Educational Institutions	15,522	8,364	—	4,935	2,166	—	57
Federal Government	3,717	1,269	1	1,133	1,296	1	17
Other Government	86	38	—	23	24	—	1
Nonprofit Organizations	882	473	1	259	145	—	4
Industry and Business	9,436	3,697	5	2,983	2,688	3	60
Self-employed	249	115	—	56	73	1	4
Military	603	104	—	305	194	—	—
Other Employers	41	27	—	5	9	—	—
Not Employed	1,132	182	—	562	382	—	6
No Report	823	42	—	515	262	—	4

TABLE A-7 (continued)

Scientific and Technical Field and Type of Employer	Total	Highest Degree					No Report of Degree
		Doctorate	Professional Medical	Master's	Bachelor's	Less Than Bachelor's Degree	
PSYCHOLOGY	23,077	14,794	14	8,000	248	—	21
Educational Institutions	12,810	8,658	4	4,039	102	—	7
Federal Government	1,443	1,069	—	360	14	—	—
Other Government	1,977	916	1	1,022	36	—	2
Nonprofit Organizations	2,318	1,410	2	870	33	—	3
Industry and Business	1,747	1,001	—	716	27	—	3
Self-employed	1,402	1,084	5	300	13	—	—
Military	256	142	1	109	3	—	1
Other Employers	176	90	1	83	2	—	—
Not Employed	744	319	—	408	15	—	2
No Report	204	105	—	93	3	—	3
SOCIOLOGY	6,638	3,396	3	2,507	698	—	34
Educational Institutions	4,827	2,866	—	1,602	333	—	26
Federal Government	240	100	—	97	42	—	1
Other Government	232	55	—	134	43	—	—
Nonprofit Organizations	343	154	1	151	35	—	2
Industry and Business	121	35	1	55	28	—	2
Self-employed	53	28	—	22	2	—	1
Military	32	11	—	17	4	—	—
Other Employers	60	23	1	26	9	—	1
Not Employed	533	77	—	298	158	—	—
No Report	197	47	—	105	44	—	1

STATISTICS	2,639	929	2	1,147	531	3	27
Educational Institutions	889	600	1	260	25	—	3
Federal Government	588	86	1	253	238	1	9
Other Government	149	20	—	64	61	—	4
Nonprofit Organizations	132	39	—	65	28	—	—
Industry and Business	692	151	—	386	147	2	6
Self-employed	21	11	—	6	3	—	1
Military	36	3	—	30	3	—	—
Other Employers	24	3	—	12	3	—	3
Not Employed	71	10	—	45	16	—	—
No Report	37	6	—	26	4	—	1

[a]Source: National Register of Scientific and Technical Personnel, 1968.[15]

TABLE A-8: The Major Nonprofit Research Institutions Employing Scientists and Engineers in the United States (Alphabetical Listing).[a]

| Institution (Address) | Research Volume Dollars/Yr times 10^{-6}(Yr) | Number of Employees | | | Major Research Interests | Means of Support |
		Research Professionals	Supporting Professionals	Technicians, Others		
Aerospace Corp. (El Segundo Calif.)	–	——— 1900 ———		2100	Systems engineering, ballistic missile space systems, etc.	U.S. govt. (air force)
Applied Physics Laboratory, Johns Hopkins Univ. (Silver Springs, Md.)	47.2(1967)[b]	——— 1126 ———		1386	Aerodynamics, electronics, guidance, control systems, etc.	U.S. govt. (Dept. Defense, navy)
Argonne National Laboratory (Argonne, Ill.)	87.3(1967)[b]	1163	239	3618	Peaceful uses of atomic energy, natural sciences, engineering, etc.	U.S. govt. (Atomic Energy Comm.)
Balcones Research Center, Univ. Tex. (Austin, Tex.)	–	174	43	183	Multidisciplinary and engineering	U.S. and State of Texas govts., industry

Institution	Budget ($ millions) (year)				Fields	Sources of support
Battelle Memorial Inst. (a) Columbus Labs. (Columbus, Ohio)	87.5(1965)	914	233	1372	Multidisciplinary science and engineering	Industry, govt, endowment income, etc.
(b) Pacific Northwest Labs (Richland, Wash.)		795	149	1243		
Brain Research Institute Univ. Calif. (Los Angeles, Calif.)	6.1(1964)	71	200	150	Brain, central nervous system	U.S. and state of Calif. govts., foundations, private institutes and donors.
Brookhaven National Lab. (Upton, N.Y.)	64.2(1967)[b]	500	350	2400	Nuclear and related sciences	U.S. govt. (Atomic Energy Comm.)
Cambridge Electron Accelerator, Harvard Univ. (Cambridge, Mass.)	10.3(1967)[b]	-	-	-	High energy and particle physics	U.S. govt. (Atomic Energy Comm.)
Cornell Aeronautical Lab. Cornell Univ. (Buffalo, N.Y.)	22.3(1965)	600	800		Aerodynamics, hypersonics, applied mechanics, etc.	U.S. govt, industry
Denver Research Institute, Univ. of Denver (Denver, Colo.)	6.6(1965)	118	6	267	Multidisciplinary, physical sciences, engineering	Univ. Denver, U.S. govt., industry
Franklin Institute of the State of Pennsylvania (Philadelphia, Pa.)	6.0(1966)	400			Multidisciplinary sciences, engineering	U.S. govt, industry foundations, etc.
Engineering Experiment Station, Georgia Institute of Technology (Atlanta, Ga.)	5.3(1965)	325 full-time 375 part-time			Engineering and technology	U.S. govt, industry, gifts, endowment income

TABLE A-8 *(continued)*

Institution (Address)	Research Volume Dollars/Yr times 10^{-6}(Yr)	Number of Employees				Major Research Interests	Means of Support
		Research Professionals	Supporting Professionals	Technicians, Others			
I.I.T. Research Institute, Illinois Institute of Technology (Chicago, Ill.)	25.4(1965)	830	570	450	Multidisciplinary sciences and engineering	U.S. govt, industry
Illinois, University of, Engineering Experiment Station (Urbana, Ill.)	14.1(1965)	–	–	–	Multidisciplinary sciences and engineering	U.S. govt, industry
Institute for Atomic Research, Iowa State Univ. (Ames, Iowa)	9.4(1967)[b]	400	100	500	Sciences and engineering devoted to peacetime uses of atomic energy	U.S. and state of Iowa govts.
Institute for Cancer Research, Columbia Univ. (New York, N.Y.)	–	100	100	300	Cancer, laboratory and clinical studies	Columbia Univ., U.S. govt., nonprofit organization donors
Institute for Defense Analyses (Arlington, Va.)	–	312	——— 298 ———		Multidisciplinary scientific and technical support to U.S. Dept. of Defense	U.S. govt., research grants

Institution	Budget (year)				Research areas	Sponsors
Institute of Science and Technology, Univ. Michigan (Ann Arbor, Mich.)	12.2(1965)	390	——— 370 ———		Acoustics, seismics, science, technology	U.S. and state of Mich. govts., industry
Jet Propulsion Lab., Calif. Institute of Technology (Pasadena, Calif.)	222(1967)[b]	1304	674	2100	Physics, propulsion, electronics, related to unmanned space program	U.S. govt, (NASA)
Lawrence Radiation Lab., Univ. Calif. (Berkeley, Calif.)	174.7(1967)[b]	——— 643 ———		2514	High energy physics, nuclear chemistry, etc., related to controlled fusion, high energy particles	U.S. govt, (Atomic Energy Comm.)
Lincoln Lab., Massachusetts Institute of Technology (Lexington,)	67.0(1967)[b]	606	——— 1200 ———		Multidisciplinary emphasis on national defense, space, etc.	U.S. govt, (Dept. Defense, air force)
Livermore Radiation Lab., Univ. Calif. (Livermore, Calif.)	118(1966)	——— 1162 ———		3777	Nuclear weapons, reactors, other applied research	U.S. govt
Los Alamos Scientific Lab., Univ. Calif. (Los Alamos, N.M.)	102(1967)[b]	1553	——— 2546 ———		Multidisciplinary nuclear sciences, engineering	U.S. govt
Massachusetts Institute of Technology, Instrumentation Lab. (Cambridge, Mass.)	–	700	——— 1100 ———		Guidance systems for space, surface, underwater travel and missiles	M.I.T., U.S. govt.

TABLE A-8 (continued)

Institution (Address)	Research Volume Dollars/Yr times 10^{-6}(Yr)	Number of Employees			Major Research Interests	Means of Support
		Research Professionals	Supporting Professionals	Technicians, Others		
Mayo Foundation, Univ. Minnesota (Rochester Minn.)	–	54	150	325	Biomedical sciences	Univ. Minn, U.S. govt., industry, endowment income
Mellon Institute (Pittsburgh, Pa.)	6.3(1965)	117	118	324	Research primarily in physical sciences and engineering	U.S. govt., industry, foundations, endowment income
Midwest Research Institute (Kansas City, Mo.)	5.5(1966)	224	——— 153 ———		Multidisciplinary sciences and engineering	Industry, U.S. govt.
Mitre Corp. (Bedford, (Mass.)	33(1966)	800	400	700	Comand, control systems; planning, design, development primarily for U.S.A.F.	U.S. govt.
National Center for Atmospheric Research (Boulder, Colo.)	12.5(1966)	140	——— 262 ———		Atmospheric sciences including a broad range of disciplines	U.S. govt. (NSF)
New Mexico State Univ., Physical Science Lab. (Univ. Park, N.M.)	–	175	80	340	Space systems engineering	U.S. govt., industry

Institution						
New York State Psychiatric Institute, Columbia Univ. (New York, N.Y.)	-		———— 500 ————		Psychiatry, including research in basic science	N.Y. State Dept. Mental Hygiene
New York Univ. Engineering Research Division (Bronx, N.Y.)	6.0(1965)	271 (+97 part-time)	————256————		Areas of engineering and technology	U.S. govt., industry, foundations
The Ohio State Univ. Engineering Experiment Station (Columbus, Ohio)	5.3(1965)	-	-		Areas of engineering and technology	U.S. and state of Ohio govts., industry
Rand Corp. (Santa Monica, Calif.)	22.2(1965)	473	115	529	Programs focused on national security	U.S. govt., foundations
Research Analysis Corp. (McLean, Va.)	-	310	————300————		Operations and systems analysis, scientific studies of military problems	U.S. govt. (Dept. Defense, primarily)
Research Triangle Institute Duke Univ. North Carolina State Univ., Univ. North Carolina (Durham, N.C.)	4.2(1966)	180	————100————		Multidisciplinary programs in science, engineering	U.S. govt., foundations, industry
Roswell Park Memorial Institute (Buffalo, N.Y.)	-	159	298	1344	Cancer research and treatment	U.S. and state of N.Y. govts., foundations, health agencies, gifts

TABLE A-8 *(continued)*

Institution (Address)	Research Volume Dollars/Yr times 10^{-6}(Yr)	Number of Employees			Major Research Interests	Means of Support
		Research Professionals	Supporting Professionals	Technicians, Others		
Sloan-Kettering Institute for Cancer Research Cornell Univ. (New York, N.Y.)	9.3(1966)	203	381	260	Cancer research	U.S. govt., foundations, etc.
Stanford Electronics Labs., Stanford Univ. (Stanford, Calif.)	6.5(1965)	150	150	150	Plasma theory, systems techniques, trainable systems, electronic devices, etc.	U.S. govt., industry
Stanford Linear Accelerator Center, Stanford Univ. (Stanford, Calif.)	30.9(1967)[b]	87	401	669	High energy physics	U.S. govt. (Atomic Energy Comm.)
Stanford Research Institute (Menlo Park, Calif.)	51.5(1965)	1500	———1500———		Multidisciplinary research in science and engineering	U.S. govt., industry
Syracuse Univ. Research Corp. (Syracuse, N.Y.)	5.0(1966)	122	———132———		Electronics, applied engineering, etc.	U.S. and state of N.Y. govts., industry
Tufts-New England Medical Center, Tufts, Univ. (Boston, Mass.)	5.0(1965)	400	———3300———		Basic and clinical biomedical and dental areas	U.S. govt., industry

| Washington, Univ. of, Applied Physics Lab. (Seattle, Wash.) | 5.7(1966) | 73 | —— 91 —— | Antisubmarine warfare, military oceanography, etc. | U.S. govt. |

---

[a] Data from Palmer (1968),[47] abstracted from his complete listings which describe over 4500 research centers in the U.S. and Canada; only those institutions with an annual volume of research exceeding $5 million or those hiring more than 175 research and supporting professionals are shown here.

[b] Represents total federal government funding to the institute as reported in *Federal Support to Universities and Colleges, Fiscal Year 1967*.[53]

References

1. K.S. Pitzer, "Science and Society: Some Policy Changes Are Needed," *Science*, **172**, 223 (1971).

2. Anonymous, "NAS Aims at Social Issues," *Chemical and Engineering News*, **49**, (18), page 7 (May 3, 1971).

3. F.S. Perls, *In and Out the Garbage Pail*, Real People Press, Lafayette, California (1969).

4. B. Nelson, "A Surplus of Scientists? The Job Market Is Tightening," *Science*, **166**, 582 (1969).

5. B. Vetter, "National Scientific Manpower Problems," *The Chemist*, **48**, (6), 138. (June, 1971).

6. D. Shapely, "Job Prospects: Science Graduates Face Worst Year in Two Decades," *Science*, **172**, 823 (1971).

7. Anonymous, "Job Outlook: Dim and Growing Dimmer," *Chemical and Engineering News*, **48**, (30), 22 (July 20, 1970).

8. Anonymous, "Grim Job Outlook for Class of 1971," *Chemical and Engineering News*, **49** (15), 16 (April 12, 1971).

9. A.M. Cartter, "Scientific Manpower for 1970-1985," *Science*, **172**, 132, (1971); Copyright 1971 by the American Association for the advancement of science.

10. F.E. Terman, "Supply of Scientific and Engineering Manpower: Surplus or Shortage?" *Science*, **173**, 339 (1971).

11. R.C. Graber, F.K. Erickson, W.B. Parsons, "Manpower for Environmental Protection," *Environmental Science and Technology*, **5** (4), 315 (1971).

12. D.A.H. Roethel, "1971 Salary Survey," *Chemical and Engineering News*, **49** (25), 64 (June 21, 1971).

13. The interested student is referred to the texts, *Advanced Tests for the Graduate Record Examination*, Edward C. Gruber, ed., Arco Publishing Company. These are now out of print but most libraries have them available in the areas of biology (1963), chemistry (1967), geology (1963), physics (1963), and psychology (1965). Sample tests and helpful hints are given on how to show your true capabilities on the examination.

14. An exception to this generalization occurs in many colleges of engineering. Here the traditional pattern of the M.S. degree preceding the Ph.D. degree may be followed. It appears to the authors that the departments which choose this plan commonly have a rather low graduate student to faculty ratio.

15. *American Science Manpower, 1968,* a report of the National Register of Scientific and Technical Personnel, Washington, D.C.: U.S. Government Printing Office.

16. The data used are rough estimates derived from: (a) The review of A.F. Scott, "The Crisis in Chemical Education," *Chemical and Engineering News,* **43** (17), 94 (April 26, 1965).
(b) *American Science Manpower, 1966,* a report of the National Register of Scientific and Technical Personnel, NSF 68-7, Washington, D.C.: U.S. Government Printing Office.
(c) Private communication from D.A.H. Roethel, Office of Professional Relations, the American Chemical Society, Washington, D.C.
(d) D*irectory of Graduate Research, 1967,* The American Chemical Society, Washington, D.C. The estimate of the percentage of Ph.D. graduates taking postdoctoral work is very approximate and based on the data of this reference and the assumptions (based on our experience largely) that a postdoctoral student spends an average of two years in postdoctoral work and that about one-half of all postdoctoral students are from abroad.

17. R.F. Moore, "Self Appraisal– A First Responsibility," *Chemical and Engineering News,* **41** (48), 68 (Dec. 2, 1963).

18. *Scientific and Technical Societies of the United States, Eighth Edition,* Publication 1499, National Academy of Sciences, Washington, D.C. (1968).

19. (a) A.M. Cartter, *An Assessment of Quality in Graduate Education,* American Council on Education, Washington, D.C. (1966).

(b) K.D. Roose and C.J. Anderson, eds., *A Rating of Graduate Programs*, American Council on Education, Washington, D.C. (1970).

20. *Federal Support to Universities and Colleges, Fiscal Year, 1968*, National Science Foundation, Washington, D.C.: U.S. Government Printing Office.

21. A. Renetzky and P.A. Kaplan, eds., *Annual Register of Grant Support, 1969*, Academic Media Inc., Los Angeles, Calif. (1969).

22. *Graduate Student Support and Manpower Resources in Graduate Science Education, Fall 1969*, N.S.F. 70-40, Superintendent of Documents, U.S. Government Publications Office, Washington, D.C. (1970).

23. H.E. Carter, chairman, Committee on Professional Training, American Chemical Society, *Chemical and Engineering News*, 76 (May 4, 1964).

24. W.G. Young, "Is Chemical Education at the Crossroads?" 1968 Priestley Medal Address, April 1, 1968, 155th National American Chemical Society Meeting, San Francisco, Calif., *Chemical and Engineering News*, 82 (April 8, 1968).

25. There are many very good, old and new books which provide a review of the special features of rapid translation of scientific literature in French, German, and Russian, for example see:
(a) W.N. Locke, *Scientific French*, New York, John Wiley and Sons, 1957.
(b) G.E. Condoyannis, *Scientific German*, New York: John Wiley and Sons, 1957,
(c) N.D. Gershevsky, *Scientific Russian Reader*, New York: Pitman Publishing Corp., 1948.

26. A.A. Frost and A.S. Hussey, *Journal of Chemical Education*, 35, 599 (1958).

27. G.R. Robertson, *Journal of Chemical Education*, 35, 212 (1964).

28. G.S. Hammond, "Relevance of Pure Research Today," *Journal of Chemical Education*, **48** (6), 382 (1971).

29. E. Bright Wilson, Jr., *An Introduction to Scientific Research*, New York: McGraw-Hill Book Co., Inc., 1952, also available in a paperback edition (1969).

30. J. Hadamard, *The Psychology of Invention in the Mathematical Field*, Princeton University Press, 1945. Reprinted Dover Publications, Inc., New York, N.Y. 1954.

31. H. Poincare, translated by G.B. Halstead, "Mathematical Creation," *Foundations of Science*, New York: The Science Press, (1913).

32. "General Information Concerning Patents," bulletin issued by the U.S. Patent Office (1967).

33. "Do You Know Your Economic ABC's? Patents: Spur to American Progress," published by U.S. Department of Commerce (1969).

34. W.T. Lippincott, "The Major Critical Problem in the American University: Quality Teaching in the Freshman and Sophomore Years," *Chemical and Engineering News*, **43** (20), 45 (May 17, 1965).

35. J.R. Hayes, "Research, Teaching, and Faculty Fate," *Science*, **172**, 227 (1971).

36. C.F. Cullis, "Chemistry Research and Teaching in a New University," *Chemistry in Britain*, **3**, 370 (1967).

37. C.E. Rothwell, chairman, Committee on Undergraduate Teaching, *The Importance of Teaching: A Memorandum to the new college teacher.* Copies available on request to the Hazen Foundation, 400 Prospect St., New Haven, Conn. 06511.

38. *International Financial Statistics*, **24**, No. 3, March 1971, published by the International Monetary Fund.

39. Anonymous, "The Fortune Directory of the 500 Largest Corporations," *Fortune Magazine*, 172 (May 1971).

40. Anonymous, "Industry Backing for R & D Faces Further Decline," *Chemical and Engineering News*, **48** (7), 40 (February 16, 1970).

41. Anonymous, "Companies Disclose New Financial Information," *Chemical and Engineering News*, **49** (23), 17 (June 7, 1971).

42. Anonymous, "CPI's Faltering Profits Stall R & D Funding," *Chemical and Engineering News*, **47** (2), 18 (Jan. 13, 1969).

43. T.M. Schmitz and R.K. Davies, "Safety in the Chemical Laboratory. XLI. Laboratory Accident Liability: Academic and Industrial," *Journal of Chemical Education*, **44**, A654 (1967).

44. J.D. Watson, *The Double Helix*, New York: Atheneum, 1968.

45. E.W. Lindveit, *Scientists in Government*, Washington, D.C.: Public Affairs Press, 1960.

46. F.P. Kilpatrick, N.M.C. Cummings, Jr., and M.K. Jennings, *Source Book of Study of Occupational Value and the Image of the Federal Servant,*" Washington, D.C.: The Brookings Institute, 1964.

47. *Research Centers Directory*, Second Edition, Ed. A.M. Palmer and A.T. Kruzco, Gale Research Co., Detroit, Mich., 1965; *New Research Centers*, a periodic supplement, Ed. A.M. Palmer, Gale Research Co., Detroit, Mich., No. 1, 1965; No. 2, August 1965; No. 3, November 1965; No. 4, February 1966; No. 5, May 1966, No. 6, September 1966; No. 7, February 1967; No. 8, January 1968.

48. Anonymous, "Women Chemists: Concerned over Rights," *Chemical and Engineering News*, **48** (45), 26 (October 26, 1970).

49. Anonymous, "Few Women in Academia," *Chemical and Engineering News*, **49** (19), 21 (May 10, 1971).

50. Benjamin Linsky, "Case Histories for Teaching Environmental Concern," *Engineering Education,* **60** 269 (1969); a telephonic lecture entitled, "Social Responsibilities of Engineers with Especial Regard to the Environment," presented to the A.S.E.E. North Central Section Meeting, April, 1969, at the University of Windsor, Windsor, Ontario, Canada.

51. Paul F. Chenea, "Man's Greatest Challenge: To Learn to Live with Himself," speech delivered at the symposium, "Chemical Reactions in the Urban Atmosphere," General Motors Corporation, Research Center, (October 6, 1969).

52. K.S. Pitzer, "Effecting National Priorities for Science," Priestly Award Address, *Chemical and Engineering News,* **47** (17), 72 (April 21, 1969).

53. *Federal Support to Universities and Colleges, Fiscal Year 1967,* National Science Foundation, U.S. Government Printing Office, Washington, D.C.

Index